NUCLEAR POWER AND NONPROLIFERATION

Written under the auspices of the Center for International and Strategic Affairs, University of California, Los Angeles.

A list of other center publications appears at the end of this book.

Nuclear Power
and
Nonproliferation

An Interdisciplinary
Perspective

William C. Potter

Center for International and Strategic Affairs
University of California, Los Angeles

 Oelgeschlager, Gunn & Hain, Publishers, Inc.
Cambridge, Massachusetts

International Standard Book Number: 0-89946-019-4

Library of Congress Catalog Card Number: 81-14220

Printed in West Germany

Library of Congress Cataloging in Publication Data

Potter, William C.
  Nuclear power and nonproliferation

  Bibliography:
Includes index.
  1. Nuclear nonproliferation.   2. Atomic power.
3. Atomic weapons.   I. Title.
JX1974.73.P67   327.1'74   81-14220
ISBN 0-89946-019-4   AACR2

Contents

Glossary of Acronyms

ACDA	Arms Control and Disarmament Agency
AEC	Atomic Energy Commission
AGR	Advanced gas-cooled reactor
AIF	Atomic Industrial Forum
AVLIS	Atomic vapor laser isotope separation
BWR	Boiling-water reactor
CANDU	Canadian deuterium-uranium reactor
CTB	Comprehensive Test Ban
EEC	European Economic Community
ERDA	Energy Research and Development Administration
FBR	Fast breeder reactor
FRG	Federal Republic of Germany
GCFB	Gas-cooled fast breeder reactor
GW$_e$	Gigawatt (10^9 watts) of electric power
HEU	Highly enriched uranium
HTGR	High-temperature gas-cooled reactor
IADA	International Atomic Development Authority
IAEA	International Atomic Energy Agency

INFCE	International Nuclear Fuel Cycle Evaluation
KWU	Kraftwerk Union
LEU	Low enriched uranium
LMFBR	Liquid-metal fast breeder reactor
LWBR	Light-water breeder reactor
LWR	Light-water reactor
MFCF	Multinational fuel cycle facility
MLIS	Molecular laser isotope separation
MOX	Mixed-oxide
MSBR	Molten-salt breeder reactor
MW	Megawatt (10^6 watts)
MW_e	Megawatt of electrical power
NASAP	Nonproliferation Alternative Systems Assessment Program
NNPA	Nuclear Non-Proliferation Act of 1978
NNWS	Non-nuclear weapon state
NPT	Treaty on the Non-Proliferation of Nuclear Weapons
NRC	Nuclear Regulatory Commission
NWS	Nuclear weapon state
PNE	Peaceful nuclear explosion
PRC	People's Republic of China
PRW	Pressurized-water reactor
ROC	Republic of China
ROK	Republic of Korea
SIPRI	Stockholm International Peace Research Institute

List of Tables

List of Figures

Preface

Since the first nuclear explosion in 1945, we have stood in awe and fear of the atom. Anxious to atone for our violent heritage, we have sought to exploit the atom for peace while controlling, if not eliminating, the atom for war. In pursuit of the first objective, the U.S. government has promoted research on and development of the peaceful applications of nuclear technology and has exported the products of that research abroad. At the same time, in deference to the second goal, it has sought to restrict the proliferation of nuclear weapon capabilitites to other states. Intent on distinguishing between "atoms for peace" and "atoms for war," American decision-makers have frequently ignored the relationship between the world-wide growth of nuclear power and the proliferation of nuclear weapons.

A number of recent developments, however, have aroused public and governmental interest in the nuclear power–nuclear weapons proliferation dilemma. The 1973 oil embargo and the quadrupling of world oil prices, the subsequent increase in demand by developing states for nuclear energy production capabilitites, the 1974 explosion of a "nuclear device" by India, the appearance in the 1970s of increasingly sophisticated and worldwide terrorist groups, and, most recently, the Israeli destruction of Iraq's nuclear reactor, have combined to raise the intensity of the nuclear power–nuclear proliferation debate between those who emphasize the promise of nuclear energy and those who fear its consequences. What tends to unite adherents of both views is the feeling that time is running out and that decisive action must be taken shortly if energy independence is to be assured and/or if extensive and uncontrolled proliferation is to be prevented. This concern was reflected in the Carter administration's decision to give high priority to proliferation control and the outpouring since the mid-1970s of government and foundation-funded reports on a myriad of nuclear power and proliferation topics. Unfortunately, the intensity of public debate today over the merits and deficiencies of alternative nuclear power–nonproliferation choices often is not matched by an understanding of the complex and wide range of issues involved. These issues encompass nuclear physics, engineering, history, economics, and domestic and international politics. For example:

How critical is nuclear power to future U.S. and global energy requirements?

What are the social, economic, and environmental costs of increased reliance on nuclear power?

Is nuclear proliferation inevitable or likely?

What are the consequences of the proliferation of nuclear weapons?

What are the incentives and disincentives to "go nuclear"?

What influence can the United States exert on the likelihood of proliferation?

Is the threat or use of sanctions against would-be proliferators apt to be effective?

How reversible is the diffusion of nuclear technology process?

Can effective nonproliferation strategies avoid an undesirable level of North/South discrimination?

How effective are International Atomic Energy Agency safeguards?

Can nuclear waste be disposed of safely?

Are there feasible alternatives to a plutonium-based nuclear fuel cycle?

What are the economic and proliferation implications of alternative nuclear fuel cycles?

Would deployment of fast breeder reactors be compatible with nonproliferation objectives?

Can the Non-Proliferation Treaty or other arms control measures make a meaningful contribution to containing proliferation?

Has the nonproliferation dam already burst and thus should we now concern ourselves principally with managing rather than halting the proliferation process?

Although many of these individual questions have received attention in government and foundation-sponsored research, dissemination of the researchers' findings often has been impeded by the narrow and very technical focus of the inquiries and the assumption, implicit in many of the studies, that the target audience already is familiar with basic nuclear power principles and hardware and/or the political and economic incentives and disincentives for proliferation. Most of these studies also lack the broad interdisciplinary and analytical perspective necessary to assess the political, economic, and social trade-offs posed by alternative nuclear power–nonproliferation strategies. The absence of a broad, interdisciplinary framework frequently leads to the exaggeration of the role of economic rationality in the nuclear power decision-making process and the neglect of relevant psychological and political factors. In addition, most studies of nuclear proliferation pay little attention to non-American perspectives on major nuclear power issues and fail to distinguish between the causes of proliferation that are unalterable and the causes that are susceptible to manipulation and cure.

This volume is designed to provide a broad, interdisciplinary perspective on the major issues of nuclear power and proliferation. It is intended to serve as an introduction to the field and to provide a reference source for the non-specialist. Historical, technical, economic, and political components of the nuclear power–proliferation dilemma are described and analyzed, and alternative strategies for nonproliferation are assessed. An extensive annotated bibliography on nuclear proliferation also is provided to assist in further study of the topic.

W. C. P.

Acknowledgments

This book is indirectly the product of many minds and hands. I am especially indebted to Philip Farley of Stanford University, Michael Intriligator and Bennett Ramberg of UCLA, and Thomas Graham of MIT for their thoughtful reading and criticisms of earlier drafts of the entire manuscript. I also benefited enormously from the advice of Dan Caldwell (Pepperdine University), Stephen Meyer (MIT), Peter Zimmerman (Louisiana State University), Paul Jabber (UCLA), Neil Joeck (UCLA), and Ciro Zoppo (UCLA), who read and criticized individual chapters.

Gerri Page and Linda Bidasio typed a difficult manuscript with care and efficiency. Their efforts are greatly appreciated, as is the diligent research assistance provided by Etel Goldman.

Finally, I wish to thank the UCLA Center for International and Strategic Affairs for its support.

This book is dedicated to my son, Benjamin, who was convinced it would never be completed.

Chapter 1

An Overview

THE NATURE
OF THE PROBLEM

For better or for worse, nuclear power is now a fact of international life. Six nations vie with the United States for nuclear power reactor sales on the international market, and another four states produce power reactors for domestic use.[1] Today approximately 240 commercial nuclear power reactors are in operation in 22 states and account for more than 130,000 megawatts of electric capacity (MW_e).[2] About 40 percent of this nuclear power capacity resides in the United States, most of the remainder being distributed among other industrialized nations.[3]

The nuclear power output of the United States and other industrialized countries appears more modest when nuclear-generated electricity is compared to the total electric capacity for these countries. The contribution, at present, averages about 12 percent.[4] Current nuclear power capacity as a percentage of total energy production (i.e., including energy for transportation and heating as well as electric power) is even less imposing, amounting to approximately 2 percent in the United States.[5] Worldwide nuclear power growth, on the other hand, was very substantial in the 1970s; nuclear-generated electricity increased more than sevenfold during the decade.[6] Despite this impressive growth rate, the future of nuclear power, especially in the United States, is uncertain. This

1

uncertainty is due in part to forecasts of a reduced economic growth rate and lower energy demand, as well as escalating capital costs for nuclear power facilities, and is reflected in the repeated downward revisions of estimates of future U.S. nuclear power capacity by most government and industry sources. Under the Nixon energy program, Project Independence, as updated by President Ford, U.S. nuclear capacity was to double every four to five years until the turn of the century. According to this schedule, 90,000 megawatts (MW) was set as the nuclear power capacity base for 1980, growing to 1,250,000 MW of installed capacity by the year 2000.[7] In April 1976, however, the Energy Research and Development Administration (ERDA) revised these estimates for the year 2000 downward to range from 450,000 to 800,000 MW$_e$.[8] At the beginning of 1978, when estimates of nuclear power capacity for the year 2000 were presented to the International Nuclear Fuel Cycle Evaluation (INFCE), the high- and low-case projections for the year 2000 dropped still farther in 1979 to a high of 300,000 and a low of 235,000 MW$_e$, and in January 1980 they were once again deflated to a high of 200,000 and a low of 150,000 MW$_e$.[10] Recent forecasts for nuclear power growth in most other states also have been revised downward, although these revisions generally have not been as great as those for the United States.

Although economic variables including recession, rising capital costs, projections of lower energy demand, and a renewed interest in alternative energy sources have contributed to the uncertainty of future U.S. nuclear power growth, a number of noneconomic factors also have been influential. Principal among these are increased public concern over nuclear power safety since the 1979 accident at Three Mile Island and political considerations related to the link between civilian nuclear power and the proliferation of nuclear weapons.

The major worry with respect to the link between nuclear power and proliferation derives from the fact that nuclear power reactors, in addition to producing electricity, generate substantial quantities of plutonium. It has been estimated, for example, that for each year of operation of a 1000-MW nuclear electric plant, enough plutonium is generated to equip 20 to 25 nuclear bombs.[11] Although none of the present nuclear weapon states acquired weapons capability via nuclear power reactors, the potential for misuse of civilian nuclear power facilities to produce nuclear weapons remains a major risk associated with the spread of nuclear power technology.

There have been no additions to the nuclear weapons club since India exploded a nuclear device in 1974. At least no other states have joined India and the original club of five—the United States, the Soviet Union, the United Kingdom, France, and China—in demonstrating both the inclination and ability to construct and actually detonate a nuclear explosive. An increasing number of states, however, have advanced to the nuclear "twilight zone" in which the absence of operational nuclear weapons is more a function of political will than of technical knowhow. One prominent analyst, for example, suggests that for many countries, a time schedule rather than a formal nuclear or non-nuclear designation best describes nuclear weapons status.[12] If a country's time schedule is such that it could manufacture or deploy a nuclear bomb within a short period (e.g., during a crisis), other states would have to regard that country as having a nuclear option. Israel is the state most frequently cited in this connection, but Pakistan, South Korea, South Africa, and Taiwan also are candidates for inclusion, in terms of their perceived security incentives as well as their probable possession of or access to the requisite technical skills and nuclear materials.[13]

Indeed, if one extends the time frame slightly to the mid-1980s, more than 20 currently non-nuclear weapon states can be expected to have nuclear power reactors in operation, each capable of generating enough by-product plutonium annually for over a dozen nuclear weapons.[14] Six of these countries are not parties to the 1968 Non-Proliferation Treaty (Israel, South Africa, Brazil, Spain, Argentina, and Pakistan), and others, although formal parties to the treaty, are "pariah" states isolated from much of the world and/or plagued by domestic and regional security problems (e.g., Taiwan and South Korea).

Capability, it should be emphasized, does not imply the likelihood that it will be exercised. Germany and Japan, for example, are representatives of a larger body of states with very sophisticated nuclear technologies which have chosen for political reasons to forgo exercising an autonomous nuclear weapons option. This restraint may be due simply to the absence of perceived advantage for "going nuclear." Fear of hostile domestic reaction and international public opinion, disruption of present military security guarantees, adverse reaction by regional adversaries, and diversion of economic resources may also serve as disincentives for nuclear proliferation. Altogether, over 100 states formally have renounced their intention of acquiring nuclear weapons by ratifying the Non-Proliferation Treaty (NPT). These states also have pledged under Article III of the NPT to accept international safeguards for the explicit purpose of preventing diversion of nuclear energy and material from peaceful use to the production of nuclear weapons. The adequacy of these safeguards is subject to much debate and most likely would not deter a state, intent on deception, from obtaining the nuclear material and technology necessary to manufacture nuclear explosives. Support for the nonproliferation objectives of the NPT, nevertheless, is widespread, as is the belief that international safeguards are a useful, if imperfect, means to deter the diversion of nuclear materials.

Most attention, until recently, has been directed toward containing the spread of nuclear weapons to additional national governments. A new proliferation concern, however, has developed that subnational or transnational groups, including terrorist organizations, could attain the capability to manufacture independently a nuclear explosive from stolen plutonium or highly enriched uranium. Much of the requisite technical knowledge for bomb design is available in the public literature. There is also a growing cadre of individuals familiar with nuclear technology who, theoretically, could help a dissident group assemble a crude nuclear bomb with an explosive force in the subkiloton range. The principal impediment to building such a bomb, it generally is assumed, is acquisition of the nuclear material. At present this is a major obstacle for would-be nuclear terrorists since the current generation of nuclear power reactors in most of the world uses a uranium fuel that is well below the level of enrichment required for weapons purposes.[15] The spent fuel produced by these reactors also is not conducive to weapons fabrication since it is highly radioactive and difficult to handle and because it normally contains substantial amounts of plutonium isotopes that are undesirable for weapons purposes. Although the latter difficulty, especially for would-be national proliferators, has been exaggerated in the past, it is unlikely that a terrorist organization, without access to costly and sophisticated reprocessing or enrichment facilities, could safely obtain the nuclear material necessary for an explosive. This situation could change, however, if reprocessing and recycling of plutonium is introduced as a major part of the nuclear power fuel cycle. This is one of the fears expressed by those opposed to the commercial development of a plutonium-dependent breeder reactor program.

COMMON MISCONCEPTIONS ABOUT PROLIFERATION

The debate over nuclear power and nonproliferation is intense and often has been characterized by impassioned pleas, dire warnings, and bitter accusations. This is understandable given the violent heritage of nuclear energy and the aura of mystery that has surrounded both military and peaceful application of nuclear power since the Manhattan Bomb Project of the 1940s. Passion, however, may distort perspective and lead to the proposal of deceptively simple solutions for extremely complex problems. Unfortunately, this often has been the case in the issue area of nuclear power and proliferation, a subject for which one astute observer has noted "there are no simple solutions that are feasible, no feasible solutions that are simple, and no solutions at all that are applicable across the board."[16] In order to better appreciate the nature of the problems surrounding nuclear power and proliferation, and to assess alternative policy options intelligently, it is useful to identify a number of common misconceptions regarding nuclear energy and the causes and cures for proliferation.

Good Atoms and Bad Atoms

Few popular and misleading ideas have proved more resilient than the belief that there exist clearly distinguishable good "atoms for peace" and bad "atoms for war." In fact, U.S. nuclear policy for most of the past twenty-five years has nurtured this misconception by actively promoting the development of civilian, and presumably safe, nuclear activities with little regard for their military or dangerous implications. Implicit in this policy was the philosophy that these dual activities were in some sense mutually exclusive and that "the more we used atoms for peace, the less we would use them for war."[17] This false dichotomy between peaceful and military atoms also is expressed in the 1968 Non-Proliferation Treaty, which simultaneously commits the nuclear powers to provide non-nuclear weapon states with civilian nuclear technology for peaceful purposes in exchange for the latter's pledge to forgo a military nuclear capability. This ambiguous division between peaceful and military nuclear activity was further reinforced by language in the treaty that distinguished between peaceful and military nuclear explosive capabilities. Benefits from the former, it was promised, would be made available to non-nuclear parties to the treaty at a low cost.[18]

It does *not* follow that, because there are no clearly distinguishable "peaceful" or "military" nuclear technologies or "good" or "bad" atoms, all nuclear activities are equally dangerous. Nor is it correct to assume that all aspects of civilian nuclear power contribute equally to the development of a nuclear weapons potential.[19] What is apparent, however, is the fundamental dilemma of trying to deter the proliferation of nuclear weapons capabilities while at the same time promoting the benefits of nuclear energy when the basic raw materials and technology for both is essentially the same.[20]

The Myth of Denaturing

Faith in the ability to segregate safe from dangerous nuclear activities has been reinforced by the widespread belief that nuclear power reactors do not produce weapons-grade plutonium. This misconception has been prevalent since the 1946 Acheson-Lilienthal Report suggested that plutonium could be "denatured" (i.e., rendered ineffective as an explosive) by mixing in other isotopes of the same element. This could be achieved, it was suggested, through the standard operation of nuclear power reactors since the presence of "contaminating" isotopes accumulate in nuclear reactor fuel rods as a consequence of irradiation. The longer the irradiation time or operation of the reactor, the greater the concentration of plutonium isotopes undesirable for weapons fabrication.[21] Since a long irradiation time is desirable for the economic production of electric power, people hoped that a kind of invisible hand would operate to encourage economic, yet safe, nuclear power production.[22]

As Albert Wohlstetter has pointed out, this hope, although still commonly expressed, is ill founded. In the first place, "it is neither illegal nor uncommon to operate reactors uneconomically."[23] Governments intent upon acquiring relatively pure plutonium via the operation of power reactors could thus do so without much visibility. Numerous public sources have also made it apparent that weapons can be based on plutonium with an isotopic content that is common to power-reactor operation.[24] Thus, although utilization of power-reactor plutonium in a weapon will most likely reduce the efficiency of the explosive and the predictability of its yield—considerations of major importance for a nuclear weapons state such as the United States—it probably will not deter a potential proliferator from producing a crude but formidable nuclear explosive.[25]

The Limits to Economic Rationality

Implicit in most discussions of nuclear power choice is the assumption that national decisions to acquire nuclear power reactors, recycle plutonium, and otherwise develop nuclear energy capabilities are based on careful consideration of the economic costs and benefits of nuclear power. Great attention in debates over nuclear power, therefore, is directed toward such issues as the availability of alternative energy sources, future energy demand, the assurance of uranium supplies, and the economic dividends from recycling plutonium. Nuclear power proponents, for example, frequently cite the continued rise in worldwide energy demand, the skyrocketing of fluid fuel prices after the 1973 oil embargo, recent downward revisions of estimated U.S. oil reserves, alleged lower economic costs of nuclear-generated electricity compared to alternative sources of power (based on estimates of high-capacity nuclear plant operation), and the economic necessity of nuclear power for energy-poor developing nations.[26] These arguments, in turn, often are countered with reference to the declining growth rate of U.S. and global electricity demand, the limited contribution of nuclear power to overall electricity-generating capacity, the enormous increase in capital costs of nuclear plants (relative to coal-fired facilities), the failure of nuclear plants to operate at expected output levels, the ample supply of fossil fuels in the foreseeable future, and the economic irrationality of nuclear power for developing nations which lack concentrated energy demands.[27] Although both schools of thought tend to emphasize the role of economic rationality in the nuclear power decision-making process, it is likely that psychological and political considerations are just as important in national decisions to develop or expand nuclear power capabilities. This is particularly apparent with respect to less developed countries (LDCs).

It is clear, for example, that Pakistan's efforts to acquire a plutonium reprocessing facility make little sense on economic grounds. Recycling of plutonium generally is not assumed to be economical for civilian purposes unless a ratio of 20 to 1 or better exists between power reactors and reprocessing facilities,[27] and yet Pakistan presently has only one power reactor in operation and no additional reactors on order.[29] A similar situation exists for Argentina, which expects to have no more than three nuclear power plants in operation by 1985. Both Argentina and Pakistan, moreover, not only seek to develop domestic recycling facilities, but plan to rely on a reactor type (the CANDU heavy-water reactor) for which recycling is especially uneconomical.[30] More generally, those countries most attracted to nuclear power are frequently the ones for whom civilian nuclear programs are least promising economically. This appears to be the case, for example, for both capital-rich nations such as Kuwait and Libya, which have large supplies of fossil fuel and small energy demands, and capital-poor countries such as Mexico, Thailand, the Philippines, and Yugoslavia. As a representative of the International Atomic Energy Agency (IAEA) acknowledges in a major nuclear trade journal, factors such as technical and organizational infrastructure, grid size, generating unit size, and financing conditions tend to "adversely affect the competitiveness of nuclear power, particularly in developing countries."[31] Although investing in nuclear energy might not seem to make economic sense for most less developed countries,[32] this is precisely the energy route a number of LDCs have taken.

Alternative explanations for the decision by developing and developed nations to adopt nuclear power are explored later in this volume. It is appropriate here simply to note that psychological factors can override strict economic analyses of the costs and benefits of nuclear power. Such factors are, for example, "the need" to share advanced nuclear technology, the fear of missing the nuclear revolution, an unwillingness to accept a "have not" status in an openly discriminatory nuclear–non-nuclear world order, and, in the case of the more economically advanced states, the desire to be a leader in the development of a new technology.[33]

The Technological Imperative

Immediately after Hiroshima, again in the late 1950s, once more after the first Chinese nuclear explosion in 1964, and most recently following the Indian nuclear demonstration in 1974 a global alarm was sounded forecasting the rapid proliferation of nuclear weapons. Underlying these prophecies was the assumption, not always explicit, that a kind of domino theory or chain reaction was in effect whereby the violation of the nuclear weapons taboo by one nation undermines nuclear inhibitions for regional adversaries, leading ultimately to the global diffusion of nuclear weapons (the so-called *N*th country problem).

There are very real and compelling reasons to be concerned about nuclear weapons proliferation in the future. The failure of past proliferation prophecies to materialize, however, highlights the need to avoid deterministic thinking about proliferation and the mistake of equating proliferation of nuclear capabilities with the decision to exercise those capabilities. This problem of misconception, sometimes referred to as the technicist fallacy, is particularly detrimental if it leads one to conceptualize proliferation primarily in terms of technological causes and solutions rather than political incentives and disincentives.[34] Stated somewhat differently, a technicist perspective directs attention toward the *necessary* rather than the *sufficient* conditions for proliferation.[35] It also obscures the significant number of cases in which the technological imperative has, to date, been inoperative. Study of the politics of nonproliferation in countries which have refrained from proliferation despite the requisite technical and industrial capability (e.g., Canada, Sweden, Switzerland, West Germany, Japan, and Italy) can provide useful insights into alternative strategies for containing proliferation.

Grand Designs and Great Expectations

There is a tendency for individuals to attribute major events to large and discrete causes. In the realm of nuclear weapons proliferation this tendency is manifest in the search for a few underlying precipitants in national decisions to "go nuclear" and the quest for permanent, universally applicable restraints. Most studies of the nuclear power-nonproliferation dilemma and policy proposals for nonproliferation, consequently, suffer from a tendency to ignore the context-dependent nature of proliferation problems and the distinction between the causes of proliferation that cannot be altered and those contributing factors which are susceptible to manipulation and cure. Explanations, for example, which stress status-related incentives for acquiring nuclear weapons may be compelling and yet may not identify conditions over which the United States or other interested parties have substantial influence. Alternatively, although hypotheses which focus on "supply-push" factors involving, for example, the spread of nuclear technology and the development of plutonium-recycling facilities are probably not sufficient to explain weapons proliferation, they may be more deserving of policy attention if they afford the opportunity for corrective action to reduce the temptation to "go nuclear" or to manage the proliferation process better. The success or failure of alternative nonproliferation policies, in any case, will probably vary substantially across nations and will depend to a large extent on whether the primary motivation for seeking nuclear weapons is to achieve strategic autonomy, deter a regional adversary, divert domestic attention, attain international prestige, possess a weapon of last resort, or perhaps, simply a desire to gain something in return for the promise not to acquire actual weapons.[36]

An additional problem is associated with conceptualizing proliferation policy in terms of the universally applicable and single-minded goal of halting any further spread of nuclear weapons. This type of conceptualizing inclines one to divorce proliferation policy objectives from broader foreign policy considerations, and to ignore the trade-offs between specific nonproliferation policies and other important domestic and foreign policy goals. Diminishing the role of nuclear weapons in U.S. military strategy, for example, might contribute to the erosion of the prestige associated with nuclear weapons and thereby act as a proliferation disincentive. At the same time, it could conceivably undermine the credibility of U.S. alliance guarantees. Increased conventional arms transfers also might initially restrain a potential proliferator's quest for a nuclear arsenal. This might simultaneously trigger, however, a regional arms race while leading states to escalate demands in return for their future nuclear abstinence. Increased restrictions on technology transfer and the threat of or imposition of sanctions by nuclear supplier states, similarly, may have the mixed effect of erecting temporary obstacles in the path of proliferation candidates and increasing the incentive to acquire independent nuclear capabilities.

THE CONSEQUENCES
OF PROLIFERATION

Implicit in almost all discussions of proliferation is the assumption that the spread of nuclear weapons to additional states is undesirable and to be avoided, if possible. That is also the perspective shared in this analysis. It is important, however, to make explicit the logic underlying this perspective and to recognize alternative assessments. Only after the issue of the probable consequences of proliferation has been addressed, can one properly turn attention to the question of what priority the United States should give to antiproliferation efforts.

Although U.S. decision-makers and scholars have generally viewed the spread of nuclear weapons negatively, a minority viewpoint questions the assumption that an increase in the number of nuclear powers is necessarily hazardous. Fred Iklé, former director of the U.S. Arms Control and Disarmament Agency and a high-ranking official in the Reagan administration's Department of Defense, for example, at one time suggested that the spread of nuclear weapons might actually reduce the risk of nuclear war by making the superpowers less likely to intervene in local conflicts.[37] The international relations scholar Morton Kaplan has also described a theoretically possible "unit veto" international system in which deterrence results from the fact that each actor in the system possesses the capability to destroy any other actor.[38] A similar argument sometimes expressed is that the spread of nuclear weapons may create favorable conditions for regional balances which approximate the relatively stable U.S.–Soviet strategic relationship.[39] It has been suggested, for example, that the possible existence of Israeli nuclear weapons may have had a moderating effect on Arab decision-makers in 1973, and that "an overtly nuclear-ized Middle East strategic balance might facilitate a future political settlement between the Arabs and Israelis."[40] Nuclear proliferation, from this perspective, is viewed as inducing governments to behave in a more prudent fashion. It is also sometimes suggested that nuclear weapons may act as a great equalizer in international relations, enabling middle-range states to achieve a form of minimal deterrence against the superpowers. This is one effect, some argue, that the small British and French nuclear forces have vis à vis the Soviet Union.[41] Finally, there is an additional minority viewpoint which denies that the development of nuclear weapons has had any major impact, good or bad, on international politics. Possession of nuclear weapons, according to this perspective, does not induce more prudent behavior among nations, but merely reinforces existing patterns of international conduct.[42]

The anticipated consequences of nuclear proliferation have, at times, probably been exaggerated. The arguments of those who regard proliferation as benign, if not favorable, however, can be challenged on a number of grounds.

The argument that nuclear weapons would have a stabilizing influence on regional balances analogous to their alleged effect on U.S.-Soviet relations ignores the fact that to the extent that a deterrence relationship characterizes U.S.-Soviet relations, it is probably more properly described as delicate than stable and represents a theoretical goal not yet violated rather than a description of the actual relationship.[43] Moreover, the political and technical conditions usually cited as responsible for stability in U.S.-Soviet relations (e.g., invulnerable second strike forces, established systems of command and control, domestic political stability, and relative satisfaction with the status quo) are conspicuously absent in most potential Nth country strategic situations.[44] In their stead are apt to be small and vulnerable nuclear forces with tenuous systems of command and control. The existence of nuclear weapons under these circumstances, rather than enhancing deterrence stability, would probably serve as an incentive for preemptive attack and promote crisis instability. As illustrated by the Israeli raid on Iraq's nuclear facility, the danger of preemption can also be acute for a state that has not yet developed or deployed nuclear weapons but is perceived by its adversary to have embarked on a nuclear weapons program.

Even if new nuclear forces were modeled, at great expense or with superpower assistance, after the relatively secure U.S. and Soviet strategic arsenals, the proliferation of nuclear weapons would increase the statistical probability of their use through the greater opportunity for mechanical accidents, unauthorized demonstration, strategic miscalculation, and the escalation of conventional conflict to nuclear war.[45] Indeed, the record of U.S. and Soviet experiences with nuclear weapons provides little reason for optimism regarding nuclear safety or the ability of states to learn nuclear restraint.

A further problem posed by the proliferation of nuclear weapons is that negotiating meaningful international restraints on nuclear arms will probably be more difficult. The record of the past decade of the Strategic Arms Limitation Talks (SALT) indicates the difficulty of negotiating restraints between even two relatively equal nuclear powers. An increase in the number of nuclear armed states would almost certainly compound the problems of arms control negotiations, even if the proliferators did not partake directly in the negotiating process. This would likely result from the creation of new ambiguities in the superpower strategic relationship. The spread of nuclear weapons, for example, might encourage the Soviets and the Americans to reconsider the logic of a mutual hostage relationship—the theoretical underpinning of the most significant arms control accord to date, the 1972 ABM Treaty. The increased risk of nuclear weapons use due to accident, unauthorized firing, or miscalculation by parties with little experience in the management of nuclear force and poorly developed systems of command and control also might give new impetus to civil defense efforts that are destabilizing from the standpoint of mutual deterrence.[46]

Identification of the major hazards of proliferaton does not by itself provide an answer to the question of whether the potential gains from a vigorous antiproliferation effort by the United States outweigh the political costs of the effort. An answer to that question requires additional information about the objectives of U.S. proliferation policy and their place in the broader scheme of domestic and foreign policy strategy. One also can argue that the question of selecting an effective nonproliferation strategy is academic, if by nonproliferation one means the permanent and absolute curtailment of the spread of nuclear weapons. Some analysts would contend, for example, that the real proliferation issue is not *if* the nuclear dam will burst but *when* and *in what fashion*.[47] In any case, however, the risks of proliferation are substantial. Although it may be impractical to halt permanently or reverse the process of nuclear proliferation, there appears to be merit in the argument that the fewer the number of proliferators and the longer the delay in proliferation, the better.[48]

MAJOR POLICY ISSUES:
AN AMERICAN PERSPECTIVE

Since the 1973 oil embargo and the 1974 Indian nuclear test, nuclear power and nonproliferation issues have emerged as priority items on both the domestic and foreign policy agenda of the U.S. government decision-makers. Although the government's nuclear policies have not been perfectly consistent or constant and, in mid-1981, appear to be undergoing considerable review and partial revision, the key issues remain the same. They involve plutonium reprocessing and recycling, breeder reactor development, uranium-enrichment capacity, nuclear waste management and disposal, nuclear fuel exports, and technology transfer.

Plutonium Reprocessing and Recycling

At the center of the controversy is the issue of plutonium reprocessing and recycling and President Carter's decision in April 1977 to defer indefinitely the commercial reprocessing and recycling of plutonium produced in the United States on the grounds that they were not essential for a viable and economic nuclear power program.[49] Essentially, reprocessing refers to the chemical and mechanical processes by which plutonium and uranium are separated out and recovered from a nuclear reactor's spent fuel. The reuse of these products to fuel a reactor is known as recycling or recycle.

Since the early days of the U.S. nuclear weapons program, it generally was assumed that spent nuclear fuels would be reprocessed and the recovered plutonium and uranium reused as fuel. To do otherwise, it appeared, would be wasteful, especially given early Atomic Energy Commission projections of rapid nuclear power growth and concern that uranium reserves would soon be depleted.[50] The reprocessing and recycling of plutonium, moreover, were widely believed to be indispensable to the development and operation of the reactor of the future—the breeder—a reactor which produces more fissile material than it consumes and offers the promise of an almost unlimited nuclear fuel supply. Until recently, therefore, there was little doubt among U.S. nuclear policy planners about the need for the eventual development of reprocessing and recycling facilities; it was only a question as to when it would become economically feasible. Developments in the early 1970s, however, have raised disturbing questions about the inevitability and the desirability of plutonium reprocessing and recycling. These questions pertain principally to economic costs and proliferation safeguards.

The economic track record of U.S. experiments with commercial reprocessing is not impressive. The first commercial reprocessing plant was opened in West Valley, New York in 1966 and closed after six years of operation at well below capacity level and before it had recovered its original capital costs.[51] A subsequent effort by General Electric to build a reprocessing facility in Morris, Illinois also was unsuccessful and was abandoned in 1974 after an investment of $64 million. The projected cost of a third facility, under construction since 1970 in Barnwell, South Carolina, already has increased ten fold over the original estimate of $70 million.[52] Initially scheduled to begin operation in 1973, the Barnwell plant now is not expected to be ready for operation before the mid-1980s, even assuming favorable action by the Nuclear Regulatory Commission.

A number of factors have contributed to the skyrocketing costs of reprocessing facilities, including more stringent health and safety requirements for radioactive waste management and seismic protection, increased security against theft, and the difficulty and great expense of repairs. These increased costs, in combination with projections of a decline in the energy growth rate and revision upwards of estimates of uranium reserves, have led some experts to conclude that reprocessing and plutonium recycling can, at best, make only a marginal contribution to the economic attractiveness of nuclear power.[53]

Although critics of plutonium reprocessing may cite economic arguments, their opposition centers on the alleged impetus that plutonium reprocessing and recycling provides for nuclear weapons proliferation. To critics of reprocessing, plutonium is not only a potent fuel, but the stuff of atomic bombs. From their perspective, anything which increases the availability of plutonium in the nuclear fuel cycle increases the risk of diversion or theft of material directly usable for nuclear weapons.

Adherents to this position emphasize that in contrast to the present situation in which the high radioactivity of spent fuel affords protection against easy diversion of plutonium, introduction of a plutonium reprocessing and recycling economy would make plutonium vulnerable to theft and rapid fabrication into nuclear weapons following its separation at reprocessing plants. It has been estimated, for example, that a single reload of mixed oxide fuel (containing easily separable plutonium) for a standard 1000 MW light-water reactor might contain as much as 1000 kg of plutonium—sufficient for the production of as many as fifty nuclear weapons.[54] The danger of proliferation in this scenario resides not just in the increased quantity of available plutonium, but in the availability of plutonium which could be quickly accessible and relatively easily used to manufacture nuclear bombs. The reduction in early warning which would result from a quickly available source of weapons material, it is feared, would deprive international safeguards of much of their political value by reducing the time available for deterrent action or efforts to relieve or counter the pressures motivating a nation to acquire nuclear weapons.

Critics of the Carter administration's decision to defer indefinitely the commercial reprocessing and recycling of plutonium tend to view the policy as a sign of government opposition to nuclear power in general and the plutonium-dependent breeder reactor in particular. They also are less inclined to view commercial reprocessing of spent fuel as a likely avenue to weapons proliferation and they express concern that efforts to defer reprocessing will not only have unfortunate domestic economic repercussions, but will be counterproductive internationally. According to this latter argument, U.S. denial of reprocessing technology at home will undermine other nations' confidence in the ability of the United States to guarantee nuclear fuel and fuel cycle services and may actually stimulate proliferation by encouraging the development of foreign reprocessing capabilities.[55]

Both proponents and critics of recent U.S. nuclear policy acknowledge that reprocessing in the United States and other nuclear weapons states is not directly an issue of proliferation (except regarding terrorists). They also appear to recognize that pursuit of domestic reprocessing to meet U.S. energy needs while simultaneously discouraging the nuclear efforts of other states would create an undesirable double standard. Subject to debate, however, is the effect a U.S. decision to postpone the commercial development of reprocessing facilities will have on other states.[56] Many analysts are skeptical about whether the United States will achieve much nonproliferation success by setting an example which is widely opposed by nuclear supplier and recipient states alike.[57] To date, this skepticism appears to be justified. A U.S. decision to proceed with plutonium reprocessing and recycling, on the other hand, might well reinforce interest abroad in a plutonium fuel cycle and undermine U.S. efforts to contain the spread of nuclear weapons.[58]

Breeder Reactors

The issue of plutonium reprocessing and recycling is closely linked to the controversy over development and deployment of the breeder reactor. This is because the breeder, as presently conceived, and unlike the standard light-water reactor, is dependent upon a plutonium fuel cycle which includes fuel reprocessing and recycling.[59] The American decision in 1977 to defer the date of introduction of commercial breeders, therefore, raised many points of contention that resemble those of the debate over plutonium reprocessing and recycling. They include the issue of resource depletion and assurance of supply, economic costs, and proliferation risks.

Anticipation of energy resource scarcity is a major impetus behind breeder-reactor development. Incentives for rapid breeder development are provided by the knowledge that breeders are in principle capable of extracting about 70 times more energy from uranium stock than can current light-water reactors,[60] and the assumption that a continued rise in energy demand and nuclear power capacity will soon lead to the depletion of moderately priced uranium reserves. Alternatively, assumptions of continued uranium availability, the presence of alternative energy resources and technologies, and a decline in the growth rate of energy demand and nuclear power capacity are consistent with a pro-deferral position.

Although much less a problem for the United States than for other nations not so well endowed, a lack of confidence that energy supplies will not be disrupted also can provide strong motivation for breeder development. The concentration of known reserves of low-priced uranium in a relatively few countries and the fear of political and economic manipulation via international energy overdependence, for example, often are cited as arguments in favor of breeder development, even though breeder construction and fuel processing may require substantial reliance on foreign manufacturers.[61]

Because of the major uncertainties associated with projections of future energy sources and with construction and maintenance costs of various electricity-generating facilities, both proponents and critics of rapid breeder development are apt to cite economic arguments in support of their position.

The capital costs of commercial breeders are generally recognized to be substantially greater than those of light-water reactors. Advocates of breeder reactor development, however, maintain that these capital charges will be more than offset by savings in fuel cycle costs. Although few assert that breeders are presently economically competitive, breeder supporters contend that high energy growth and escalating uranium prices will make commercial breeders economically attractive by the end of the century.[62]

Those favoring deferral of the breeder, on the other hand, point to the pattern of cost overruns in U.S. reactor construction, the likelihood of additional costs for safeguarding plutonium and for environmental protection, and the utility industry's own reluctance to commit additional capital to the Clinch River breeder reactor project as evidence of the economic imprudence of rapid breeder development. In response to the argument that foreign breeder reactor progress will undermine U.S. export opportunities in the absence of an active domestic program, those favoring deferral note that the large deployment of breeder reactors necessary to justify full fuel cycle facilities (estimated to be between 50 and 100 breeders) is economically unrealistic for most countries, as is the expectation that a large export market for breeder reactors will soon develop.[63]

Recent U.S. nuclear policy has proceeded from the premise that while the economics of breeder reactors may be uncertain, the proliferation risks of the plutonium-fueled breeder are real and great. Introduction of breeder reactors, it was argued, would frustrate efforts to deter nuclear proliferation by infusing vast sums of weapons-grade plutonium into the domestic and international market and providing a vehicle by which other state, and even nonstate, actors could move quickly and relatively inconspicuously to the threshold of nuclear weapons acquisition.[64] It has been estimated, for example, that annual civilian commerce in plutonium within the United States alone would surpass by a factor of ten the total amount of plutonium produced in the entire U.S. military program to date once breeder reactor deployments reach the 1000 GW$_e$ level.[65] No matter how carefully this traffic in plutonium is regulated, it is argued, the opportunity for diversion, theft, and misuse is bound to increase.

Most supporters of rapid development of the breeder reactor acknowledge the possibility that the breeder fuel cycle could be exploited for military purposes. They insist, however, that emerging global energy needs do not permit the luxury of inefficient nuclear fuel use. They argue, moreover, that denying a state access to the breeder reactor and its associated fuel cycle does not provide a major obstacle or delay in implementing a decision to produce nuclear weapons.[66] They also dispute the ease of terrorist diversion and suggest that technological safeguards such as colocation of fuel reprocessing and fabrication facilities, "spiking" of fuel for transport (by adding other radioactive materials), and creation of multinational fuel centers could substantially reduce, if not eliminate, the hazards of diversion or theft of plutonium for weapons production.[67]

The Carter administration, it should be noted, maintained that its deferral announcement did not represent a decision to abandon the breeder program. Its expressed purpose, rather, was to "restructure the U.S. breeder reactor program to emphasize safer fuel cycle technologies rather than early commercialization."[68] Among other options it wished to consider were more resource efficient, "once through" nonbreeder reactors that would avoid the proliferation risks of plutonium reprocessing and recycling and breeder reactors with a nonplutonium fuel cycle. This reassessment effort was undertaken domestically under the Nonproliferation Alternative Systems Assessment Program (NASAP) and internationally through U.S. participation in the International Nuclear Fuel Cycle Evaluation (INFCE).[69]

Uranium-Enrichment Capacity

The need for expanded uranium-enrichment facilities and the proliferation implications of their absence were not widely recognized prior to 1974. Until then most attention to nuclear power and proliferation problems focused on plutonium as the fissionable material for explosives rather than on uranium 235 (U-235).[70] This was because the enormous cost and extreme complexity of uranium-enrichment facilities were assumed to provide a greater barrier to would-be proliferators than did access to plutonium at the "back end" of the nuclear fuel cycle (i.e., separation of plutonium from spent reactor fuel).[71] This assumption, however, was challenged following the 1974 decision by the U.S. Atomic Energy Commission to suspend the signing of contracts to supply fuel for new reactors abroad and the decision by Brazil to purchase both uranium-enrichment and plutonium-reprocessing facilities from West Germany. The reason given by the AEC for its cessation of fuel export commitments was that projected commercial demands for enriched uranium were outstripping the capacity of its three enrichment plants.[72]

The decline in nuclear power plant construction and the increase in foreign enrichment services (including those of the USSR) have relieved pressure for immediate expansion of U.S. enrichment capabilities. Basic questions related to uranium enrichment policy, however, remain unsettled, including the pace at which expansion should proceed, the kind of enrichment technologies to be pursued, and the role of the private sector in enrichment expansion.

The problematic nature of projections about future rates of growth for energy demand and nuclear power production cautions against too rapidly expanding uranium-enrichment facilities. Another principal argument voiced for delaying the rapid expansion of enrichment capabilities is the economic and proliferation uncertainties associated with alternative enrichment technologies.

Currently all large-scale enrichment facilities operating in the United States and abroad use a gaseous diffusion method which requires a very large industrial installation and an enormous supply of electricity.[73] Alternative enrichment technologies, however, are being developed that promise to lower the costs of constructing enrichment facilities and, in some instances, also reduce electric energy consumption.[74] They include the gas centrifuge process (presently at the pilot stage level of development and selected by President Carter for use in the next enrichment plant addition);[75] the so-called nozzle, or aerodynamic, enrichment process under development in West Germany and South Africa; and laser technologies, successfully demonstrated on a laboratory scale in the U.S., the USSR, West Germany, Italy, Japan, and France. Because of their low energy demand and very efficient enrichment capability, laser techniques appear to offer, in the long run, the greatest economic advantage. The same factors which make laser technology very attractive for incorporation in the nuclear power fuel cycle, however, also enhance its attractiveness for weapons proliferation.[76] U.S. decision-makers contemplating the kind and pace of enrichment plant construction, therefore, must assess a complex set of factors which involve difficult trade-offs between early expansion (probably gas centrifuge) and delayed, but potentially less costly, deployment (probably lasers), and choices between facilities which are relatively energy inefficient but proliferation resistant (gas diffusion) and highly energy efficient processes (laser and also centrifuge) which may extend uranium supplies, but at the cost of making highly enriched uranium more accessible for weapons construction.

Decisions regarding the future of U.S. enrichment policy have also been complicated by disagreement over the proper role of private industry in the expansion of uranium-enrichment capacity. Currently, all domestic enrichment facilities are owned by the government but operated under contract by private companies. Recently, however, many large industrial firms and conglomerates have made proposals to construct and operate a number of new enrichment facilities, contingent on their securing extensive governmental assistance and investment guarantees. Despite support by the Ford administration, the vehicle for meeting industry demands (the proposed Nuclear Fuels Assurance Act) failed to pass Congress. The issue of privatization, however, remains alive.

The major arguments for relinquishing government ownership is that this would encourage plant efficiency through competition and would reduce federal spending. These claims are disputed by opponents of privatization who view the arrangement of governmental guarantees sought by private industry as unlikely to encourage plant efficiency, while leaving the burden of financial risk for plant mismanagement with the government. Critics of privatization also think that diminished governmental control over enrichment technology decisions might entail substantial foreign policy costs (e.g., failure to weigh adequately the proliferation implications of promoting gas diffusion, centrifuge, or laser-enrichment technologies). These fears of conflicting private and public nuclear interests were reinforced by events in 1975, when a representative of one of the private American firms interested in building enrichment facilities in the United States approached Brazilian nuclear energy officials about the possibility of constructing an enrichment plant in Brazil at the same time that U.S. officials were in Bonn trying to persuade the West German government not to supply Brazil with enrichment technology.[77]

Nuclear Waste Management and Disposal

One of the most controversial issues, domestically, regarding nuclear power has been that of nuclear waste disposal and management. Difficulties associated with the interim handling and storage of nuclear wastes (i.e., management) and their permanent storage (i.e., disposal) have emerged as major political obstacles to nuclear power growth and have also become entangled with the issues of breeder reactor development and plutonium reprocessing.

Waste products are generated at each stage of the nuclear fuel cycle. Those of greatest concern, however, are found in spent reactor fuel. Even if the products of uranium and plutonium are removed by reprocessing, dangerous wastes remain. Management and disposal of these wastes present a problem, since the waste products are highly radioactive and contain materials with half-lives sometimes in excess of 10,000 years.

To date, management of commercial waste has been limited to storage of spent fuels in pools of water at reactor facilities and, in the case of spent fuel which was chemically reprocessed at the West Valley plant in New York between 1966 and 1972, storage in both liquid and solid form at the plant site.[78] Over 1200 tons of spent fuel already are stored at these facilities. Although interim storage at reactor sites is relatively inexpensive and expandable, the large amount of spent fuel produced domestically—about 30 metric tons annually per light-water reactor—necessitates a longer term solution. Resolution of the waste disposal issue, moreover, has been made a prerequisite for construction of additional reactors in California as well as in a number of foreign countries.

Selecting an appropriate strategy for waste management and disposal is complicated by indecision over the issue of breeder reactor development and plutonium reprocessing. Because breeder reactors require substantial quantities of plutonium to begin operation, and since until recently it was generally assumed that plutonium reprocessing would be exploited for that purpose, spent fuel was allowed to accumulate at reactor sites.[79] Until the issues of plutonium reprocessing and breeder reactor development are resolved, no decision can be made as to whether spent fuel should be permanently and irretrievably stored. The method of waste disposal also is contingent on reprocessing and breeder deployment decisions, since reprocessing alters the physical characteristics of nuclear waste elements, as well as their level of radioactivity. Alternative waste disposal methods which have been suggested include permanently storing waste in underground salt mines, embedding it in chemically inert glass, dumping it deep in the ocean, injecting liquid waste into hydrofractured rock, and disposing of it extraterrestrially.

Because of its high radioactivity and need for reprocessing, nuclear waste does not pose a major risk of theft and illicit weapons manufacture. A country with a reprocessing facility, however, would be in a position to separate plutonium from retrieved waste for use in nuclear weapons.

Nuclear Fuel Exports and Technology Transfer

The United States traditionally has been the leader in the development of nuclear technology for export as well as domestic use. For most of the period since 1954, after President Eisenhower introduced his Atoms for Peace proposals and signed the Atomic Energy Act, U.S. export policy has been guided by the philosophy that nuclear energy is an asset to humanity in general and nuclear exports a boon to the U.S. economy in particular.[80] Consequently, although the export of certain sensitive technologies—most notably those of enrichment and reprocessing—were prohibited, licenses for export of most nuclear facilities, fuel, and technology were granted routinely. This situation changed during the last half of the 1970s when an effort was made to tighten U.S. export policy. Movement toward more stringent export controls, however, has not proceeded without controversy, and has provoked harsh criticism from both the domestic U.S. nuclear industry and foreign nuclear supplier and recipient states.

The basic premise underlying recent U.S. nuclear export policy has been that although the diffusion of nuclear weapons technology cannot be entirely prevented, restraints on the transfer of sensitive technologies and materials directly usable in weapons manufacture can slow the diffusion process and provide time for the development of more proliferation-resistant technology and more effective international institutions.[81] A major manifestation of this nonproliferation perspective is the Nuclear Non-Proliferation Act (NNPA). Among the important provisions of this act, signed by President Carter in March 1978, are: (1) a requirement that all parties receiving U.S. nuclear exports place all their nuclear facilities under International Atomic Energy Agency safeguards (so-called full-scope safeguards);[82] (2) a cutoff of nuclear exports to nonweapon states that detonate a nuclear explosive device, terminate or abrogate IAEA safeguards, or engage in activities having direct significance for the manufacture or acquisition of nuclear explosives; (3) preclusion of reprocessing or retransfer of U.S. exported material without prior U.S. approval; (4) cooperation with developing countries to help them meet their energy needs through the development of indigenous non-nuclear energy resources; and (5) the requirement of presidential renegotiation of outstanding agreements to meet the new export criteria.[83]

The 1978 act states that it is intended in part to ensure that the United States "will act reliably in meeting its commitment to supply nuclear reactors and fuel to nations which adhere to effective nonproliferation policies."[84] President Carter also avowed that the United States had no intention of forcing other nations to adopt our nuclear policies. Critics of the new U.S. nuclear export policy, however, have not been impressed with these assurances, and tend to portray U.S. policy as naive, costly, and likely to be counterproductive. Although by mid-1981 the Reagan administration had not yet altered the major tenets of President Carter's nonproliferation strategy, spokesmen for the administration indicated that it might support revision of the 1978 NNPA to bring the United States more into line with other Western nuclear exporters.[85] No direct mention of the NNPA, however, was contained in President Reagan's first major policy statement on nuclear proliferation made on July 16,

1981. Indirect reference was limited to the President's appeal for reestablishing the United States "as a predictable and reliable partner for peaceful nuclear cooperation under adequate safeguards" and his instructions to executive branch agencies "to undertake immediate efforts to insure expeditious action on export requests under agreements for peaceful nuclear cooperation when the necessary statutory requirements are met." The statement also emphasized that the United States would "continue to inhibit the transfer of sensitive nuclear material, equipment and technology, particularly where the danger of proliferation demands, and to seek agreement on requiring IAEA safeguards on all nuclear activities in a nonnuclear-weapon state as a condition for any significant new nuclear supply commitment."[86]

A major criticsm of the 1978 nonproliferation legislation is that it does little to forestall access by other states to material needed for weapons proliferation, but further polarizes the international politics of nuclear energy. According to this argument, it is naive to expect that states which have flouted the NPT and the principle of full-scope safeguards in the past (e.g., Argentina, Brazil, India, and South Africa) will suddenly reverse their position and defer to U.S. requests as long as they can meet their nuclear demands from other suppliers. Whatever leverage the United States currently possesses, it is argued, is apt to erode in the near future when a number of "high risk" states acquire fuel cycles that are essentially independent of U.S. exports (e.g., South Africa).[87] It is in fact possible, some critics warn, that excessive U.S. restrictions on the supply of nuclear materials and services will accelerate the development abroad of indigenous fuel cycle capabilities which will further reduce the effectiveness of international safeguards and will exacerbate proliferation tensions.[88] The counterproductive nature of the new U.S. export policy, critics maintain, is already apparent in strained U.S. relations with both Europe and Japan. U.S. relations with members of the European Economic Community (EEC), for example, are alleged to have suffered unnecessarily from the U.S. moratorium on shipments of enriched uranium to the EEC in April 1978—an action mandated by the 1978 Nuclear Non-Proliferation Act.[89] Although advocates of a more flexible U.S. export policy do not deny the potential link between certain nuclear power technologies and weapons proliferation, they are apt to de-emphasize the role of technology diffusion as a major proliferation hazard, and to point instead to the need to reduce the economic, political, and military insecurities of potential nuclear weapon states as the preferred nonproliferation strategy.

Most supporters of stringent export controls acknowledge that the ability of the United States to influence proliferation developments unilaterally through export policy is limited.[90] They also recognize the fallacy of viewing the proliferation danger as a simple function of the availability of nuclear technology. They are convinced, however, that what the United States does can have an important demonstrative effect.[91] What is essential, they contend, is not to view U.S. export policy in isolation, but rather as part of a broad nonproliferation strategy which includes self-restraint in domestic nuclear development, the promotion of more effective international safeguards, creation of nonproliferation incentives through guarantees of fuel supply, reduction of security or prestige motives to acquire nuclear weapons, and development of an international consensus on how to manage the nuclear fuel cycle and inhibit weapons proliferation.[92] These initiatives, it generally is acknowledged, may at times cause friction among states with different energy requirements and security concerns and will not guarantee the containment of nuclear weapons proliferation. Supporters hope, however, that prudent restraints on the transfer of sensitive technologies and material can play an important role as part of a long-term nonproliferation strategy whose immediate objective is to buy time for the development of more effective safeguards and more proliferation-resistant technology.

MAJOR POLICY ISSUES:
THE INTERNATIONAL CONTEXT

U.S. concern over the dangers of nuclear proliferation is shared by many nations. More than 100 states are parties to the Non-Proliferation Treaty and other non-NPT states have agreed to abide by International Atomic Energy Agency safeguards. Indeed, what is surprising, one observer has noted, is not the growth of potential nuclear weapons capabilities, but the degree to which this has occurred within a nonproliferation regime of NPT commitments and international safeguards.[93] Since 1975, key nuclear supplier states also have shown a willingness to cooperate on guidelines for the export of sensitive nuclear materials and technologies, and no new state since 1974 has chosen to emulate India in demonstrating a nuclear weapons capability. These developments suggest the possibility of constructing a broad international agreement, if not consensus, on nuclear energy and nonproliferation objectives.

Wide acceptance of the desirability of assuring global energy needs and limiting the spread of nuclear weapons, however, should not be confused with agreement on the means to achieve those objectives. Disagreement over means is apparent in the serious reservations a number of states have expressed about recent U.S. nuclear policy developments. These misgivings relate mainly to the fairness, effectiveness, and practicality of U.S. policy.[94]

A major source of resentment toward U.S. nuclear policy on the part of non-nuclear weapon states involves the discriminatory nature of the present two-tiered nuclear order and the perceived reinforcement of the international status quo by U.S. nonproliferation policy. Although proliferation itself usually is not condoned as a means to reduce international inequities, there is a tendency on the part of the developing states to view U.S. nuclear policy in terms of North–South politics in which the less-developed Southern nations are denied their fair share of the product of the nuclear technology revolution. According to this perspective, recent U.S. initiatives seek to void the one significant concession made to non-nuclear weapon states in the otherwise discriminatory Non-Proliferation Treaty—the pledge that "all the parties to the Treaty undertake to facilitate, and have the right to participate in, the fullest possible exchange of equipment, materials and scientific and technological information for the peaceful use of nuclear energy.[95]

Nuclear supplier states have also voiced concern over the fairness of U.S. nuclear policy. Some suppliers, for example, argued initially that U.S. opposition to the development of the breeder reactor and the sale of reprocessing and enrichment facilities abroad was influenced by economic as well as nonproliferation considerations. The United States, according to one variant of the argument, sought to prevent European and Japanese export advances in areas of technology in which the U.S. lagged behind (e.g., breeder reactors).[96]

Accusations of ulterior U.S. economic motives have subsided since the nuclear supplier states reached tentative agreement in September 1977 on a code of conduct governing the export of sensitive nuclear materials and technology.[97] Until recently, however, both France and West Germany have continued to express resentment over what they regard as unnecessary U.S. interference in their nuclear policy. West Germany, in particular, has been upset with U.S. condemnation of its agreement to supply uranium enrichment and reprocessing facilities to Brazil, since it maintains that the deal requires Brazil, a non-NPT state, to accept safeguards which go far beyond those required by the IAEA.[98] More generally, the nuclear supplier countries feel that the United States continues to change the nuclear "rules of the road" without considering the legitimate concerns of other supplier club members. The Europeans and

Japanese, for example, were reportedly furious about the immediate implementation of portions of the 1978 Nuclear Non-Proliferation Act, following indications by the Carter administration that existing nuclear arrangements would remain in effect until the conclusion of the International Nuclear Fuel Cycle Evaluation.[99]

Other nations have expressed doubts not only about the fairness of U.S. nuclear policy, but about its effectiveness. These reservations include skepticism that would-be proliferators would select the relatively costly civilian nuclear power route to weapons acquisition and concern that an embargo on the shipment of fuel cycle facilities might stimulate indigenous programs which would be subject to no international safeguards. Providing nuclear assistance in return for imposing rigorous safeguards on imported nuclear facilities, it is argued, may be a more effective means to curtail proliferation than a strategy of denial.[100]

Regular meetings among the members of INFCE during 1977 and 1978 helped make the United States more sensitive to charges that it was overbearing in its pursuit of nonproliferation objectives. The resultant U.S. adoption of more flexible tactics in the conduct of its international nuclear policy and the demonstration of nuclear self-restraint domestically has apparently convinced many states that the United States is sincere in its dual commitment to strengthen fuel assurances and contain proliferation. Fundamental reservations, however, persist regarding U.S. awareness of the extent of other nations' very different energy and security needs—differences which undermine the practicality of U.S. nonproliferation proposals.

U.S. insensitivity to other nation's energy requirements, it is often alleged, stems from the vast discrepancy between the energy resources of the the United States and other countries. Unlike Japan and the industrially developed states of Europe, the United States possesses large reserves of oil, natural gas, and coal, as well as substantial uranium reserves. From an international perspective, this explains why the United States appears ready to postpone or even forgo plutonium reprocessing and breeder development. This luxury of choice, however, it is argued, is not available to other states which face immediate problems of reliable energy supply. Substantial consensus on this point of view among policy makers in Japan and West Europe is apparent in the conclusions of the International Nuclear Fuel Cycle Evaluation,[101] and in the recent Rockefeller Foundation sponsored study of international perspectives on the need for immediate development of the breeder reactor.[102] It is simply not practical, from this non-American perspective, to delay development of nuclear energy, and especially the breeder reactor. The critical nuclear policy issue for Japan and most West European countries is not primarily a question of economics or nonproliferation, but one of reducing their energy dependence to a manageable degree.[102]

Doubts regarding the practicality of U.S. nuclear policy in many industrially advanced states center on energy insecurities. Policy makers in a number of states, however, are apt to have misgivings because of other real or imagined physical security needs which may be threatened by U.S. nonproliferation policy. One can discern, for example, three kinds of security-motivated candidates for nuclear weapons proliferation that could be expected to contest U.S. nonproliferation policy. They are the pygmy states that are threatened by much larger and in some instances nuclear armed neighbors (e.g., Pakistan and Yugoslavia); paranoid states, which are relatively secure militarily and yet behave as if they were under imminent attack (e.g., South Korea and India); and pariah states that not only confront serious regional military threats but are isolated internationally (e.g., South Africa, Taiwan, and to a lesser degree, Israel).[104] For a number of these states the critical nuclear policy issue is preservation or extension of existing U.S. security guarantees. U.S. willingness to extend security assurances may produce a strong nonproliferation incentive. Alternatively, U.S. policy makers confront the possibility that retraction of security commitments, for example in South Korea or Taiwan, may prompt those countries to acquire nuclear weapons regardless of U.S. promises to assure fuel supply or impose economic sanctions.

This brief overview of the major nuclear power issues facing U.S. and foreign decision-makers indicates the magnitude of the nuclear power—nonproliferation dilemma and the lack of consensus at home and abroad as to how to proceed. This situation, however, did not develop suddenly. It can be traced to a number of prior decisions and "non-decisions" regarding nuclear power. In order to understand better the current predicament and to assess intelligently the prospects for a future national and international nuclear power consensus, it is useful to examine in the next chapter the historical context of today's nuclear problems.

NOTES

1. Useful background information on the international nuclear power market is provided by Paul L. Joskow, "The International Nuclear Industry Today, *"Foreign Affairs* (July 1976), pp. 788–803; Irwin C. Bupp, "The Actual Growth and Prob-

able Future of the Worldwide Nuclear Industry," *International Organization* (Winter 1981), pp. 59–77; Pierre Lellouche and Richard K. Lester, "The Crisis of Nuclear Energy," *Washington Quarterly* (Summer 1979), pp. 34–48; Mans Lonnroth and William Walker, *The Viability of the Civil Nuclear Industry*, Working Paper of the International Consultative Group on Nuclear Energy (The Rockefeller Foundation/Royal Institute of International Affairs, 1979); and *Nuclear Proliferation Factbook*, 3rd edition (Washington, D.C.: U.S. Government Printing Office, 1980), pp. 275-320.

2. "World List of Nuclear Power Plants," *Nuclear News* (February 1981), pp 75-94. These figures are for power reactors of 30 MW$_e$ or larger. Slightly higher figures are suggested by the Atomic Industrial Form in *INFO News Release*, March 13, 1981.

3. Despite great interest on the part of many developing states in nuclear energy, only five developing countries at the end of 1980 had nuclear power plants in operation. See "World List of Nuclear Power Plants."

4. Atonic Industrial Forum, *INFO News Release*, March 13, 1981. The figure for the United States in 1980 was 11 percent.

5. Nuclear Energy Policy Study Group, *Nuclear Power Issues and Choices* (Cambridge, Massachusetts: Ballinger, 1977), p. 5.

6. Derived from the biannual "World List of Nuclear Power Plants," *Nuclear News*. Most of this increase, incidentally, occurred between 1970 and 1976.

7. Gerald Garvey, *Nuclear Power and Social Planning* (Lexington, Massachusetts: Lexington Books, 1977), p. 27.

8. *Nuclear Proliferation Factbook*, 2nd edition (September 1977), p. 231.

9. Ibid., and "INFCE Estimates of Nuclear Power Growth in the World," reprinted in *Uranium: Resources, Production and Demand*, A Joint Report by the OCED Nuclear Energy Agency and the IAEC (Paris, 1979), p. 29.

10. Department of Energy projections reported in *Nuclear Proliferation and Civilian Nuclear Power*, Report of the Nonproliferation Alternative Systems Assessment Program, U.S. Department of Energy (June 1980), Vol. 1, pp. A-5-A-6.

11. Philip J. Farley, "Nuclear Proliferation," in Henry Owen and Charles Schultze, eds., *Setting National Priorities: The Next Ten Years* (Washington, D.C.: The Brookings Institution, 1976), p. 132.

12. Thomas C. Schelling, "Who Will Have the Bomb?" *International Security* (Summer 1976), p. 79.

13. For a much larger list of potential proliferators emphasizing technical capabilities rather than security incentives see *Nuclear Proliferation Factbook*, 3rd edition, p. 325.

14. "World List of Nuclear Power Plants," *Nuclear News* (February 1981), pp. 75-94. This calculation assumes the annual yield of 200 kg/plutonium per 1000 MW$_e$.

15. Natural uranium found in ores is not suitable for nuclear explosives. It consists of over 99 percent of the isotope U-238 and approximately 0.7 percent of the isotope U-235. The concentrate of U-235 must be increased (i.e., enriched) to about 3 percent for use in most power reactors and to about 90 percent for weapons purposes. Many research reactors, however, do use highly enriched uranium and are a potential target for diversion. For a list of research reactors, by country, that use highly enriched uranium, see Albert Wohlstetter et al., *Swords from Plowshares* (Chicago: University of Chicago Press, 1979), p. 169.

16. Richard K. Betts, "Paranoids, Pygmies, Pariahs & Nonproliferation," *Foreign Policy* (Spring 1977), p. 178.

17. Albert Wohlstetter, *The Spread of Nuclear Bombs: Predictions, Premises, Policies* (Los Angeles: Pan Heuristics, 1977), p. 32.

18. See Treaty on the Non-Proliferation of Nuclear Weapons, Article V.
19. See the discussion on distinguishing between safe and dangerous nuclear activities in Vince Taylor, "Is Plutonium Really Necessary?" (Los Angeles: Pan Heuristics, 1976), p. 1.
20. This dilemma is emphasized by Michael A. Guhin, *Nuclear Paradox: Security Risks of the Peaceful Atom* (Washington, D.C.: American Enterprise Institute for Public Policy Research, 1976).
21. The process by which different isotopes of plutonium are generated in the nuclear fission process is described more fully in Chapter 3, "The Technology of Nuclear Power."
22. See the discussion of denaturing in William Van Cleave, "Nuclear Technology and Weapons" in Robert M. Lawrence and Joel Larus, eds., *Nuclear Proliferation Phase II* (Lawrence: University Press of Kansas, 1974), pp. 42–43, and Albert Wohlstetter et al., *Moving Toward Life in a Nuclear Armed Crowd?* (Los Angeles: Pan Heuristics, 1976), pp. 9–10 and Chapter 3.
23. Albert Wohlstetter, "Spreading the Bomb Without Quite Breaking the Rules," *Foreign Policy* (Winter 1976–77), p. 159.
24. See Van Cleave, p. 43. According to the summary volume of the International Nuclear Fuel Cycle Evaluation, "The United States government has declared that commercial-grade plutonium can be used for weapon purposes and that this statement has not been challenged by other nuclear-weapon states." See *INFCE Summary Volume* (Vienna: IAEC, 1980) pp. 29–30.
25. Handling and reprocessing of the spent fuel, however, still would pose serious obstacles for nuclear terrorists as opposed to many national actors. The likely effect of power reactor plutonium on weapons efficiency and the predicability of yield is discussed in Van Cleave, p. 43.
26. Cf. Fred H. Schmidt and David Bodansky, *The Fight Over Nuclear Power* (San Francisco: Albion Publishing Co., 1976) and Chauncey Starr, "Nuclear Power and Weapons Proliferation—the Thin Link," *Nuclear News* (June 1977), pp. 54–57. See also Sivgard Eklund, "We Must Move Forward with All Deliberate Speed," *Bulletin of the Atomic Scientists* (October 1977), pp. 42–47.
27. Cf. R. Michael Murray, Jr., "The Economics of Electric Power Generation—1975–2000" in Arthur W. Murphy, ed., *The Nuclear Power Controversy* (Englewood Cliffs, New Jersey: Prentice-Hall, Inc., 1976), pp. 55–85; Wohlstetter et al., *Moving Toward Life in a Nuclear Armed Crowd?"* p. 4; and *Nuclear Power Issues and Choices*, pp. 7–16.
28. Betts, pp. 159–160.
29. "World List of Nuclear Power Plants," *Nuclear News* (February 1981), p. 82.
30. Betts, p. 160.
31. George Woite, "Can Nuclear Power Be Competitive in Developing Countries?" *Nuclear Engineering International* (July 1978), p. 46.
32. See Wohlstetter et al., *Moving Toward Life in a Nuclear Armed Crowd?"* pp. 4–5 and 74–75 on this point.
33. For a similar expression of the importance of psychological factors and the limits of economic rationality, see Lewis A. Dunn, "The Proliferation Policy Agenda: Taking Stock," Report of the World Peace Foundation Conference on Managing in a Proliferation-Prone World, Dedham, Massachusetts, December 9–11, 1977, pp. 6–7.
34. See Betts, pp. 162–164, for a discussion of the technicist fallacy.
35. Ibid., p. 163.
36. Betts, p. 178, suggests the importance of the latter incentive.
37. Fred C. Iklé, "Nth Countries and Disarmament," *Bulletin of the Atomic Scientists* (December 1966), p. 391. Iklé subsequently adopted a more con-

ventional perspective and, in fact, acquired the reputation as a strong nonproliferation advocate during the Ford administration. See his introduction to Wohlstetter et al., *Swords from Plowshares*.

38. Morton A. Kaplan, *System and Process in International Politics* (New York: John Wiley & Sons, 1957), pp. 50–52. According to Kaplan, this system is governed by the "negative golden rule of natural law"—do not do unto others what you would not have them do unto you. (p. 50)

39. See, for example, Michael D. Intriligator and Dagobert L. Brito, "Nuclear Proliferation and the Probability of War," *Public Choice,* No. 37, 1981; Harold W. Maynard, "In Case of Deluge: Where Nuclear Proliferation Meets Conventional Arms Sales" (Mimeo, USAF Academy, July 29, 1977); and Kenneth Waltz, "What Will the Spread of Nuclear Weapons Do to the World?" in John Kerry King, ed., *International Political Effects of the Spread of Nuclear Weapons* (Washington, D.C.: U.S. Government Printing Office, 1979), pp. 165–197.

40. Reported by Dunn, p. 12. See also Steven Rosen, "Nuclearization and Stability in the Middle East," *Jerusalem Journal of International Relations* (Spring 1976), pp. 1–32, and Robert W. Tucker, "Israel and the United States: From Dependence to Nuclear Weapons," *Commentary* (November 1975), pp. 29–43.

41. See Farley, pp. 136–137, for a discussion of this point.

42. This point of view is expressed most clearly by A. F. K. Organski, *World Politics,* 2nd edition (New York: Alfred A. Knopf, 1968), pp. 334–337.

43. See Farley, p. 137.

44. See, for example, Dunn, p. 12; Farley, p. 138; and Joseph S. Nye, "Nonproliferation: A Long-Term Strategy," *Foreign Affairs* (April 1978), p. 602.

45. For a discussion of U.S. government views on this point, see James E. Dougherty, *How to Think about Arms Control and Disarmament* (New York: Crane Russak & Co., 1973), p. 146.

46. A discussion of the possible impact of proliferation on the superpower strategic relationship is provided by David C. Gompert, "Introduction: Nuclear Proliferation and the 1980s Project," in Ted Greenwood et al., *Nuclear Proliferation: Motivations, Capabilities and Strategies for Control* (New York: McGraw-Hill Book Co., 1977), pp. 12–15.

47. Cf. Maynard and Dunn.

48. This is a major argument of Wohlstetter in *The Spread of Nuclear Bombs.* See p. 83.

49. "Remarks by President Carter on Nuclear Power Policy," April 7, 1977, reprinted in *Nuclear Proliferation Factbook* (1977), pp. 112–119.

50. A discussion of the early history of reprocessing is provided in Wohlstetter et al., *Moving Toward Life in a Nuclear Armed Crowd?* p. 96.

51. Simon Rippon, "Reprocessing—What Went Wrong?" *Nuclear Engineering International* (February 1976), p. 24.

52. *Nuclear Power Issues and Choices,* p. 322.

53. Cf. Wohlstetter et al., *Moving Toward Life in a Nuclear Armed Crowd?* p. 99; Taylor, "Is Plutonium Really Necessary?" p. 6; and *Nuclear Power Issues and Choices,* pp. 31–32.

54. Taylor, p. 3.

55. This argument is made cogently by Starr, pp. 54–57.

56. At the time of this writing, the Reagan administration had yet to announce formally its policy on domestic reprocessing, although the President appeared likely to lift the U.S. reprocessing ban and to bring U.S. policy more in line with its European allies.

57. The Ford-MITRE Nuclear Policy Study Group, however, was optimistic about

the influence the U.S. example may have internationally. See *Nuclear Power Issues and Choices*, p. 31.

58. This argument is made forcefully in *Nuclear Power Issues and Choices*, p. 31.
59. Although breeders can be designed to operate on either of two fuel cycles, using uranium-238 and plutonium or thorium and uranium-233, almost all breeder reactor development to date has emphasized the uranium-238/plutonium cycle. The technical aspects of these alternative fuel cycles and their economic and proliferation implication are discussed in Chapter 3.
60. *Nuclear Power Issues and Choices*, p. 335.
61. A good discussion of the assurance of supply issue is provided in John E. Gray et al., *International Cooperation on Breeder Reactors* (New York: The Rockefeller Foundation, 1978), pp. 4-8–4-10.
62. Cf. T. R. Stauffer et al., *Breeder Reactor Economics* (Breeder Reactor Corporation, July 1975), and J. C. Scarborough, *Comparative Capital Costs for the Prototype Large Breeder Reactor* (NUS Corporation, November 1977) (both reprinted in part in Gray et al., Appendix J). See also *Nuclear Power Issues and Choices*, pp. 344–356.
63. This point is made persuasively in *Nuclear Power Issues and Choices*, pp. 336 and 338.
64. For an excellent summary of the proliferation implications of the breeder reactor, see *Fiscal Year 1979 Arms Control Impact Statements* (Washington, D.C.: U.S. Government Printing Office, June 1978), pp. 253–268.
65. *Nuclear Power Issues and Choices*, p. 357. One GW_e is the equivalent of 1000 ME of electricity.
66. See C. Starr and E. Zebroski, "Nuclear Power and Weapons Proliferation," paper presented to the American Power Conference, April 18–20, 1977, pp. i and 15.
67. Gray et al., p. 4-19.
68. Nye, p. 609.
69. It is not yet apparent what impact, if any, on U.S. nonproliferation policy will follow from INFCE's finding that fuel cycles cannot be ranked in terms of their relative proliferation risk based on whether or not they employ reprocessing of spent fuel. See *INFCE Summary Volume*.
70. See note 15.
71. See Ted Greenwood, George Rathjens, and Jack Ruina, "Nuclear Power and Weapons Proliferation," Adelphi Paper no. 130 (London: International Institute for Strategic Studies, Winter 1976), p. 21.
72. Norman Gall, "Atoms for Brazil—Dangers for All," *Bulletin of the Atomic Scientists* (June 1976), p. 8. The U.S. decision to suspend the signing of enrichment contracts also had the unfortunate effect of fostering the image of the United States as an unreliable nuclear supplier.
73. It has been estimated that when the three U.S. enrichment plants are used simultaneously at peak output they account for over 10 percent of the total electric power consumption in the United States (Van Cleave, p. 49).
74. These alternative enrichment technologies are discussed in Chapter 3.
75. *Nuclear Proliferation Factbook*, p. 171.
76. To some extent this proliferation risk may be balanced by the ability of laser techniques to extend uranium supplies and thereby undermine a major rationale for the rapid development of breeder reactors and plutonium reprocessing and recycling. See Chapter 3 for a discussion of some of the technical difficulties recently encountered in laser development which may make laser isotope separation less of a proliferation danger than originally feared.

77. Edward F. Wonder, *Nuclear Fuel and American Foreign Policy: Multilateralization for Uranium Enrichment* (Boulder: Westview Press, 1977), p. 64.
78. *Nuclear Power Issues and Choices,* p. 244. Nuclear Wastes from the military program also have been stored in both liquid and solid form at three sites: Idaho Falls, Idaho; Aiken, South Carolina; and the Hanford Reservation near Rushland, Washington.
79. Ibid., p. 247.
80. The U.S. Energy Research and Development Administration estimated that the United States might earn as much as $2.3 billion annually by 1980 through exports of reactors and fuel cycle services. (Reported in *Nuclear Power Issues and Choices,* p. 377). This estimate proved to be extremely optimistic.
81. This assumption was expressed clearly by a major spokesman for the Carter administration's nonproliferation policy, Joseph S. Nye, "Nonproliferation: A Long-Term Strategy," *Foreign Affairs* (April 1978), pp. 601–623.
82. Under the terms of the NPT, non-nuclear weapon state ratifiers of the treaty must place all their nuclear facilities under full-scope safeguards. Non-NPT states who receive nuclear products, however, need place only the imported material under safeguards.
83. See Public Law 92-242, March 10, 1978. In most instances the President is given authority to waive export cutoff criteria if he determines that cessation of such exports would be prejudicial to the achievement of U.S. noproliferation objectives or otherwise jeopardize U.S. security. The Congress, however, reserves the right to override a waiver decision by concurrent resolution.
84. Section 3, Part 6, Public Law 95-242.
85. See, for example, the speech by James Malone, Assistant Secretary of State for Oceans and International Environment and Scientific Affairs, at the Arms Control Conference at Lawrence Livermore National Laboratory, May 27, 1981.
86. "Reagan Statement on Spread of Atomic Arms," *The New York Times* (July 17, 1981).
87. See, for example, Dunn, p. 6, and Charles K. Ebinger, "International Politics of Nuclear Energy," *The Washington Papers,* no. 57 (Beverly Hills: Sage Publications, 1978), p. 81.
88. Starr and Zebroski, p. iii.
89. See "Fuel Reprocessing Still the Focus of U.S. Nonproliferation Policy," *Science* (August 1978), p. 693, and "EEC Ready to Talk to U.S.," *Nuclear News* (August 1978), pp. 52–54. The moratorium was lifted only in late June after the EEC apparently agreed to renegotiate terms of the Euratom Treaty under which the United States serves as a nuclear supplier.
90. See, for example, *Nuclear Power Issues and Choices,* p. 387.
91. Cf. Nye; Wohlstetter, *The Spread of Nuclear Bombs;* and *Nuclear Power Issues and Choices.*
92. See Nye, pp. 611–620, for a detailed discussion of the Carter administration's six-pronged nonproliferation strategy.
93. Farley, p. 147.
94. These categories of misgivings are suggested by Gray et al., Appendix L., p. 40.
95. Article IV, Section 2, Treaty on the Non-Proliferation of Nuclear Weapons.
96. The argument also is sometimes applied to the light-water reactor market where the U.S. share of sales has declined markedly. U.S. export prohibitions on the sale of reprocessing and enrichment facilities, it can be argued, undermine U.S. conventional reactor sales, since European suppliers can tie the sale of a small reprocessing plant to a purchase agreement for their nuclear power reactors (John Goreham Palfrey, "Nuclear Exports and Nonproliferation Strategy,"

in Murphy, ed., *The Nuclear Power Controversy,* p. 138). Supplier acceptance of U.S. export criteria, presumably, would eliminate this U.S. export disadvantage.

97. Background on the "Nuclear Suppliers Group" is provided in Chapter 2.

98. See Gall, p. 6. The agreement does not, however, require Brazil to place all its nuclear facilities under safeguards. The German position also is inconsistent with the spirit of the NPT in that it provides special benefits to a non-NPT state.

99. See Ebinger, p. 82, and "Fuel Reprocessing Still the Focus of U.S. Nonproliferation Policy," *Science* (August 25, 1978), p. 693. For a more recent review of European perspectives on U.S. nuclear policy see Karl Kaiser, ed., *Reconciling Energy Needs and Non-proliferation* (Bonn: Europa Union Verlag GMBH, 1980).

100. Gray et al., Appendix L., pp. 40–41.

101. See *INFCE Summary Volume.*

102. Gray et al. See especially Chapter 5.

103. See, for example, Gray et al., Appendix L, p. 41, and J. P. Mustelier, "Plutonium Fuels," *Nuclear News* (July 1977), pp. 67–69.

104. The three types of potential proliferators are suggested by Betts, pp. 165–167.

Chapter 2

Historical Context

For over two decades the United States has promoted the development of peaceful nuclear energy in this country and abroad. This policy, however, represents a significant departure from the initial U.S. response to the splitting of the atom and recognition of its dual potential for military and peaceful purposes. That response was essentially to try to put the genie back in the bottle by keeping information about atomic energy secret.

Characteristic of this initial secrecy/denial approach to control proliferation was a bill introduced in the U.S. Congress in September 1945 by Senator Brian McMahon. It sought "to conserve and restrict the use of atomic energy for the national defense" and "to preserve the secret and confidential character of information concerning the use and application of atomic energy."[1] Eventually enacted as the Atomic Energy Act of 1946, the McMahon legislation acknowledged the desirability of disseminating scientific information about the peaceful uses of nuclear energy, but prohibited the international exchange of such information until Congress had established that effective and enforceable international safeguards existed against the use of atomic energy for destructive purposes.

At the same time that the McMahon legislation was being drafted in Congress, the United States proceeded at the international level to give priority to preventing the spread of nuclear weapons. In November 1945, three months after the bombing of Hiroshima and Nagasaki, the United States, Canada, and the United Kingdom announced, in a joint declaration, that because "the military exploitation of atomic energy depends, in large part, upon the same methods and processes as would be required for industrial uses," dissemination of information regarding atomic energy should be deferred until adequate international safeguards against the military applications of atomic energy were developed.[2] The three nations also proposed that a commission be set up under United Nations auspices to submit recommendations for ensuring that atomic energy be used exclusively for peaceful purposes and that inspection safeguards against the hazards of proliferation be developed. Essentially the same proposal for creation of a UN Commission was endorsed the following month by the United States, the United Kingdom, and the Soviet Union at a meeting of foreign ministers in Moscow, and in January 1946 a draft resolution creating the UN Atomic Energy Commission (UNAEC) was adopted unanimously by the General Assembly.

THE BARUCH PLAN

The United States took advantage of the new UNAEC forum in June 1946 to propose what became known as the Baruch Plan, the first comprehensive effort by the United States to address the dilemma of how to attain the potentially peaceful benefits of nuclear energy while avoiding the dangers of nuclear proliferation. Based on an internal U.S. government report directed by Undersecretary of State Dean Acheson and Tennessee Valley Authority Chairman David Lilienthal, the Baruch Plan called for the creation of an International Atomic Development Authority (IADA) to which would be entrusted all phases of the development and use of atomic energy. More specifically, the IADA was to have "managerial control or ownership of all atomic energy activities potentially dangerous to world security," "power to control, inspect, and license all other atomic activities," and "the duty of fostering the beneficial uses of atomic energy."[3] The Baruch Plan also called for ending the manufacture of atomic bombs and disposing of existing atomic stockpiles. These latter steps, however, were to be taken only after the IADA was in operation and an adequate system for control of atomic energy in effect. Finally, the Baruch Plan specified that punishment for violations of the plan was *not* to be subject to the usual Security Council veto procedure.[4]

From the American perspective the Baruch Plan was a magnanimous proposal involving the promised surrender of the U.S. nuclear monopoly in the interests of world peace. The plan, however, was viewed very differently from the Soviet vantage point. Elimination of the veto power, rather than guaranteeing swift and sure punishment for guilty parties, was seen as an attempt by the United States to facilitate mobilization of the Western-dominated United Nations against the Soviet Union. The Baruch proposal for international control over atomic energy, similarly, was seen by the Soviets as a maneuver by which the West might gain control over the Soviet economy, at least to the extent that it became dependent upon nuclear power. Inspection procedures called for by the Baruch Plan also probably raised in Stalin's mind the spectre of Western intelligence operations within the Soviet Union and possible espionage directed at Soviet military industrial facilities. Since the Soviets had yet to test a nuclear explosive, they also had some reason to regard the Baruch Plan as a strategem to perpetuate Soviet nuclear inferiority. In short, from the Soviet perspective, to have accepted the Baruch Plan's approach to placing the development of atomic energy under UN control would have been tantamount to placing it under the control of the United States.[5]

Given these reservations by the Soviets about the Baruch Plan it is not surprising that their response to the plan was a counterproposal which reversed the sequence of control and disarmament. Whereas the U.S. proposal envisioned first the creation of inspection and control machinery and then disarmament, the Soviets insisted that the destruction of all atomic weapons precede introduction of an international control system. This meant, in practice, nuclear disarmament by the United States alone. Although discussions over the alternative proposals continued for several years, fundamental differences between the U.S. and Soviet approaches to the control of atomic energy made agreement impossible.

ATOMS FOR PEACE

The passage of the Atomic Energy Act of 1946 following the Soviet's negative response to the Baruch Plan marked the height of U.S. efforts to prevent the spread of nuclear technology by "secrecy/denial." Even exchanges of information with those U.S. allies which had cooperated in the development of the first U.S. atomic bomb were prohibited. By the end of 1953, however, it was apparent that the policy of secrecy/denial had failed. The Soviet Union had joined the United States as an atomic weapon state and both the U.S. and USSR had tested hydrogen bombs. In addition to the development of more sophisticated nuclear weapons, research also had progressed on the peaceful uses of nuclear power, especially in the commercial applications of nuclear reactors for generating electricity. Moreover, it was no longer clear whether a U.S. policy of strict secrecy would encourage or discourage indigenous nuclear development programs in other states. As Secretary of State John Foster Dulles noted during testimony before the Joint Committee on Atomic Energy, knowledge about atomic energy was growing in so much of the world that it was impossible for the United States to "effectively dam . . . the flow of information." Even if we did try to do it, he observed, "we [would] only dam our influence and others [would] move into the field with the bargaining power that that involves."[6]

This change of perspective was accompanied by a shift in U.S. policy from secrecy/denial to active promotion of the peaceful applications of atomic energy. This shift was most clearly expressed in President Eisenhower's famous "Atoms for Peace" speech before the United Nations in December 1953. Eisenhower acknowledged in his address that the secret of the atom eventually would be acquired by other states and emphasized the need to exploit those properties in the atom which were good rather than evil. More specifically, he proposed that the governments principally involved in nuclear research and development make joint contributions from their stockpiles of fissionable materials to an International Atomic Energy Agency (IAEA). The agency was to be set up under the jurisdiction of the United Nations and would be responsible for the storage and protection of contributed fissionable materials. The IAEA also was to have the important responsibility for devising methods to distribute fissionable material for peaceful purposes, especially electrical energy production. Contribution of fissionable products to the IAEA, it was hoped, would also assist arms control by diverting the stockpile of fissionable materials from military to peaceful purposes. The contributing powers would, in Eisenhower's words, "be dedicating some of their strength to serve the needs rather than the fears of mankind."[7]

It took nearly four years before Eisenhower's Atoms for Peace proposals found fruition in the establishment of the International Atomic Energy Agency. Not only did the Soviet Union's opposition to the proposals need to be overcome, but substantial revisions had to be made in the very restrictive 1946 U.S. Atomic Energy Act. These changes were incorporated in the Atomic Energy Act of 1954 and included removing most controls on the classifications of information regarding nuclear research, approving ownership of nuclear facilities and fissionable material by private industry, and authorizing the government to enter into agreements for cooperation with other nations on the peaceful uses of nuclear energy. Although these agreements required guarantees by the recipient of nuclear materials or equipment that they forswear their use for military purposes, the 1954 act clearly signaled a basic reordering of U.S. nuclear power priorities. As one observer of the change in U.S. policy points out, "while the idea of safeguards and protective requirements was by no means foresaken, it now took a backseat to the promotion of atomic energy domestically and internationally.[8]

Implementation of Eisenhower's Atoms for Peace proposals required the cooperation of the USSR in addition to the revision of domestic law. Although the initial Soviet response was negative and sought to link the proposed new IAEA plan to a comprehensive general disarmament scheme, the United States was in a strong bargaining position. Passage of the 1954 Atomic Energy Act clearly signalled a new U.S. commitment to the development of peaceful nuclear applications. The United States also proceeded vigorously after 1954 to extend nuclear assistance unilaterally to a large number of countries, including some nonaligned, less developed states. Members of the European Coal and Steel Community in 1955 also had indicated their intent to create a European organization for atomic energy as a step toward the integration of their markets.[9] Unable to halt the nuclear assistance Western nations were providing to other nations, the Soviets, who were themselves reluctant to export nuclear technology with military applications, tempered their opposition to the IAEA proposals. In October 1956, after a long series of negotiations, the Statute of the International Atomic Energy Agency was opened for signature and finally came into force on July 29, 1957.

As stated in Article II of the statute, the primary objectives of the IAEA were "to accelerate and enlarge the contribution of atomic energy to peace, health and prosperity throughout the world."[10] In pursuit of these objectives the IAEA was authorized to perform a number of functions which can be divided into two basic categories: promoting peaceful uses of nuclear energy and controlling its use. Authorized functions in the former "assistance" category entail: (1) encouragement and assistance with research, development, and application of atomic energy for peaceful purposes; (2) provision of necessary nuclear-related materials, services and equipment, with special consideration for the needs of the underdeveloped countries; (3) promotion of the exchange and training of personnel; and (4) fostering the exchange of information. With respect to "safeguard" functions, the IAEA is authorized to create and administer safeguards to ensure that materials designated for peaceful purposes are not diverted to military use, and also to design and possibly administer a set of atomic energy safety standards.

The IAEA which finally emerged in 1957 was a far cry from the kind of international agency on atomic energy initially proposed by the United States in 1946. Unlike the Baruch Plan which had emphasized international ownership, management, and control of all aspects of atomic energy, the IAEA had no enforcement powers and could only detect, but not prevent, diversions. IAEA safeguards prior to the Non-Proliferation Treaty of 1968, moreover, were applied in a very limited fashion—essentially only to projects which the IAEA itself had initiated or to already existing projects at the host state's request. Finally, as one longtime participant-observer in proliferation matters points out, there was nothing in the IAEA statute which prohibited a state, having "tasted of the hitherto forbidden fruit of nuclear technology in an assisted and safeguarded project, ...from applying that 'know-how' in any way it saw fit to its own, otherwise acquired materials and facilities."[11]

President Eisenhower's Atoms for Peace program ushered in a period of relaxed control over nuclear information which, ironically, allowed the development of a U.S.-Soviet peaceful nuclear energy and prestige race in tandem with the superpower arms race. One aspect of the former competition was the rush by both the United States and the Soviet Union to declassify and disseminate a large volume of technical nuclear information. By 1958 this competition resulted in the adoption of new guidelines for information declassification in the United States which made it possible for any nation to gain access to almost all basic scientific information on research, development, and operation of plants and equipment in the field of nuclear fission.[12] During this same period in the 1950s, the United States moved to the forefront in the international nuclear export race, exploiting its lead in the field of enriched uranium-fueled research reactors to capture the market abroad. As Bertrand Goldschmidt points out, the U.S. position as the only supplier of enriched uranium for these reactors gave it an invaluable political as well as commercial advantage, and enabled the United States "to require that the reactors be used only for peaceful purposes, and be inspected first by Americans and then by the IAEA."[13]

FIRST STEPS TOWARD A NONPROLIFERATION REGIME

It would be unfair to characterize U.S. arms control policy during the Eisenhower years as unconcerned about the problems of nuclear proliferation. Eisenhower's preferred approach to nonproliferation, however, was to shun partial arms control measures such as a test ban moratorium in favor of international controls over fissionable products from which bombs could be made. Such controls, he believed, would check the proliferation of nuclear weapons until a comprehensive disarmament scheme could be negotiated replete with verifiable control and inspection procedures.[14] The Eisenhower administration's reluctance to support a partial test ban or nonproliferation treaty also was reinforced by the desire to retain flexibility in the development and deployment of the U.S. nuclear arsenal and the fear that a test ban or nonproliferation agreement might undermine the nuclear weapons programs of both the United States and its allies.[15]

U.S. opposition to the cessation of nuclear testing lasted until 1958, when the Eisenhower administration abandoned its insistence on linking a test ban to a more comprehensive disarmament program. Test ban discussions, however, continued to founder on American demands for adequate verification.[16]

The general desire of President Kennedy and his secretary of defense to put the nuclear genie back into the bottle enhanced the prospects for formal test ban and nonproliferation agreements.[17] President Kennedy, for example, explicitly linked the conclusion of a test ban with nonproliferation and admitted to being "haunted by the feeling that by 1970, unless we were successful in negotiating [a treaty], there may be ten nuclear powers instead of four...."[18] Public pressure for a test ban also increased during 1962 and 1963 as more scientific evidence accumulated on the biological effects of radioactive fallout. The main impetus for the partial test ban agreement that was finally reached in August 1963, however, was probably the October 1962 Cuban missile crisis—an event which dramatized the dangers of nuclear war and the need for arms control.[19]

Both the Kennedy administration and its successor were interested in following up the Partial Test Ban Treaty with another international accord more directly curtailing the proliferation of nuclear weapons. A major stumbling block, however, existed in Washington's commitment to the idea of a multilateral nuclear force (MLF) in Europe. Although the MLF was regarded by its proponents as a means to deter the proliferation of nuclear weapons in Western Europe by providing weapons sharing under a form of NATO control, the Soviet Union saw the MLF as a blatant attempt to give the West Germans access to nuclear arms. The Soviets therefore insisted that any nonproliferation treaty include comprehensive nontransfer and nonacquisition clauses which would have forbidden the MLF. By 1967, however, both American and West German enthusiasm for an MLF had waned and the superpowers were ready to move ahead on a nonproliferation treaty.[20]

The final major obstacle that had to be overcome was opposition on the part of the non-nuclear weapon states (NNWS), many of whom regarded the draft treaties prepared by the Soviet Union and the United States in August 1967 as one-sided and discriminatory. In particular the NNWS called for more positive obligations on the part of the nuclear weapon states (NWS) in the form of assistance in developing the peaceful applications of nuclear energy. They also sought acceptance by the NWS of a package of "purposeful measures" that included the renunciation of nuclear weapons use against NNWS, security guarantees for NNWS, and a legal commitment by the NWS to definite disarmament measures.[21] The superpowers revised portions of the treaty drafts to take account of some of these criticism by the NNWS, and on June 12, 1968 the UN General Assembly, by a vote of 95 to 4 with 21 abstentions, adopted a resolution commending the revised draft of the treaty.[22] On July 1, 1968 the Treaty on the Non-Proliferation of Nuclear Weapons was opened for signature in London, Washington, and Moscow.

The NPT went into effect on March 5, 1970.[23] By that time 97 states had signed the treaty and 47 had ratified it. These figures are indicative of both the significance of the treaty and some of its limitations.

Symbolically, the NPT was a milestone in U.S.–Soviet relations. If not the "first actively cooperative venture between the United States and the Soviet Union since 1945," as George Quester asserts, it certainly was the most significant.[24] As Quester points out, it proved "that superpower cooperation was possible and established a bureaucratic group with a vested interest in continuing it."[25] Among the five states with a demonstrable nuclear weapons capability in 1970, however, only three (the U.S., the USSR, and the UK) ratified the treaty. Most of the non-nuclear weapon powers that had or were planning significant nuclear industries also had major reservations about the treaty and were not party to it when it came into force in 1970. This group included India, Argentina, Brazil, West Germany, Japan, Italy, South Korea, Switzerland, Israel, Pakistan, South Africa, and Egypt.[26]

The support of the superpowers for the NPT and the abstention of so many would-be nuclear powers stemmed in large part from the fundamental distinctions made in the treaty between a nuclear weapon state and a non-nuclear weapon state and the differential treatment accorded them. This distinction was spelled out in Article IX, paragraph 3 of the treaty where a nuclear weapon state was defined as one that had "manufactured and exploded a nuclear weapon or other nuclear explosive prior to January 1, 1967."

The core of the NPT, from the standpoint of the superpowers, was the prohibitions and obligations in the first three treaty articles. These articles forbid the transfer "to any recipient whatsoever" of nuclear weapons or other nuclear explosive devices, prohibited NNWS parties to the treaty from manufacturing or otherwise acquiring nuclear weapons or explosive devices, and obliged all NNWS parties to the treaty to accept safeguards for the purpose of verification of their obligations under the treaty "with a view to preventing the diversion of nuclear energy from peaceful uses to nuclear weapons or other explosive devices." Nuclear weapon states, however, were not required to place any of their nuclear activities under international safeguards.

The NPT was thus discriminatory in several respects. It was inherently discriminatory in the sense that it recognized the distinction between NWS and NNWS and specified that the latter must remain non-nuclear. Most states accepted the necessity of this form of strategic discrimination, at least in the short term, if it were coupled with progress toward nuclear disarmament or at least the curtailment of "vertical proliferation." Much less acceptable to the non-nuclear weapons states was the requirement of international safeguards in the area of peaceful nuclear activities. To many NNWS, especially those with a developed civilian nuclear industry, the NPT seemed designed to confer commercial advantage to the NWS. The charge of commercial discrimination was therefore added to the list of grievances of the NNWS and ranged from very general assertions by the Argentine, Brazilian, and Spanish governments that the NPT interfered with the full utilization of nuclear technology for peaceful purposes, to more specific accusations by Switzerland, South Africa, West Germany, and Japan that Article III's safeguard requirements were unnecessarily burdensome and constituted instrusions into the peaceful nuclear activities of NNWS which might jeopardize industrial secrets.[27]

THE NTH COUNTRY PROBLEM REVISITED

Despite the reservations of many NNWS and the abstentions of several nuclear weapon powers, the NPT's entry into force in 1970 appeared to signal the emergence of a set of rules, widely shared norms, and institutions to regulate an important dimension of interstate behavior—what political scientists sometimes refer to as an international regime. The impression of a viable international nonproliferation regime was reinforced by the freeze in the membership in the nuclear weapons club for nearly a decade after the Chinese nuclear explosion, superpower progress in the strategic arms control arena, and a widely shared impression that the domino effect of nuclear proliferation had been effectively contained if not broken. This impression was severely tested on May 18, 1974 when India exploded a nuclear device and demonstrated that even a relatively poor, developing country could, with sufficient political will, circumvent the proliferation barriers imposed by the NPT and "leapfrog" into the ranks of the nuclear weapons club.[28] The deficiencies of the regime were further highlighted by the relatively mild public responses of most states to the explosion and by India's insistence that her detonation was a "peacful nuclear explosion," a claim facilitated by the NPT's unfortunate affirmation of a distinction between peaceful and nonpeaceful nuclear explosions.[29] What was particularly worrisome for nonproliferation advocates was the demonstration effect the Indian explosion might have on the many countries which had initiated or accelerated nuclear power programs in the aftermath of the 1973–1974 oil crisis.

Although Washington's public rebuke of India was very mild, the Indian explosion intensified U.S. diplomatic efforts to establish strict guidelines for the major nuclear exporting states covering the transfer of nuclear fuel and sensitive technology and facilities. Two multinational bodies meeting in secret—the Nuclear Exporter's Committee and the London Suppliers Group—were mobilized for this purpose.

The Nuclear Exporter's Committee, or Zangger Committee as it is usually known, was set up in 1970 to interpret the safeguards clause of the NPT (i.e., the provision of Article III designed to prevent the unsafeguarded transfer of nuclear supplies).[30] Although the committee of over a dozen industrialized states met periodically from 1970 to 1974, it was not until June 1974, one month after the Indian explosion, that a formal decision was reached to adopt a trigger list.[31] This list specified those items (e.g., heavy water, reprocessing plants, and enrichment equipment) whose export would trigger the application of IAEA safeguards to the facility for which items were supplied. Items on the trigger list, in other words, were not supposed to be exported to nonsignatories of the NPT unless the recipient state accepted IAEA safeguards designed to detect (but not prevent) the diversion of nuclear material from peaceful to military purposes.

Despite the adoption of the major components of its programs by the Zangger Committee, Washington felt that a more comprehensive trigger list and more stringent safeguards were necessary to reduce the risk of diverting nuclear material and technology. Consequently, in late 1974, the United States moved to organize a new multilateral body for the purpose of regulating international nuclear commerce. This body, which started meeting in London during 1975, was known as the London Suppliers Group (or Club), and initially consisted of the seven major suppliers of nuclear materials and equipment (Canada, France, West Germany, Japan, the United Kingdom, the United States, and the USSR).[32] In January 1976, these seven states exchanged letters endorsing a uniform code of conduct for international nuclear exports. The major provisions of the code, which is essentially a gentlemen's agreement rather than a treaty, require that before sensitive nuclear materials, equipment, or technology are transferred, the recipient state must:

1. pledge not to use the transferred materials, equipment, or technology in the manufacture of nuclear explosives;
2. accept, with no provision for termination, international safeguards on all transferred materials and facilities employing transferred equipment or technology, including any facility that replicates or otherwise employs transferred technology;
3. provide adequate physical security for transferred nuclear facilities and materials to prevent theft and sabotage; and
4. agree not to retransfer the materials, equipment, or technology to third countries unless they too accept the constraints on use, replication, security, and transfer, and unless the original supplier concurs in the transactions.[33]

The London Suppliers Group Agreement of 1976, it should be noted, does not ban nuclear transfers to nonparties of the NPT or to states which refuse to accept "full-scope safeguards" (i.e., to place all of their nuclear facilities under IAEA safeguards). Nor are members of the group legally bound to act according to the trigger list guidelines. Unlike the Zangger list, which has legal standing because of its direct association with the NPT, the London Suppliers' list is simply a multilateral statement of national policy. In other words, rather than prohibiting the export of sensitive reprocessing and enrichment equipment, the London Agreement attempts to minimize the proliferation risk of such exports by imposing safeguards and government promises.

One observer has noted that "in a sense, the very existence of the London Club is an admission of the failure of the NPT to establish a viable non-proliferation regime."[34] As the same source points out, "the fact that non-nuclear weapon parties to the NPT are subject to more stringent safeguards than are states outside the treaty is an absurd and intolerable discrimination."[35] Both the Zangger Committee and London Supplier Group have also evoked criticism from developing countries who regard them as the vehicle of industrialized states anxious to establish a nuclear cartel for the purpose of assuring the continued economic dependency of Third World nations.[36]

NUCLEAR REVISIONISM AND THE FORD AND CARTER ADMINISTRATIONS

Surprisingly little has been written on the politics of U.S. nonproliferation policy after the May 1974 Indian explosion.[37] Between 1974 and 1976, however, the Arms Control and Disarmament Agency (ACDA) appears to have acquired greater intragovernmental influence over nonproliferation policy. ACDA also was successful in goading the Ford administration into attaching much greater priority to nonproliferation matters, including the international implications of domestic nuclear activities.[38] This task was facilitated by a number of developments in addition to the Indian blast. Among the more significant were the none-too-subtle efforts by Pakistan, South Korea, Taiwan, and South Africa to move closer to a nuclear weapons capability; the "nuclear deal of the century" between West Germany and Brazil; congressional alarm over these developments; dissemination of the findings of a number of reports by outside experts under contract with ACDA which emphasized the deficiencies of U.S. nuclear export policy; and dwindling congressional support for the Energy Research and Development Administration (ERDA), an offshoot of the Atomic Energy Commission and a staunch opponent of restrictive nuclear export legislation.[39] The strong stand on nonproliferation taken by Jimmy Carter during the 1976 election campaign also raised the domestic political salience of the issue of nonproliferation and particularly the link between domestic nuclear policy and proliferation.

This link was forcefully acknowledged by President Ford in a major policy statement on October 28, 1976—the first presidential declaration devoted exclusively to nuclear proliferation since Nixon's brief statement accompanying the submission of the NPT for Senate ratification.[40] In his statement, President Ford announced that the United States would no longer regard reprocessing of spent nuclear fuel as a "necessary and inevitable step in the nuclear fuel cycle;" that "the reprocessing and recycling of plutonium should not proceed unless there is sound reason to conclude that the world community can effectively overcome the associated risks of proliferation"; and that the terms of existing agreements for U.S. cooperation in nuclear energy with other nations would be re-examined.[41] President Ford also directed the Energy Research and Development Administration to seek new means to meet U.S. energy needs which did not require the separation of plutonium from spent fuel and proposed an international three-year moratorium on the sale or purchase of enrichment and reprocessing facilities.

If Gerald Ford's administration initiated the trend in U.S. nonproliferation policy away from reliance upon the efficacy of the NPT and the existing nonproliferation regime, the Carter administration completed the return to an earlier American approach to nonproliferation which emphasized technology denial. The Carter approach, however, departed from past policy in emphasizing not only denial of nuclear technology to others, but self-denial. This dual denial posture was most clearly expressed in the seven point nuclear program announced by President Carter in April 1977. The program entailed:

1. indefinitely deferring the commercial reprocessing and re-cycling of plutonium produced in the United States on the grounds that reprocessing and recycling were not essential for a viable and economic nuclear program;
2. deferring the date of introduction of breeder reactors into commercial use, and restructuring of the U.S. breeder reactor program to give greater priority to alternative designs;
3. refocusing U.S. nuclear research and development programs to accelerate research into alternative nuclear fuel cycles which do not involve direct access to materials usable in nuclear weapons;
4. expanding U.S. production capacity for enriched uranium to provide an adequate and timely supply of nuclear fuels to other states in order to reduce their incentives to develop indigenous enrichment facilities;
5. revising the nuclear export licensing process to permit the United States to conclude nuclear fuel supply contracts with other countries and to guarantee delivery of such fuels in order to reduce pressure for the reprocessing of nuclear fuels by other states;
6. continuing the embargo of U.S. uranium enrichment and chemical reprocessing equipment and technology; and
7. continuing discussions with supplier and recipient states on means to achieve mutual energy objectives without contributing to the proliferation of nuclear weapons.[42]

The most significant and controversial measure taken by the United States to implement President Carter's nonproliferation program was the Nuclear Non-Proliferation Act (NNPA), passed in 1978. This legislation, based on the faulty premise that other states would remain dependent on U.S. nuclear assistance, required a cutoff, after 24 months, of all U.S. nuclear exports to non-nuclear weapon states lacking full-scope safeguards. It also (1) prohibited the reprocessing or retransferring of U.S. exported material without prior U.S. approval; (2) called for the cutoff of nuclear exports to non-weapon states that detonate a nuclear device or engage in activities "having direct significance for the manufacture or acquisition of nuclear explosive devices"; and (3) obliged the President to renegotiate existing agreements to meet the new criteria.[43] These requirements could only be waived if the President determined that failure to approve an export would be "seriously prejudicial to the achievement of U.S. nonproliferation objectives or otherwise jeopardize the common defense and security."[44] Even if such a judgment were made, the President's decision could be vetoed if within a 60-day period Congress chose to oppose the export.[45] The complexity of the NNPA and its limitations were soon highlighted by U.S. nuclear controversies with India and Pakistan.[46]

The dispute with India involved the question of whether the United States should continue to supply nuclear fuel for use in India's Tarapur light-water reactors. The dispute, however, was both intranational as well as international and pitted the Nuclear Regulatory Commission (which argued that India did not meet the NNPA export requirements for shipments already contracted because of its refusal to accept full-scope safeguards) against President Carter's foreign policy advisors (who maintained that the export license application was within the Act's grace period). Ultimately, President Carter authorized shipment of the fuel, but only narrowly avoided a congressional veto when an override resolution carried in the House but failed by a close vote in the Senate. As President Carter's own Special Representative for nonproliferation matters notes, "The issue sharply divided the Administration from its own congressional allies in the drafting of the NNPA [and] did little to improve either the U.S. image as a reliable supplier or its overall nonproliferation posture."[47]

Pakistan's efforts to build reprocessing plants and to obtain advanced enrichment technology underscored a different problem—the difficulty of stopping a nation determined to acquire nuclear weapons even when there exists "timely warning." As Gerard Smith and George Rathjens point out, "The United States and other nations became fully aware of what Pakistan was doing well in advance of the program's fruition (now expected to be in several years), but were unable to mount any concerted program that could dissuade the Pakistani government."[48]

The Pakistan case also directs attention to the hazards of substituting narrow considerations of nonproliferation policy for a broad foreign policy perspective. Having initially adopted an inflexible stance toward Pakistan, involving withholding military and economic assistance, the United States sought to reestablish closer ties after the Soviet invasion of Afghanistan. The result of this foreign policy flip-flop has been an estrangement between the United States and Pakistan without a commensurate slowing of the Pakistani nuclear weapons program.[49]

Although most U.S. public attention on the provisions of the NNPA has focused on implications for nuclear exports to India and Pakistan, the foreign policy implications of the act have probably been greatest with respect to our European allies and Japan. Indeed, despite President Carter's recognition at the beginning of his administration that U.S. proliferation policy entailed the "risk of some friction with our friends," it is doubtful that he anticipated the magnitude of friction his proliferation policies would produce.[50]

With the principal exceptions of Australia and Canada, reaction to the Carter administration's nuclear revisionism was emphatically negative. France resented but eventually acceded to U.S. pressure to cancel its March 1976 agreement to provide Pakistan with a reprocessing capability; West Germany and Brazil resented but successfully resisted similar U.S. efforts to cancel their June 1975 agreement involving the sale to Brazil of a complete nuclear fuel cycle; Japan resented U.S. attempts to block the commissioning of the Tokai Mura reprocessing plant, but agreed to compromise after protracted and bitter negotiations; and the less developed countries almost uniformly resented what they perceived to be a cavalier and callous U.S. attitude toward their energy problems and aspirations.[51]

As noted in the conclusion to Chapter 1, the negative reaction overseas to the Carter administration's nonproliferation policy can be traced in large part to a basic skepticism abroad about the efficacy of a nonproliferation strategy which restricts energy in an energy-hungry world. The resource-poor Europeans and Japanese simply do not regard it as practical to follow the U.S. example of delaying nuclear energy development, especially commercial reprocessing and the breeder reactor. They also question the reliability of the United States as a provider of either "front end" (uranium ore supply, preparation, and enrichment) or "back end" (waste treatment and storage) services and point out that despite frequent expressions of support regarding fuel assurances and spent fuel storage, there has been little in the way of policy implementation. Finally, they suspect that the anti-breeder bias in U.S. nonproliferation policy may have commercial as well as security origins since U.S. industry has a major economic stake in the future of the light-water reactor and lags behind competitors in breeder technology.

THE INTERNATIONAL NUCLEAR FUEL CYCLE EVALUATION

At the same time that President Carter announced his plans in 1977 to initiate legislation culminating in the Nuclear Non-Proliferation Act, he sought to promote international acceptance of his nonproliferation policy by proposing an International Nuclear Fuel Cycle Evaluation (INFCE). As described by Joseph Nye, one of the architects of the Carter administration's nonproliferation policy, the idea behind INFCE was "to have both the supplier countries and the consumer countries come together to study the technical and institutional problems of organizing the nuclear fuel cycle in ways which provide energy without providing weaponry."[52]

Although INFCE oficially was defined as a "technical and analytical study" and not a negotiation, procedural disputes reflecting political stands often dominated discussions of the 8 working groups in the 61 meetings held over a 2-year period.[53] This was not surprising given the extraordinarily broad range of views represented by the 46 countries and 5 international organizations which participated in the working group sessions.[54] It was also to be expected that in evaluating alternative fuel cycles and their proliferation risks the values attached to energy self-sufficiency and nonproliferation would vary according to a country's military and energy security needs. The Communiqué of the Final INFCE Plenary Conference, issued in February 1980, clearly reflects those competing national perspectives in announcing that the INFCE findings simultaneously have strengthened the views that (1) "nuclear energy is expected to increase its role in meeting the world's energy needs and can and should be widely available to that end"; (2) "effective measures can and should be taken to meet the specific needs of developing countries in the peaceful uses of nuclear energy"; and (3) "effective measures can and should be taken to minimize the danger of the proliferation of nuclear weapons without jeopardizing energy supplies or the development of nuclear energy for peaceful purposes."[55]

It is probably correct, as Joseph Nye contends, that no country "won" at INFCE and that nearly all countries, including the United States, achieved support for a portion of their position.[56] Most pleasing to the United States were the findings that: (1) the projected demand for uranium was much less than had been generally accepted prior to INFCE; (2) recycling in thermal reactors was not apt to promote substantial economic savings; (3) safe storage or disposal of spent fuel did not require reprocessing; and (4) breeder reactor programs did not make sense for countries with small electrical power grids. These findings might be interpreted as reducing pressures for the widespread and premature use of plutonium and as supporting U.S. policy.[57] A contrary and, from the U.S. perspective, less optimistic interpretation, however, also may be drawn from a major conclusion of INFCE that fuel cycles cannot be ranked in terms of their proliferation risk. This finding that once-through fuel cycles are not necessarily more proliferation resistant than those based on the reprocessing of spent fuel is directly at odds with the fundamental premise of U.S. nonproliferation policy between 1976 and 1981.[58]

THE STATUS OF THE NUCLEAR NONPROLIFERATION REGIME

One significant effect of INFCE was to focus international attention on what previously was primarily a North American concern—the nuclear power/nonproliferation linkage. In a number of governments this increased attention probably resulted in the readjustment upwards of the priority nonproliferation objectives received in competition with other foreign policy goals. It remains to be seen, however, whether this heightened global interest in nonproliferation will be long lasting and whether INFCE will provide much assistance in reestablishing the basis for a consensus on a revitalized nonproliferation regime.

On the one hand, it can be argued that as a result of INFCE the U.S. nonproliferation posture has moved toward the mainstream of international thinking (i.e., away from the extreme position of repudiating altogether reprocessing and breeders toward a position of acknowledging that the problem of proliferation "is not sensitive materials and technologies as much as sensitive countries.")[59] This shift in U.S. policy appears to have accelerated under the Reagan administration and may bring the United States into line with other nuclear exporting states. The change in nuclear policy is reflected domestically through support for the Clinch River breeder reactor (a project President Carter unsuccessfully sought to kill throughout his four year term of office,[60] and internationally through efforts to improve ties with such near-nuclear and non-NPT-party states as Pakistan, Argentina, Brazil, and South Africa.[61]

Some observers, like Joseph Nye, also credit INFCE with having strengthened the fuel cycle aspects of the nonproliferation regime. They maintain, for example, that "INFCE helped to build [international] agreement that safeguard improvements are feasible and necessary if the basic bargain of the nuclear regime is to be kept."[62] They also perceive the emergence of an "evolving consensus on the reservation of plutonium for breeders," the need for international spent fuel storage, and the provision of long-term fuel supply assurances.[63]

Other analysts, like George Quester, Ted Greenwood, and Robert Haffa, also are optimistic that maintenance of an effective nonproliferation regime today is possible, although they are less inclined to credit INFCE as the source of their optimism.[64] For Quester, the basis for optimism about regime maintenance is simply the perception that the global community increasingly regards proliferation as a bad and avoidable phenomenon.[65] He is thus inclined not to attach much importance to the failure of the Second NPT Review Conference in August 1980 to produce a final declaration reaffirming support for the value of the treaty's principles and provisions and is more impressed with the relatively small number of states actively pursuing a nuclear weapons capability today.[66] For Greenwood and Haffa, the basis for optimism is the belief that the market mechanism itself (i.e., reduced electricity demand, reduced rate of expansion in the nuclear power industry, excess global uranium-enrichment capacity, and the high cost of reprocessing and breeder reactors) will provide the key to achieving broad acceptance of a revitalized nonproliferation regime. The promise of a "global nuclear bargain," to use their words, is viewed as the cornerstone for a regime in which assurances of access to economically justifiable nuclear-fuel-cycle materials and services would be coupled with the limitation of weapons-sensitive reprocessing, enrichment, and breeder facilities to those countries that already have domestic programs.[67]

A rather different and more pessimestic view of the international nonproliferation regime in the 1980s, however, can also be discerned. It regards U.S. nonproliferation policy as based on an inflated view of American leverage and points to the increasing balkanization of nuclear politics. It is skeptical that either INFCE or any other multinational arrangement can reverse that process of fragmentation and believes that we are witnessing a global nuclear-industry depression in the post-hegemonic era of the United States in international economics and technology. Under such conditions, it is argued, a real danger exists that rather than promoting a revitalized nonproliferation regime based on a "global nuclear bargain," a new era of competition among nuclear exporting states will emerge, fueled by the domestic economic plight of nuclear industries.[68] In other words, it is possible to make the plausible and pessimistic forecast for the post-INFCE decade that because of domestic nuclear difficulties, governments will act first to protect their national industries and will pursue unilateral advantage and national economic solutions before they consider multinational economic interest or the promotion of a viable, international non-proliferation regime.[69] Before we can adequately discuss the economic and political factors which determine the prospects for regime maintenance and decay, however, we must examine the technology of nuclear power.

NOTES

1. The text of the bill is provided in Richard G. Hewlett and Oscar E. Anderson, *The New World: 1939-1946: A History of the U.S. Atomic Energy Commission,* volume 1 (University Park: Pennsylvania State University, 1962), Appendix 1.
2. See "Joint Declaration by the Heads of Government of the United States, the United Kingdom, and Canada, November 15, 1945," in *Documents on Disarmament, 1945-1959,* volume 1 (Washington, D.C.: Department of State, 1960), pp. 1-3.
3. Statement by Bernard Baruch, U.S. Representataive to the United Nations Atomic Energy Commission, June 14, 1946 in *Documents on Disarmament, 1945-1959,* vol. 1, pp. 7-11.
4. Unlike the Baruch Plan, the Acheson-Lilienthal Report had not recommended granting the IADA powers to impose sanctions because of Acheson's conviction that formal sanctions were ineffective in the absence of superpower accord. Bernard Baruch, Truman's choice to present the substance of the report to the UNAEC, however, was able to convince Truman that the plan must provide for "immediate, swift, and sure punishment" for violators and that the permanent members of the Security Council should not be allowed to veto sanctions approved by the council majority. For a discussion of the intra-U.S. bargaining which preceded the formulation of the Baruch Plan see John H. Barton and Lawrence D. Weiler, eds., *International Arms Control* (Stanford: Stanford University Press, 1976), pp. 70-71.
5. William Epstein reports that Nikita Khrushchev said precisely that in discussing Soviet reaction to the Baruch Plan in 1962 with a group of American journalists.

See William Epstein, *The Last Chance* (New York: The Free Press, 1975), p. 12. See also Barton and Weiler, p. 71, and William B. Bader, *The United States and the Spread of Nuclear Weapons* (New York: Pegasus, 1968), pp. 19-20.

6. Cited in Michael A. Guhin, *Nuclear Paradox: Security Risks of the Peaceful Atom* (Washington, D.C.: American Enterprise Institute, 1976), p. 10.

7. The text of the "Atoms for Peace" speech may be found in *The Congressional Record,* volume 100 (January 7, 1954), pp. 61-63.

8. Guhin, p. 11.

9. The European Atomic Energy Community (EURATOM), formally came into being in March 1957 at the same time as the establishment of the European Economic Community.

10. Statute of the International Atomic Energy Agency reported in *Nuclear Proliferation Factbook,* 2nd ed. (Washington, D.C.: U.S. Government Printing Office, 1977), p. 43.

11. Epstein, p. 16. In terms of budgetary and manpower allocations, the nuclear assistance functions of the IAEA clearly dominate those of proliferation watchdog. The breakdown for the 1977 IAEA budget reveals the following distribution among promotion and development and control functions:

	Budget	Manpower
Promotion and development	68%	67%
Control	32%	33%

These figures assume that the resources for administration are equally apportioned to the fields of substance. Data is reported by Christian Loeck, "The Present International Nuclear Regime: Survey and Evaluation of Selected International Organizations," paper presented at the Annual Meeting of the International Study Association, March 21-24, 1979, p. 13.

12. See Harold Neiburg, *Nuclear Secrecy and Foreign Policy* (Washington, D.C.: Public Affairs Press, 1964), pp. 89-101.

13. Bertrand Goldschmidt, "A Historical Survey of Nonproliferation Policies," *International Security* (Summer 1977), p. 73. See also Peter deLeon, *Development and Diffusion of the Nuclear Power Reactor* (Cambridge, Massachusetts: Ballinger, 1979).

14. See Bader, pp. 23-25.

15. See Bader on this point, pp. 24-25.

16. See Bader, pp. 25-26 and Barton and Weiler, pp. 101-103.

17. See Bader, p. 45 and George Quester, *The Politics of Nuclear Proliferation* (Baltimore: The Johns Hopkins Press, 1973), p. 21.

18. President Kennedy as quoted by Arthur Schlesinger, *A Thousand Days,* cited in Jonathan E. Medalia, "Problems in Formulating and Implementing Effective Arms Control Policy: The Nuclear Test Ban Case," *Stanford Journal of International Studies* (Spring 1972), p. 138.

19. For the text of the Treaty Banning Nuclear Weapons Tests in the Atmosphere, in Outer Space and Under Water, see Barton and Weiler, pp. 355-357.

20. See Barton and Weiler, pp. 296-301, and Quester, pp. 22-23.

21. A useful discussion of the clash between the NWS and the NNWS over the making of the NPT is provided by Epstein, pp. 70-85. Among the more active NNWS in the debate over the NPT were Brazil, Canada, India, Mexico, Romania, and Sweden.

22. Voting against the UN resolution were Albania, Cuba, Tanzania, and Zambia. Abstaining were Algeria, Argentina, Brazil, Burma, Burundi, the Central African Republic, Congo (Brazzaville), France, Gabon, Guinea, India, Malawi,

Mali, Mauritania, Niger, Portugal, Rwanda, Saudi Arabia, Sierra Leone, Spain and Uganda. See Epstein, pp. 83–84, for the text of the resolution.

23. Ratification of the treaty by the United States was delayed by the Soviet intervention in Czechoslovakia. The Soviet Union delayed ratification until West Germany had signed. See Appendix A of this book for the text of the treaty.

24. Quester, p. 23. The 1963 Partial Test Ban Treaty, one might argue, was an earlier example of active U.S.–Soviet cooperation.

25. Ibid.

26. West Germany, Italy, Japan, South Korea, and Switzerland had signed but not ratified the treaty by March 1970.

27. For a discussion of the charges of commercial discrimination see Ian Smart, "Nonproliferation Treaty: Status and Prospects," in Anne W. Marks, ed., *NPT: Paradoxes and Problems* (Washington, D.C.: Arms Control Association, 1975), pp. 22–25.

28. Although India's entry into the nuclear explosives club was a shock to many, the term "leapfrog" may obscure the twenty year technical effort which preceded the Indian nuclear explosion.

29. Although not incorporated into the NPT, a number of statements were made by the United States and other nations during the negotiation of the treaty which disclaimed any technical difference between a PNE and a nuclear weapon. The United States gave the Indians a diplomatic note on this subject in 1971. (Personal memorandum, Thomas Graham, July 1981.)

30. Little information is available on the origin or work of the Zangger Committee whose sessions are conducted in secret. The most detailed discussion, at odds with some other accounts, is provided in Ashok Kapur, *International Nuclear Proliferation* (New York: Praeger, 1979), pp. 69–80. See also Charles Ebinger, "International Politics of Nuclear Energy," *The Washington Papers*, No. 57 (1978), pp. 52–53, and *SIPRI Yearbook 1977* (Cambridge, Massachusetts: MIT Press, 1977), pp. 20–21.

31. The initial members of the Zangger Committee were Austria, Belgium, Canada, Denmark, France, West Germany, Italy, Japan, the Netherlands, Norway, Sweden, Switzerland, the United Kingdom, and the United States. The few available public accounts differ on the significance of the May 1974 Indian test for the timing of the Zangger Committee decision to adopt a trigger list.(Cf. Kapur, p. 76, and Ebinger, p. 52.) At a minimum, the Indian explosion lent urgency to the committee's decision.

32. The club was expanded in 1976 to include Belgium, Czechoslovakia, East Germany, Italy, the Netherlands, Poland, Sweden, and Switzerland. For a discussion of the club see *SIPRI Yearbook 1977,* pp. 20–24, and The Office of Technology Assessment, *Nuclear Proliferation and Safeguards* (New York: Praeger 1977), pp. 220–223.

33. *Nuclear Proliferation and Safeguards,* p. 221.

34. *SIPRI Yearbook 1977,* p. 23.

35. Ibid.

36. For a discussion of this point, see Munir A. Khan, "Nuclear Energy and International Cooperation: A Third World Perception of the Erosion of Confidence," Working Paper for the International Consultative Group on Nuclear Energy, Rockefeller Foundation/Royal Institute of International Affairs (September 1979).

37. One of the best accounts is provided by Duncan L. Clarke, *Politics of Arms Control: The Role and Effectiveness of the U.S. Arms Control and Disarmament Agency* (New York: Free Press, 1979). See also Michael J. Brenner, "Nuclear

Non-Proliferation: Policy Choices and Government Organization," Occasional Paper No. 4, Center for Arms Control and International Studies, University of Pittsburgh, 1977.
38. See Clarke, p. 83.
39. Ibid, pp. 83–85.
40. Ibid, p. 83. For the text of President Ford's remarks see "Statement by the President on Nuclear Policy," Press Release, Office of the White House Press Secretary, October 28, 1976. President Ford's policy statement was largely based upon the Fri Report, a comprehensive study of domestic nuclear activities ordered by the National Security Council.
41. "Statement by the President on Nuclear Policy."
42. See "Remarks by President Carter on Nuclear Power Policy," April 7, 1977, reprinted in *Nuclear Proliferation Factbook*, pp. 112–119.
43. See Public Law 95-242, March 10, 1978. Useful discussions of the Non-Proliferation Act of 1978 are provided by Leonard Weiss, "Nuclear Safeguards: A Congressional Perspective," *Bulletin of the Atomic Scientists* (March 1978), pp. 27–33; Frederick Williams, "The United States Congress and Nonproliferation," *International Security* (Fall 1978), pp. 45–50; Thomas I. Neff and Henry D. Jacoby, "Nonproliferation Strategy in a Changing Nuclear Fuel Market," *Foreign Affairs* (Summer 1979), pp. 1123–1144; Warren H. Donnelly, "The Nuclear Non-Proliferation Act of 1978, Public Law 95-242: An Explanation," Congressional Research Service Report No. 78-1985, October 28, 1978; and Ronald Bettauer, "The Nuclear Non-Proliferation Act of 1978," *Law and Policy in International Business* (1978), pp. 1105–1180.
44. Public Law 95-242, "Conduct Resulting in Termination of Nuclear Exports."
45. If Congress objects to the nuclear export, no further exports can be made to the state in question during the remainder of that term of Congress unless the state agrees to full-scope safeguards, the president notifies Congress that he or she has determined that "significant progress has been made in getting such agreement," or the president determines that U.S. foreign policy interests dictate reconsideration and Congress removes its objection.
46. Useful discussions of the Indian and Pakistani nuclear export controversy are provided by R. Jeffrey Smith, "Fight Brewing Over Reactor Fuel for India," *Science* (June 6, 1980), pp. 1124–1125; Lewis Dunn, "Half Past India's Bang," *Foreign Policy* (Fall 1979), pp. 71–89; and Richard Betts, "India, Pakistan, and Iran," in Joseph A. Yager, ed., *Nonproliferation and U.S. Foreign Policy* (Washington, D.C.: The Brookings Institution, 1980), pp. 323–365.
47. Gerard Smith and George Rathjens, "Reassessing Nuclear Nonproliferation Policy," *Foreign Affairs* (Spring 1981), p. 884.
48. Ibid.
49. In fairness to the Carter administration it should be noted that the restrictive American nuclear export legislation may have been helpful in convincing the French to cancel their controversial nuclear deal with Pakistan by demonstrating that the United States was serious about nonproliferation and was prepared to pay a price in its bilateral relations.
50. President Carter's speech at Notre Dame University, May 1977 cited in *Strategic Survey 1977* (London: International Institute for Strategic Studies, 1978), p. 109.
51. An excellent discussion of European perspectives on the Carter Administration's nonproliferation policy is provided by Pierre Lellouche, "Breaking the Rules without Quite Stopping the Bomb: European Views," *International Organization* (Winter 1981), pp. 39–58. See also Karl Kaiser, "The Great Nuclear

Debate: German–American Disagreements," *Foreign Policy* (Spring 1978), pp. 83–110; and Erwin Hackel, Karl Kaiser, and Pierre Lellouche, *Nuclear Policy in Europe: France, Germany and the International Debate* (Bonn: Forschungsinstitut der Deutschen Gesellschaft fur Auswartige Politik, 1980). An extended discussion of Japanese perceptions is presented in Ryukichi Imai and Henry S. Rowen, *Nuclear Energy and Nuclear Proliferation: Japanese and American Views* (Boulder, Colorado: Westview Press, 1980). Third World perspectives are discussed by Munir A. Khan, "Nuclear Energy and International Cooperation."

52. Joseph S. Nye, "Nonproliferation: A Long-Term Strategy," *Foreign Affairs* (April 1978), p. 615. See also Nye, "Maintaining a Nonproliferation Regime," *International Organization* (Winter 1981), pp. 15–38.

53. See Final Communiqué of the Organizing Conference of the International Fuel Cycle Evaluation reprinted in *INFCE Summary Volume* (Vienna: IAEA, 1980), pp. 259–260. The eight INFCE working groups had responsibility for the following topics: (1) Fuel and Heavy Water Availability; (2) Enrichment Availability; (3) Assurances of Long-Term Supply of Technology, Fuel, Heavy Water, and Services in the Interest of National Needs Consistent with Non-Proliferation; (4) Reprocessing, Plutonium Handling, Recycling; (5) Fast Breeders; (6) Spent Fuel Management; (7) Waste Management and Disposal; (8) Advanced Fuel Cycle and Reactor Concepts. The final reports of INFCE were published by the IAEA in nine volumes and comprised the eight working group reports and a summary volume. They are distributed in the United States by UNIPUB, Inc.

54. A list of INFCE participants is provided in *INFCE Summary Volume*, p. 276.

55. Excerpted from the Communiqué of the Final INFCE Plenary Conference, February 27, 1980, reprinted *INFCE Summary Volume*, p. 276.

56. Nye, "Maintaining a Nonproliferation Regime," p. 25.

57. This is the interpretation given by Nye "Maintaining a Nonproliferation Regime," p. 26.

58. See Ted Greenwood and Robert Haffa, Jr., "Supply Side Non-Proliferation," *Foreign Policy* (Spring 1981), p. 131.

59. Mason Willrich cited in Pierre Lellouche, "Internationalization of the Nuclear Fuel Cycle and Nonproliferation Strategy," SJD Diss. (Harvard Law Sch. , 1979), p. 223.

60. See Robert Rosenblatt, "Reagan to Fund Construction of Breeder Reactor," *Los Angeles Times* (February 26, 1981).

61. See, for example, Tyler Marshall, "Better Ties with Pakistan a Defense Issue," *Los Angeles Times* (March 2, 1981).

62. Nye, "Maintaining a Nonproliferation Regime," pp. 29–30.

63. Ibid., p. 30.

64. See George Quester, "Introduction: In Defense of Some Optimism," *International Organization* (Winter 1981) and Greenwood and Haffa, pp. 125–140.

65. See Quester, "Introduction," pp. 1 and 8.

66. Quester attributes the declaration of support for the NPT at the 1975 Review Conference to the parliamentary talents of the Conference President, Inga Thorrson, rather than to greater support for the treaty in 1975 than in 1980, (Quester seminar at the University of California, Los Angeles, February 24, 1981). For analyses of the 1980 NPT Review Conference see "The NPT Review Conference," *Arms Control Today* (February 1981), pp. 3–9; K. Subrahmanyam, India's Stand Against NPT Vindicated," *Indian and Foreign Review* (November 1,

1980, pp. 8–10.
67. See Greenwood and Haffa, pp. 134–135.
68. See Lellouche, "Internationalization of the Nuclear Fuel Cycle and Nonproliferation Strategy," p. 217 on this prospect.
69. Ibid.

Chapter 3

The Technology of Nuclear Power

There is a tendency in the literature on nuclear power and nonproliferation to regulate discussion of nuclear power technology to an appendix, if the topic receives attention at all.[1] Perhaps this is due to the complexity of the issue and/or the aversion of social scientists to mixing the precision and theoretical elegance of nuclear physics and engineering with the atheoretical mode of analysis characteristic of most work in the "soft sciences." While the matter of nuclear technology is indeed complex, and although an introduction to the topic may highlight the imprecise nature of subsequent chapters on the economics and politics of nuclear power, many of the policy questions relating to nonproliferation are closely linked to the details of nuclear power technology and demand familiarity with the topic. For example, an assessment of the proliferation risks associated with the sale of alternative reactors requires knowledge of their respective fuel characteristics, on-line refueling capabilities, operation by-products, and dependence on enrichment and reprocessing support facilities. The design of one popular power reactor, for instance, enables it to be refueled without shutdown—an advantage in terms of the continuous generation of electricity, but a nonproliferation liability in terms of the increased difficulty it poses for guarding against the diversion of nuclear material. This same reactor has the nonproliferation asset of not requiring uranium enrichment or spent fuel reprocessing support facilities, but produces more plutonium as a by-product of operation than do other popular power reactors. Comparable knowledge of nuclear power technology is necessary in order to assess the proliferation resistance of alternative nuclear fuel cycles, enrichment processes, and waste disposal strategies.

NUCLEAR FISSION TECHNOLOGY: BASIC CONCEPTS[2]

Atoms and Isotopes

The *atom* is the fundamental building block of any chemical element. In the nucleus, or core, of the atom, there are two principal types of particles: protons and neutrons. All atoms of a particular chemical element have the same number of protons, but the number of neutrons present can vary. All atoms of uranium, for example, have 92 protons, but can have anywhere from 140 to 147 neutrons. Atoms of the same chemical element whose nuclei contain different numbers of neutrons are known as *isotopes*. Isotopes are denoted by the total number of neutrons and protons: U-235 is thus a uranium atom with 143 neutrons and 92 protons, while U-238 is a uranium atom with 146 neutrons and 92 protons.

Fission

Some heavy elements, particularly the isotopes of uranium and plutonium, split into atoms of lighter elements when bombarded by neutrons. Accompanying this splitting of the nucleus (i.e., fission) is the release of a tremendous amount of energy and the emission of two or more new neutrons. In order for a fission reaction to be self-sustaining, it is necessary, on the average, for at least one of the new neutrons emitted when a nucleus splits to strike another nucleus. Both nuclear reactors and fission nuclear weapons are based on this principle of chain reaction. The major difference between the two is that in reactors the rate of fission is carefully controlled.

Although many heavy atomic nuclei are fissionable, only a small portion of them are *fissile,* that is, fissionable by neutrons of all energies, including those with a relatively low velocity (low energy) as well as those that are fast-moving (high energy). Uranium-233 (U-233), U-235, and plutonium-239 (Pu-239) are fissile materials, while U-238 and thorium-232 (Th-232), both abundant in nature, are only fissionable by fast neutrons. From a practical point of view, fission weapons can only be made from fissile materials.[3]

The fissile materials U-233, U-235, and Pu-239 cannot be obtained in pure form. In nature U-235 is mixed with U-238 in the proportion of approximately 7 parts to 1000. U-233 and Pu-239 do not appear in nature but can be bred in nuclear reactors. The fertile element U-238, for example, can be converted into fissile Pu-239 by making it capture a slow-moving neutron.[4] Similarly, Th-232 can breed U-233 by neutron irradiation in a reactor.

Critical Mass

In order to sustain a chain reaction, whether in a reactor or in a bomb, a critical mass of fissile material must be present. The exact mass is dependent upon a number of factors, including the particular fissile isotope present, its concentration, and the geometrical arrangement of the material. Because a sphere has the highest volume-to-surface ratio of any solid shape and the least number of escaping neutrons per unit of material, it is the shape for which the critical mass is smallest.[5] For a sphere of U-235 the critical mass is approximately 50 kg, for U-233 about 12 kg, and for Pu-239 as low as 10 kg. If the material is surrounded by a substance capable of reflecting some of the neutrons which would otherwise escape, or if it is compressed to increase its density, a lower critical mass can be obtained. Under these circumstances, an efficient nuclear explosive can be achieved with about 4 to 5 kg of U-233 and Pu-239 (a sphere less than the size of a baseball) and 11 kg of U-235.[6]

To date, only U-235 and Pu-239 appear to have been used to manufacture stockpiled nuclear weapons, and it is not clear whether any state has actually tested a U-233 bomb.[7] With the exception of China, all of the first tests of the six states that exploded nuclear devices used explosives made from plutonium.

Although reactors designed to yield plutonium for weapons produce relatively pure Pu-239, power reactors generally produce plutonium containing significant amounts of Pu-240, an isotope which complicates the construction of nuclear explosives because of its high rate of spontaneous fission. Pu-240 is also more radioactive and hazardous to handle than Pu-239. Despite these problems, it is now generally accepted in the public literature that "the overall added complexity in bomb design and loss of efficiency resulting from use of 'reactor-grade' plutonium is not so great as to preclude its use."[8]

With respect to uranium-based nuclear weapons, most public estimates place the enrichment levels used by the present nuclear weapons states at 90 percent or more of U-235. Greenwood et al., however, suggest that "theoretically, uranium weapons can be made from mixtures of U-235 and U-238 containing about 10 percent U-235."[9]

The rate of fission in a nuclear reactor is carefully controlled at a constant speed over a long period of time. In contrast, a fission bomb is designed to release a large amount of energy in a very short time. This requires the rate of fission to multiply very rapidly.

The simplest fission weapons generally involve use of either a gun or an implosion device. For a gun device, two pieces of fissile material (usually U-235), each at subcritical mass, are suddenly forced together in a gunlike assembly by the detonation of a conventional explosive. The resulting supercritical mass produces an explosion. This was the kind of fission bomb dropped on Hiroshima.

The implosion device relies upon an increase in the fissile material's density, rather than its size, in order to achieve a supercritical condition. It involves a fissile material below critical mass formed in the shape of a sphere and surrounded by a conventional explosive. When detonated, the conventional explosive creates an ingoing shock wave or implosion which compresses the sphere into a supercritical mass by increasing its density by a factor of two or more. This was the principle used (with Pu-239) in the first U.S. nuclear test and in the bomb dropped on Nagasaki.

FISSION REACTORS

A nuclear power reactor is a heat-generating device fueled by fissionable material. It differs from a non-nuclear power plant in that it uses a nuclear "core" to produce heat for steam (which drives a turbine), rather than a boiler to burn fossil fuel. The design objective of a fission power reactor is to maintain a chain reaction at a steady, controlled rate over a long period of time.

Although considerable variations are possible in reactor design, most power reactors have the following general components:

1. A *core,* or central portion of the reactor, contains the nuclear fuel. It is in this region that the fission reactions occur.
2. *Fuel* material containing fissile nuclei. The fuel for a power reactor may consist of natural uranium (containing 0.7 percent fissile U-235 and 99.3 percent nonfissile U-238), enriched uranium in which the percentage of the isotope U-235 has been artifically increased, uranium-233 (produced by conversion

of Th-232), plutonium-239 (produced by the conversion of U-238), or a combination of these materials.

3. A *moderator* (usually ordinary water, heavy water, or graphite) that slows neutrons, thereby increasing their chances of being absorbed by a fissile nucleus.
4. A *coolant,* which is circulated through the reactor core for the dual purpose of removing the nuclear-generated heat and transferring it for use outside the core, typically for electricity production. Coolants can be fluids (generally water), liquid metals such as sodium (in breeder reactors), or gases such as helium and carbon dioxide. In many cases water serves as both the coolant and the moderator.
5. *Control elements,* which regulate the rate of fission. These are usually rods containing neutron-absorbing material which can prevent the neutrons from causing further fission.
6. A *reflector,* surrounds the reactor core and directs back into the core some of the neutrons which might otherwise escape.
7. A *reactor vessel,* contains the nuclear core and isolates radioactive parts of the reactor system.

Nuclear reactors may be categorized in a number of ways. One frequent approach is to distinguish reactors in terms of their "conversion ratio"—the ratio of fissile material produced to fissile material consumed. A reactor in which the conversion ratio is low (i.e., the amount of fissile material consumed is much higher than the amount produced) is termed a *burner.* Most commercial reactors currently operating are of this type. *Converters,* on the other hand, are reactors in which the conversion ratio approaches 1. Finally, there are reactors in which the conversion ratio exceeds 1. These are called *breeders.* What is important to bear in mind is that reactors which operate in the higher range of conversion are more efficient users of uranium resources than those operating at the lower range.[10]

An alternative method for categorizing reactors is by their coolant and/or moderator. On this basis one can distinguish among the light-water reactor (LWR)—of which there are two varieties: the pressurized-water reactor (PWR) and the boiling-water reactor (BWR)—and the heavy-water reactor (HWR), the high-temperature gas-cooled reactor (HTGR), the liquid-metal fast breeder reactor (LMFBR), the gas-cooled fast reactor (GCFR), the light-water breeder reactor (LWBR), and the molten-salt breeder reactor (MSBR). Major characteristics of these reactor types are noted in Table 3.1.

Table 3.1. Characteristics of Major Power Reactors

Reactor Type	Neutron Energy	Fuel[a]	Moderator	Coolant	Conversion Ratio	Thermal Efficiency (%)[b]
PWR	Thermal	Enriched U (3.2% U-235) and possibly recycled Pu	Water	Water	.59	33
BWR	Thermal	Enriched U (2.8% U-235) and possibly recycled Pu	Water	Water	.59	33–34
HWR	Thermal	Natural U	Heavy water	Heavy water	.72	31–32
HTGR	Thermal	Enriched U (90% U-235), recycled U-233, and Th-232	Graphite	Helium	<.7	39–40
LMFBR	Fast	Recycled Pu and U-238	None	Liquid sodium	>1.15	36–40
GCFR	Fast	Recycled Pu and U-238	None	Helium	1.40	35–37
LWBR	Thermal	Recycled U-233 and Th-232	Water	Water	1.01	33
MSBR	Thermal	Molten fluorides of U-233 and Th-232	Graphite	Molten salt	1.07	44

Source: Derived in part from Nuclear Energy Policy Study Group, *Nuclear Power Issues and Choices* (Cambridge, Massachusetts: Ballinger, 1977), p. 393. Conversion ratio and thermal efficiency figures are from *Nuclear Proliferation and Civilian Nuclear Power*, Vol. 9 (Washington, D.C.: U.S. Department of Energy, 1980); *Fast Breeders*, Report of INFCE Working Group 5 (Vienna: IAEA, 1980); *Advanced Fuel Cycle and Reactor Concepts*, Report of INFCE Working Group 8 (Vienna: IAEA, 1980); and John E. Gray et al., *International Cooperation Breeder Reactors*, Vol. 2 (New York: The Rockefeller Foundation, 1978).

[a]Reactors using Pu-239 or U-233 may be started with enriched U-235 substituting for other fissile materials.
[b]The ratio of net electrical energy produced to thermal energy released in the reactor.

Light-Water Reactors

Virtually all commercial nuclear power in the United States is generated by light-water reactors.[11] These reactors use ordinary water as the moderator and coolant and slightly enriched U-235 as fuel.

There are two basic varieties of light-water reactor, the pressurized-water reactor (PWR), and the boiling-water reactor (BWR).[12] The PWR, the reactor most widely adopted internationally, was developed in the United States as an outgrowth of the system used to power nuclear submarines. In it, water is maintained at high pressure in the core (which prevents it from boiling) and is used to transfer heat to a secondary, steam-generating system. The BWR is similar to the PWR, but simpler conceptually in that steam is actually produced in the reactor vessel itself. That is, while the PWR relies on an indirect cycle of steam generation, the BWR can directly use the steam produced by water boiling during its passage through the core to drive a turbine.

For both PWRs and BWRs it is necessary to renew the fuel about once a year.[13] At this time the reactor is shut down and between one third and one fourth of its fuel is replaced.[14] The entire process of shutting down the reactor, allowing it to cool, removing the reactor head, and transferring the spent fuel usually takes 4 to 6 weeks.[15] The need for periodic shutdown in order to refuel, in contrast to the continuous refueling procedures of some other reactor types, has the desirable nonproliferation effect of facilitating on-site inspection and the safeguarding of fission by-products. The long time required for refueling would make attempts to divert irradiated fuel during other-than-normal discharge and loading periods easily detectable.

Light-water reactor fuel of typical burnup contains about 0.8 percent plutonium. With this plutonium content about 1.4 metric tons of spent fuel in the form of uranium dixoide (UO_2) must be reprocessed in order to obtain 10 kg of plutonium.[16] Although reprocessing for weapons purposes is within the capabilities of many nations, non-state actors would face substantial difficulties in diverting nuclear material from the fuel storage pools and in extracting plutonium from the fuel rods because of the intense radiation emitted by the spent fuel.

Heavy-Water Reactors

Heavy water may be used as an alternative to ordinary water as the moderator and coolant of a thermal reactor. Because heavy water absorbs fewer neutrons than ordinary water (leaving more to carry on the chain reaction), it is possible to use unenriched (natural) uranium as fuel.

Although many heavy-water moderated reactor systems have been explored, the one which dominates the HWR market is of Canadian design and is known as CANDU (for Canadian deuterium-uranium reactor). For convenience, the CANDU uses heavy water as a coolant, although ordinary water could be used. In the CANDU design, the coolant is employed in conjunction with a secondary steam generator which drives the turbines.

In contrast to LWRs, the CANDU is designed to be refueled without reactor shutdown. Refueling takes place by pushing new fuel bundles through one end of a horizontal fuel channel while removing spent bundles at the other end. While this procedure of on-line refueling permits the CANDU to generate electricity continuously, it also makes it more difficult to guard against the covert diversion of nuclear material. By accelerating fuel consumption (i.e., pushing some fuel bundles through more rapidly so that the fuel is irradiated to less than normal burnup), it is possible to increase the weapons quality of the plutonium produced without a significant loss of power output.[17] Diversion of weapons-grade material from the CANDU is thus theoretically possible. Nevertheless, a recent study by the Office of Technology Assessment concluded that safeguard systems for the CANDU could most likely be designed and implemented "so that repeated covert diversion of fuel assemblies cannot take place undetected during either normal or accelerated refueling."[18] Although not specified in the report, one such system to detect abuse of on-line refueling has been devised by the Atomic Energy Agency of Canada, in cooperation with the IAEA. It incorporates means for counting the fuel bundles discharged from the CANDU and for verifying that the bundles in the spent fuel pool are not dummies substituted for irradiated fuel.[19]

A comparison of the proliferation resistance of the LWR and the CANDU presents mixed results. Although the use of natural uranium results in more plutonium production in a CANDU heavy-water reactor than in the reference LWR (500 kg versus 250 kg/gigawatt-year of operation), the concentration of plutonium per kilogram of fuel is lower. Since it would require 2½ times more spent fuel from a CANDU HWR than from a LWR (30 versus 12 metric tons) to obtain 100 kg of plutonium, the time required to extract it would be slightly greater.

As will be discussed in more detail in the section "Assessing Alternative Reactors and Fuel Systems," the CANDU also has the nonproliferation advantage of not requiring uranium enrichment or spent fuel reprocessing support facilities. On the other hand, the CANDU creates a need for heavy water, which is both expensive and can be used in production reactors fueled by natural uranium and designed to produce plutonium for nuclear weapons.[20]

High-Temperature Gas-Cooled Reactors

Gas-cooled thermal reactors provide an alternative to reactors that rely on water as a coolant. One which has received particular attention in the United States and West Germany is the high-temperature gas-cooled reactor (HTGR).[21]

As usually conceived, the HTGR is distinguished by its use of graphite as a moderator, helium as a coolant, and a fuel system consisting of highly enriched uranium (93 percent U-235), U-233, and Th-232 (for conversion to U-233).[22] The extremely high temperatures created in the HTGR permit direct utilization of gas turbines to generate power (in contrast to conventional steam-power generation).

A major attraction of the HTGR is its better uranium utilization due to its relatively high conversion ratio and thermal efficiency. The ability of the graphite core of the HTGR to absorb a great deal of heat without melting is also an important safety attraction.

The outstanding feature of the HTGR from a proliferation standpoint is its use of highly enriched uranium for fuel. This may make it a likely target for diversion. In order to reduce this prospect and still exploit the HTGR's other assets, a low-enriched uranium (approximately 20 percent U-235)/thorium fuel cycle has been proposed. Although this fuel cycle might slightly degrade reactor performance,[23] it could also make the HTGR more resistant to proliferation. It has been estimated that in HTGR uranium/thorium fuel cycles, fissile plutonium discharge would be about one-tenth of that of a comparably sized LWR. The need to divert increased amounts of spent fuel would thus present a more difficult logistics problem for the potential proliferator.[24]

BREEDER REACTORS

In today's commercial nonbreeder reactors, for every ten fissions a net of about six to seven fertile atoms are converted to fissile atoms. The possibility, however, has long been recognized of constructing a nuclear reactor in which each fission reaction produced enough neutrons to net more than one new fissile atom for each fissile atom burned—that is, a nuclear core in which the conversion ratio is greater than unity. In this case the conversion ratio is termed the breeding ratio and the reactors are called breeders.

Although not yet at the stage of commercialization, alternative breeder reactor designs have been the subject of technical discussions for three decades.[25] The four designs which have received most attention are: (1) the liquid-metal fast breeder reactor (LMFBR), (2) the gas-cooled fast reactor (GCFR), (3) the light-water breeder reactor (LWBR), and (4) the molten-salt breeder reactor (MSBR).[26] The LMFBR and the GCFR are usually termed *fast breeders* because they do not contain a moderator to slow neutrons down (i.e., fast neutrons are used). The LWBR and the MSBR are referred to as *thermal breeders* because they do contain a moderator (i.e., slow neutrons are used).

Liquid-Metal Fast Breeder Reactor

The type of fast breeder reactor at the most advanced stage of development, and the only breeder we will examine, is the LMFBR. It is also the breeder approach chosen for emphasis in the seven nations with the most highly developed breeder reactor programs (Britain, France, India, Japan, the Soviet Union, the United States, and West Germany).[27]

As currently conceived, the LMFBR uses Pu-239 (fissile)/U-238 (fertile) fuel elements in the core, a U-238 "breeding blanket" around the core, a liquid metal (sodium) coolant, and a fast neutron core. Fission initiated by the fast neutrons in the core releases an enormous amount of energy as heat, which is transferred by a sodium coolant to water in order to produce steam. The steam in turn feeds a turbine which generates electricity. The two major varieties of LMFBR are the so-called pool-type reactor favored by the European states and the loop-type reactor, until recently the anticipated breeder in the United States. The systems differ primarily in the components contained in the reactor vessel, the pool-type variety containing not only the core but also the primary coolant pump and the intermediate heat exchange.[28]

The LMFBR is expected to produce anywhere from 10 to 40 percent more fissile material each year than it consumes.[29] Currently, the plan is to use fissile plutonium to breed more fissile plutonium from U-238. However, since plutonium is not an element that occurs in nature, but depends on nuclear reactors for its production, its availability represents a potential constraint on the rapidity of LMFBR deployment.[30] The main difficulty with the LMFBR concept, however, stems not from the initial lack of plutonium availability, but from its abundance once the LMFBR begins operation.

It is estimated that a typical 1000 MW$_e$ LMFBR will have a total plutonium inventory in its core of 5000 to 6000 kg. Each year approximately 2000 kg of plutonium will be introduced into the reactor and about 10 percent more withdrawn. For each such LMFBR, moreover, at least 2500 kg of plutonium would be in process, storage, or transport at any given time. By comparison, only 250 kg of plutonium is discharged in spent fuel from one gigawatt-year's operation of a standard LWR.[31] The fresh fuel for the LMFBR will also probably be more more concentrated in plutonium than fresh fuel in the LWR cycle with plutonium recycle.[32] Because significant amounts of the plutonium produced in the blankets of the LMFBR will contain less than 5 percent Pu-240, the weapons utility of the material will also be increased.[33]

Unlike LWRs, where use of plutonium recycling is optional, breeders, as they are presently conceived, rely on a fuel cycle in which separated plutonium is present at many stages. Recent efforts in the United States to find other fuel cycles more resistant to proliferation have stimulated interest in the possibilities of using the LMFBR concept for breeding fissile U-233 from fertile thorium without producing plutonium. This option is discussed below in the section "Assessing Alternative Reactors and Fuel Systems."

THE NUCLEAR FUEL CYCLE

Before an attempt is made to assess the proliferation resistance of specific, alternative fuel systems, it is necessary to describe the structure of the generic nuclear fuel cycle, that is, the sequence of stages through which nuclear fuel material passes, from resource production (mining, milling, and conversion) to fuel recovery, waste management, and disposal. The first four stages—mining, milling, conversion, enrichment, and fabrication—are usually referred to as the "front end" of the fuel cycle. The stage in which the fission of the fuel takes place in the reactor is referred to as "irradiation." The remaining stages—spent fuel storage, reprocessing, and waste disposal—constitute the "back end" of the cycle. (See Figure 3.1). Each of these stages is briefly discussed below, focusing on their proliferation resistance.

Mining and Milling

The principal energy source for all commercial reactors and many research reactors is U-235, the only fissile isotope that occurs in nature.[34] Major deposits of uranium ore, consisting of about 0.7

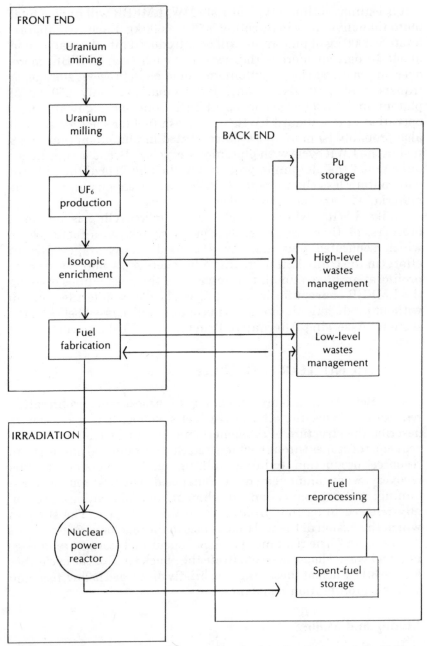

Figure 3.1. Basic elements of the nuclear fuel cycle. *(Source:* John E. Gray et al., *International Cooperation on Breeder Reactors* (New York: The Rockefeller Foundation, 1978), p. 1-8.)

percent U-235 and 99.3 percent U-238, are located in the United States, Canada, Australia, South Africa, the Soviet Union, Niger, and France.[35] At the mining and milling stage these two isotopes of uranium are inseparable. Uranium mining techniques resemble those used in coal mining, including both deep shaft and open pit methods. In the United States, commercially mined uraniam concentrations typically contain about 3 to 5 pounds of uranium per ton of ore.[36]

Following its removal from the mine, uranium ore is mechanically and chemically processed, or milled, to separate the uranium from the host rock and other minerals and to produce "yellowcake," a concentrate containing about 70 to 80 percent uranium oxide (U_3O_8). This concentrate leaves the mill for further processing in a chemical conversion plant. The portion of the ore which is rejected in the milling process is known as tailings and constitutes a safety hazard since it releases radioactive radon gas into the atmosphere.

Conversion

The nature of the next step in the fuel cycle, conversion, depends on the kind of reactor in which uranium is intended to serve as fuel. Those relying on natural uranium (i.e., the CANDU) require conversion of yellowcake to either uranium metal or uranium oxide.[37] Reactors using enriched uranium, on the other hand, require the conversion of yellowcake to the gas, uranium hexafluoride (UF_6), prior to uranium enrichment.

Enrichment

To be used as fuel in most reactors, uranium must be enriched. That is, the concentration of the fissile isotope U-235 must be increased beyond the 0.7 percent characteristic of natural uranium. For light-water reactors an enrichment level of approximately 3 percent must be achieved, while for high-temperature gas reactors (and for reactors used in ship propulsion) a U-235 concentration of about 90 percent—that is weapons grade—is required. At present, four methods of uranium enrichment are either in commercial operation or under advanced research and development: gaseous diffusion, gas centrifuge, nozzle or aerodynamic, and laser.[38]

The most developed and widely used method of enrichment is the gaseous diffusion process. This process, which was developed during the Manhattan Project in the 1940s and is responsible for almost all uranium enrichment to date for both nuclear weapons and reactors, depends on the small difference in molecular mobility between gas molecules of different isotopic species. When gaseous uranium hexaflouride (UF_6) is pumped through a porous barrier, the lighter UF_6 molecules containing U-235 pass through at a faster rate than do the heavier UF_6 molecules containing U-238. The amount of separation (i.e., enrichment) accomplished by a single barrier, however, is slight, and the process must be repeated many times in a cascadelike series in order to achieve useful enrichment levels. Thus, a gaseous diffusion plant requires many stages, approximately 1250, in order to enrich natural UF_6 to reactor fuel levels (i.e., 3 percent U-235) and about 4000 stages for enrichment to weapons standards (i.e., 90 percent U-235).[39] The process of enrichment by means of gaseous diffusion is also extremely costly due to the enormous amount of energy required to force UF_6 through the many filtering stages. Because of its high cost, large size, enormous power requirements, and need for a substantial manufacturing capability (in particular, the ability to make barrier material), it is unlikely that a gaseous diffusion facility could be clandestinely built for nuclear weapons production. If already in operation for production of highly enriched uranium for HTGRs, however, it could be a target for covert diversion.

An alternative method of uranium enrichment, only recently in operation commercially, employs gas centrifuges.[40] The gas centrifuge enrichment process makes use of a rapidly rotating cylinder filled with gaseous UF_6. Centrifugal force causes the heavier U-238 molecules to move closer to the wall of the rotor, producing partial separation of the U-235 and U-238 isotopes.[41]

The most significant difference between the gaseous diffusion and gas centrifuge processes is power use. A centrifuge plant requires only about 4 percent of the power needed for a diffusion plant of equal separarative work output.[42] The gas centrifuge process also has the advantage of obtaining a much higher degree of enrichment per stage than the diffusion technique and is less constrained by economies of scale. It is estimated, for example, that as few as 35 stages might be sufficient to produce 90 percent enrichment and that a medium-size plant with 1000 centrifuges could provide the necessary separation capacity for several nuclear weapons per year.[43] As a consequence, the same factors which make the gas centrifuge technique attractive for use in the nuclear power fuel cycle also make it suitable for a deliberate weapons program and, if used to produce highly enriched uranium for power purposes (i.e., as with HTGRs), a possible target for theft or covert diversion.

Several aerodynamic methods have also been developed to separate uranium isotopes. Best known is the "Becker Nozzle" technique, developed in West Germany, in which a gaseous mixture of UF_6 and hydrogen or helium is forced over a curved surface at high velocity. The centrifugal forces which are created tend to separate the heavier molecules containing U-238 from the lighter ones containing U-235.[44] A related aerodynamic technique known as the Helikon process has been developed in South Africa and reportedly has attained industrial demonstration.[45]

The Becker and Helikon aerodynamic processes are probably less demanding in terms of manufacturing capability and capital costs than either the gaseous diffusion or centrifuge approaches. They also require fewer stages to enrich uranium to the 3 percent and 90 percent levels than the diffusion process requires (approximately 600 stages for 3 percent enrichment and 2000 for 90 percent enrichment).[46] Because of the necessity for repeatedly compressing large amounts of hydrogen and UF_6, however, the energy requirements for the aerodynamic process are even greater than for diffusion. The aerodynamic approach to uranium enrichment, therefore, is likely to be less attractive than the centrifuge process, except where power costs are low (e.g., Brazil) or where the technological capabilities necessary for the centrifuge and diffusion processes are absent. As in the case for gaseous diffusion and centrifuge plants, the possibility of diverting materials for weapons purposes from an aerodynamic enrichment facility is most serious if the plant produces highly enriched uranium for HTGRs.

A relatively new technique for uranium enrichment which may prove to be an economic boon for nuclear power and a dilemma for nonproliferation is isotope separation by lasers. Laser techniques for uranium enrichment, now in the laboratory research stage in the United States, the Soviet Union, France, Australia, Japan, and Italy, depend on the difference in the light absorption frequencies of each isotope of an element. Using this principle, it is possible to excite only one of the isotopes (e.g., U-235) in a mixture by exposing the mixture to the light of a finely tuned laser. The excited species may then be separated.[47] Laser isotope separation can be carried out either on atomic uranium vapor or on a molecular uranium compound.[48]

A major attraction of the laser process is its potential to produce very high enrichment in one step, or at most a very few, while consuming relatively little energy.[49] The high degree of separation per stage obtainable by laser enrichment should also make possible the recovery of a larger percentage of U-235 from natural uranium than is economically feasible in conventional enrichment plants.[50] It has even been suggested that the tails remaining from years of operation of gaseous diffusion plants might serve as feed for a laser enrichment operation.[51]

Many of the factors which make laser enrichment attractive for incorporation in the fuel cycle may also make it attractive for the purpose of weapons manufacture. The possibility of very high enrichment in a single stage is particularly worrisome from the standpoint of diversion. It is not yet clear, however, whether laser enrichment processes will substantially reduce the technical barriers to proliferation, as is sometimes feared. A panel of independent experts, for example, recently concluded that the atomic-vapor laser isotope separation process, "far from being a simple technology capable of being mastered by many countries and even subnational groups, is extraordinarily complex and difficult."[52] Because of its uranium conservation potential, laser enrichment may also have the positive nonproliferation effect of reducing pressures for rapid commercialization of reprocessing, plutonium recycling, and fast breeders. A list of uranium enrichment facilities now in operation is provided in Table 3.2. Table 3.3 presents a summary of alternative enrichment techniques and their suitability for nuclear power and weapons purposes.

Fabrication

The last step in the "front end" of the fuel cycle is fabrication of the fuel elements. The form and mixture of the fuel varies with the type of reactor. For most LWRs, the enriched uranium hexafluoride (UF_6) is converted into small ceramic pellets of uranium dioxide (UO_2). These pellets are then inserted into tubes to form fuel rods. When recycled plutonium is used with uranium, plutonium oxide powder (PuO_2) is mixed with uranium oxide powder before fabricating the fuel pellets.[53] For HTGRs, the fuel is made up of particles of fertile thorium oxide (ThO_2) mixed with recycled U-233 oxide and particles of weapons-grade uranium carbide (UC).[54]

Unlike the enrichment and reprocessing steps, the fabrication stage in the nuclear fuel cycle has received little public scrutiny. It is thus important to note in regards to nonproliferation that "any facility for fabricating a mixed uranium and plutonium oxide fuel must contain pure plutonium compounds and is therefore a potential point of diversion from the fuel cycle."[55]

Irradiation

Irradiation, or fuel burn-up, occurs in the reactor core. The characteristics of each reactor determine the nature of the burn-up.

Table 3.2. Uranium-Enrichment Facilities in Operation (as of June 30, 1979)

	Gaseous Diffusion	Gas Centrifuge	Aerodynamics	Chemical	Laser	Plasma
Australia	—	C	—	—	C	—
France	A	C	—	B	C	—
Germany, West	—	A[a]	B (nozzle)	—	C	—
Italy	B,C[b]	C	—	—	C	—
Japan	C	B	—	C	C	—
Netherlands	—	A[a]	—	—	—	—
South Africa (Rep. of)	—	—	A[d] (Helikon)	—	—	—
U.K.	A	A[a]	—	—	—	—
U.S.A.	A	B	—	C	C	C
USSR	A[c]	—	—	—	—	—

Code	Typical aim of facility
A	Production
B	Industrial development
C	Laboratory and pre-industrial demonstration

Source: Derived from INFCE Summary Volume, p. 93.
— No answers supplied to the INFCE questionnaire.
[a] Joint trinational Urenco Centec plants.
[b] B: In the frame of its participation in Eurodif.
  C: In the frame of its national program.
[c] No answers were supplied to the INFCE questionnaire; data were inferred from information published elsewhere.
[d] No answers were supplied to the INFCE questionnaire but data were obtained from correspondence.

The relative concentration of Pu-240 and higher isotopes, however, always increases with time relative to Pu-239 concentration and accounts for the decreased quality of plutonium for weapons purposes as burn-up time increases.[56]

Spent Fuel Storage

After a certain period of irradiation, reactor fuel becomes too depleted in U-235 to sustain a chain reaction at the required level. Spent fuel, therefore, must be removed periodically and replaced with fresh fuel. As previously noted, LWRs must be shut down for this process, while CANDU reactors are refueled continuously. After removal from the reactor, the highly radioactive, spent fuel rods are placed (in the case of LWRs) in the fuel storage pools at the

Table 3.3. Comparison of Alternative Enrichment Technologies

	Diffusion	Centrifuge	Aerodynamic	Laser
State of art	Mature technology; proven in large-scale production; barrier technology classified	At the first stage of industrial application; substantial growth potential; some details of technology classified	Technology thoroughly demonstrated; small capacity plants are under construction; substantial growth potential. Becker nozzle technology in the public domain; South African process classified	Technology in the intensive R&D phase with emphasis on laser development and fundamental process physics. Separation in laboratory reported using U metal and UF_6, but commercial scale separation probably 10 years off. Some details of technology classified
Requirements for production	Knowledge of barrier technology needed; requires large-scale production of pumps	Mass production of precision equipment	Some precision machining capability needed; overall, requirements probably less than for diffusion or centrifuge	Expert opinion differs (cf. Greenwood et al., p. 24 and Lester, p. 24). Outstanding technical problem for MLIS process is development of suitable infrared laser. Other necessary skills and components are less demanding. For AVLIS process, technical requirements probably great for corrosive-resistant optical surfaces, uranium evaporation system, and laser itself

Stages required in ideal cascade (0.3% tails)				
3% enrichment	1086	10	600	Possibly only 1
90% enrichment	3731	35	2000	Possibly only 1
Suitability for a nuclear power fuel cycle	Not likely to be economically competitive for small or modest programs, and may not be competitive at all if pilot plant experience with other methods is satisfactory	Will probably be preferred (lasers excepted) where power costs are very high	Will probably be preferred (lasers excepted) where power costs are low, especially for small- or modest-scale operations	Likely to be particularly desirable because it will probably extend uranium supplies greatly
Adaptability of facilities developed for a power program (enrichment to 2-3%) to weapons production	Least desirable; requires construction of additional stages, or batch processing, which would be inconvenient and time-consuming because of large cascade inventory of gas	Much preferred to diffusion or aerodynamic processes because of possibility of increasing the number of stages by changing plumbing connections	Will require additional stages, or batch processing	Will probably be best; process may lead naturally to highly enriched uranium
Suitability for a small or modest deliberate weapons program	Unattractive because of large number of stages required; experience is with plants that are of large capacity	Very good; several plants are now operating or planned of a scale interesting for weapons purposes	Unattractive compared to centrifuge but probably better than diffusion, especially considering greater feasibility of batch processing	Probably preferred
Possibility of diversion of materials from power program to weapons construction	Not serious if enrichment is only 2-3%; serious for all three processes if enrichment for power purposes is 90-97% (i.e., for HTGR's)			Probably most worrisome

Source: Derived in large part from Ted Greenwood et al., "Nuclear Power and Weapons Proliferation," *Adelphi Paper* no. 130, Winter 1976, pp. 23–24. Principal revisions are under the laser heading.

plant site. The pool provides radiation shielding and continuous cooling. After several months of cooling, the fuel is either retained at the plant site pool, shipped to a reprocessing plant, or moved to an interim storage or permanent disposal facility.

Reprocessing

Following storage, during which time the most intense radioactivity decays, spent fuel can be reprocessed by chemical and mechanical means to reclaim the residual uranium and plutonium and to concentrate the radioactive fission products. This process is usually conducted in three steps.

First, the fuel assemblies are broken up and the metal cladding surrounding the fuel is removed. The fuel itself is then dissolved, along with the cladding, in a solution of nitric acid. This is called the "head end" of reprocessing.

In the second phase, plutonium and uranium are extracted from the fuel solution. This is generally done by the so-called PUREX (Plutonium Uranium Recovery by Extraction) method.[57] More than 90 percent of the uranium and plutonium present in the solution can be retrieved by this method. The uranium-thorium fuel employed in certain reactors require a somewhat different reprocessing method, called THOREX.[58]

The third step in reprocessing spent fuel is known as product purification. Uranium and plutonium recovered from the fuel solution are separated and converted to more usable forms. Recovered plutonium usually is converted to plutonium dioxide (PuO_2) and uranium is converted to UF_6.

From a nonproliferation standpoint, reprocessing is one of the most worrisome stages in the fuel cycle. It is at this stage where nuclear material directly usable for weapons is produced during normal operation. As Ted Greenwood et al. point out, "On entering a reprocessing plant uranium and plutonium are contained in irradiated fuel rods that are extremely radioactive and difficult to handle; but on coming out both are highly purified and in convenient chemical forms."[59] Although the purified uranium produced in this process would, in most instances, not be directly usable for nuclear explosives because of its high depletion in fissile isotopes, any plutonium emerging from a reprocessing plant could be used for manufacturing explosives.[60] It has been argued, moreover, that once separated at a reprocessing plant, plutonium would be vulnerable to theft, diversion, and misuse at all subsequent stages of the fuel cycle.[61] Although it may be possible to reduce these proliferation dangers by denaturing the nuclear material (i.e., mixing in other isotopes of the same element) or spiking the fuel with lethal amounts of intensely radioactive material (e.g., Cobalt-60), many experts doubt whether these approaches would constitute a significant obstacle for a national government or other technically sophisticated adversary and might have the undesirable effects of significantly increasing fuel fabrication and transportation costs and the risk to the public due to accidents.[62]

Currently, only France has an industrial-scale reprocessing plant for oxide fuel from light-water reactors in operation. The International Nuclear Fuel Cycle Evaluation (INFCE) report issued in 1980, however, lists eight more countries with plans to introduce such plants and an additional three or four countries that have expressed interest in using the services of one or more of these plants to have their spent fuel reprocessed.[63] Such commercial-scale plants designed for high burn-up oxide fuel are very expensive to construct and require extensive engineering knowhow. A reprocessing facility designed to extract plutonium for weapons from a plutonium production reactor, however, would be much easier and less expensive to construct.[64] The basic technology for reprocessing, moreover, has been in the public domain since 1955 when it was released by the United States as part of the Atoms for Peace program. Although the time and cost required to build a small reprocessing facility for weapons purposes are uncertain, it has been estimated that one could be built for as low as ten million dollars and constructed, without outside assistance, in less than one year.[65] If one accepts these figures, cost would not be prohibitive for most states and it would appear likely that "almost any state with a modest chemical industry could on its own build a reprocessing plant large enough to supply plutonium to a small explosives program."[66]

Waste Disposal

The final step in the nuclear fuel cycle is the disposal of radioactive wastes. Although waste products are generated at each stage of the fuel cycle, those of greatest concern are found in spent reactor fuel.[67] The focus of the concern is radioactive exposure and the longevity of the radioactive wastes.

At the present time, U.S. commercial spent fuel is stored in pools of water at approximately 70 power reactor facilities. When and if this spent fuel is reprocessed, uranium and plutonium will be extracted from the material and a solution consisting of 40 or more radioactive isotopes will be left as residue.[68] This high-level waste will then have to be reduced to solid form, although precise criteria have not been developed with respect to either the nuclides to be solidified or the form they would take.[69] These criteria will likely depend upon the mode of long-term or permanent disposal ultimately selected.

Numerous methods of permanent disposal of nuclear waste have been proposed.[70] They include ocean and sea bed disposal, placement in geological formations on land, ejection into outer space, and the use of multibarrier containment systems or "waste packages." According to the report of the Nonproliferation Alternative Systems Assessment Program (NASAP) issued in June 1980, of the major candidate technologies for waste disposal "mixed repository disposal (i.e., placement in geological formations) will be available soonest and is the focus of the greatest R&D effort."[71] Salt, granite, basalt, and shale are considered the most promising geological media for disposal sites, although a preferred geological environment has yet to be selected.[72]

From the standpoint of nonproliferation, waste disposal is one of the less troublesome stages in the nuclear fuel cycle. This is due in large part to the high radioactivity of spent fuel, which makes it a difficult target for theft or diversion. Waste in the form of depleted uranium oxide would also require enrichment before it would be useful for the production of nuclear weapons, and plutonium in vitrified waste or concrete would be very dispersed and difficult to recover.[73]

Although waste disposal is not a major nonproliferation problem it is perhaps the most politically sensitive issue in the realm of nuclear power politics. As one observer notes, "Many local and state officials—including the governors of certain key states—seem determined to prevent even the storage of spent fuel, to say nothing of the ultimate disposal of waste material, within their jurisdictions."[74] This problem is apt to intensify before it is resolved and to be repeated in other countries.

ASSESSING ALTERNATIVE REACTORS AND FUEL SYSTEMS[75]

Numerous alternative combinations of reactors and fuel cycles are technically possible. Indeed, as noted in the recent report of the Nonproliferation Alternative Systems Program (NASAP), "in theory any fuel cycle might be used in combination with any reactor type."[76] In practice, however, physical constraints, in addition to proliferation-resistance considerations, "dictate which combinations provide the most desirable operating characteristics with respect to reactor physics, resource utilization, safety, and operating reliability."[77] The more effective combinations and, hence, those already in use or most likely to be adopted are discussed below.

Once-Through Fuel Cycle Systems

The once-through fuel cycle system introduces nuclear materials into a reactor as fuel only once. Spent fuel is placed in storage and treated as waste rather than being recycled. This is the system currently in operation with LWRs and is the dominant fuel cycle system in the nuclear power industry today.

A typical or "reference" once-through system with a LWR is represented in Figure 3.2. The fuel cycle operations involved in this system are: mining of natural uranium ore, milling to separate U_3O_8, conversion to UF_6, enrichment to approximately 3 percent U-235, conversion to UO_2, fabrication of fuel elements, reactor operation, temporary storage of spent fuel at the reactor site, and (in principle, but not yet in practice) storage or disposal of nuclear waste.

The most significant characteristic of the once-through nuclear fuel cycle is that directly usable weapons material is never part of the fuel cycle itself. Fresh fuel contains low concentrations of U-235 (about 3 to 5 percent) diluted in U-238, while spent fuel contains low concentrations of U-235 and plutonium (each less than 1 percent), both of which are diluted in U-238 and are accompanied by high radiation fields emitted by the products of fission.[78] There are, nevertheless, three significant paths by which the reference LWR once-through system could be used to acquire material usable for weapons: (1) in-system enrichment facilities to produce highly enriched uranium (HEU); (2) out-of-system enrichment facilities to produce HEU; and (3) out-of-system reprocessing facilities to extract plutonium from the spent fuel.

The major proliferation danger with respect to in-system enrichment facilities is that the layout or operation of the enrichment plant designed to produce low-enriched uranium (LEU) can be modified to permit production of HEU. Although modification for this purpose could theoretically be accomplished for both methods of enrichment currently deployed commercially, the task would be much more difficult in a gaseous diffusion plant than in a centrifuge facility.[79] With respect to out-of-system enrichment, a potential proliferator's main task would be to build an enrichment facility capable of producing HEU. Although there is very little useful in-

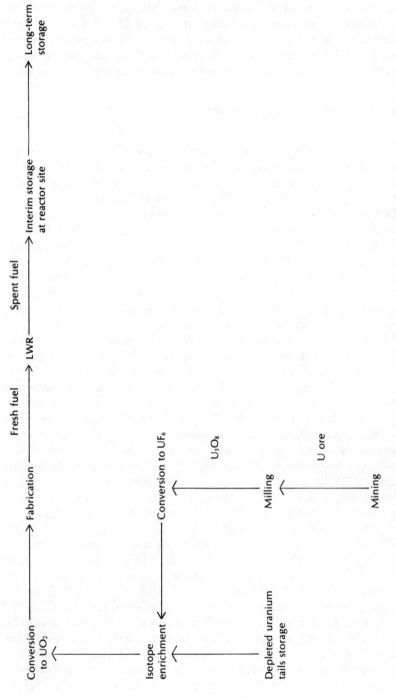

Figure 3.2. Reference once-through system for LWR.

formation on which to make a reliable estimate of the time and cost necessary to construct such a facility, one study suggests that a centrifuge plant of very low capacity capable of producing enough HEU for several weapons a year might cost as little as tens of millions of dollars.[80] The NASAP report, in contrast, refers to a figure of hundreds of millions of dollars and several years of effort for "competent personnel without specialized enrichment experience." The report, however, does not specify the kind of enrichment facility that served as the basis for its calculations.[81] Finally, with regard to the possible out-of-system reprocessing proliferation route, the main obstacle to extracting plutonium from spent fuel is building a chemical reprocessing plant. Estimates of the time and cost necessary to accomplish this task vary greatly, but almost all analyses regard the technical requirements for constructing a plutonium reprocessing facility as much less demanding than those for a uranium-enrichment facility. A diagrammatic summary of the major proliferation pathways for a LWR once-through cycle is presented in Figure 3.3.

Although the LWR once-through fuel cycle system described above is by far the most popular system today, a number of alternative once-through systems are in operation or at the advanced R&D stage. They include the Canadian deuterium-uranium (CANDU) heavy-water reactor system and the high temperature gas-cooled reactor (HTGR) system.

The once-through HWR fuel cycle is simpler than the once-through LWR cycle because it does not entail uranium enrichment. The operations involved in the fuel cycle are: mining and milling of uranium ore, converting uranium oxide to uranium dioxide, manufacturing fuel elements, operating the reactor, and storing or disposing of spent fuel. (See Figure 3.4 for a depiction of a once-through HWR fuel cycle.)

Although the once-through HWR cycle has the advantage, from the standpoint of proliferation resistance of not requiring either uranium enrichment or spent fuel reprocessing, special safeguards are needed for the on-line refueling of HWRs. As previously noted in the section on HWRs, the availability of heavy water also raises the proliferation risk that the heavy water might be used in production reactors fueled by natural uranium and designed to produce plutonium for nuclear weapons.[82]

The high-temperature gas-cooled reactor system, unlike the LWR and HWR once-through systems just described, is only at the prototype stage of development.[83] Although initially conceived as a "closed," rather than once-through, fuel cycle system employing

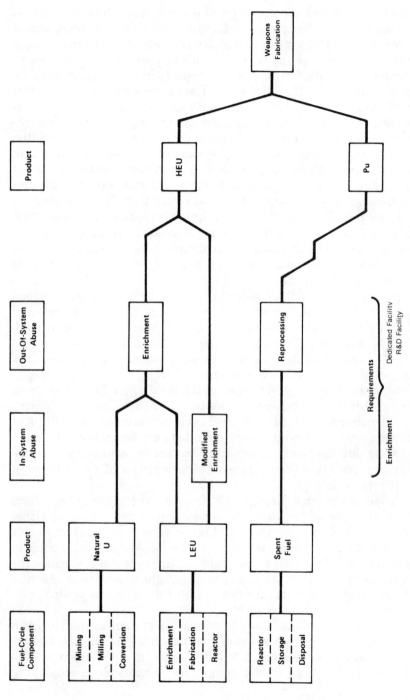

Figure 3.3. Proliferation pathways: reference once-through system. *(Source:* NASAP, vol. 2, p. 2-8.)

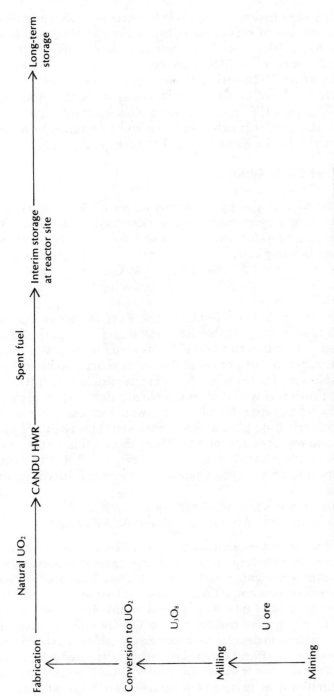

Figure 3.4. Reference once-through system for CANDU HWR.

both highly enriched uranium (over 90 percent U-235) and thorium as fuel, a number of HTGR once-through cycles that may be more resistant to proliferation have recently been considered. These include a 20 percent U-235/thorium cycle and a cycle using only low-enriched uranium.[84] In both of these cycles the uranium in the fresh fuel itself would not be usable in weapons without further enrichment. Because the HTGR allows much more burn-up of its fuel than the LWR, the once-through fuel can also be designed to minimize plutonium discharge quantities in the spent fuel.

Closed Fuel Cycle Systems

In contrast to once-through systems where nuclear materials are introduced into a reactor only once, closed systems rely upon the reprocessing and refabrication a spent fuel and its recycling to the nuclear power plant. A reference recycle system with a LWR is portrayed in Figure 3.5. The reference system consists of the currently conceived PUREX-based reprocessing method and mixed-oxides (MOX) fuel refabrication.

The key aspect of the reference recycle system regarding proliferation is that directly usable weapons material is part of the fuel cycle itself. Plutonium in various forms could be removed from the fuel cycle either in fresh or spent fuel or as separated plutonium in nitrate solution $Pu(NO_3)_4$ or oxide form (including MOX feedstocks).[85] Fresh fuel would be available at refabrication plants and at reactors, while separated plutonium would be found at reprocessing and refabrication plants. Spent fuel would be available at both reactors and reprocessing plants. Thus, in addition to the proliferation pathways shared with the reference LWR once-through system, the reference recycle system has several proliferation routes of its own.

One likely route is the out-of-system conversion of plutonium that is already separated. According to the NASAP report:

> Converting already separated plutonium in bulk storage or transport to weapons-usuable form does not involve unusual procedures and would not present significant difficulties to most nations with trained or experienced personnel. Under those circumstances, preparation activities for tens of [plutonium] metal weapons per year could be completed within a few months at a cost of a few million dollars and could be difficult to detect. Fewer resources would be required if only one or two weapons were required or if oxides were used directly. The period from the time material was first removed from the fuel cycle until significant quantities of weapons-usable material were produced could be a matter of a few days or weeks.[86]

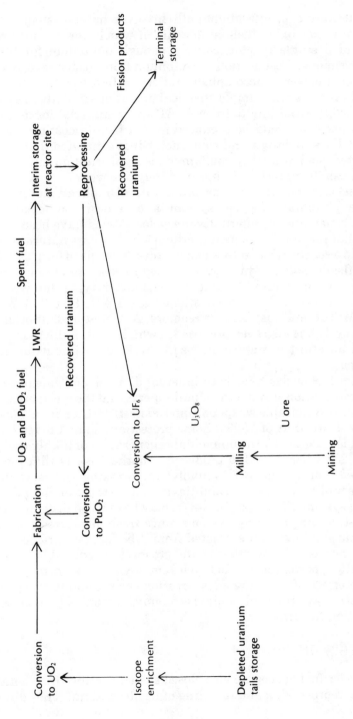

Figure 3.5. Reference recycle system for LWR.

An alternative proliferation path involves out-of-system conversion of mixed-oxide fuel—shipments of which, for a yearly reloading of a single reactor, contain enough plutonium for fifty nuclear weapons.[87] Separation of plutonium from fresh mixed oxide fuel is much easier to accomplish that separation from irradiated fuel, and involves only simple chemical operations and little radiation hazard.[88] According to the NASAP study, material for tens of weapons per year could be produced from a facility costing a few million dollars to design and construct.[89] It is estimated that once constructed, such a facility could produce significant quantities of weapons-usable material in approximately one week.[90]

Because of concern over the proliferation implications of the reference plutonium recycle system and a desire to decrease uranium consumption, alternative recycle systems have been considered that rely on the element thorium, which occurs naturally as Th-232. In a reactor, this isotope can capture neutrons to form U-233, another fissile isotope which may be used in reactors in much the same way as plutonium.[91] Among the reactor types for which thorium fuel cycles have been studied are LWR, HTGR, HWR, LWBR, MSBR, and fast breeder reactors. A "denatured" thorium-uranium cycle has also been proposed in which U-233 is diluted with U-238 in an effort to impede its use in weapons without further enrichment.

Thorium fuel cycles have both inherent dangers and safeguards from a proliferation standpoint. One danger is that the fuel it breeds, U-233, is a very suitable weapons material itself with a critical mass about one-third that of U-235. Some protection against diversion, however, is afforded by the unavoidable generation of highly radioactive U-232 when U-233 is produced. Another risk is that most envisioned thorium fuel cycles involve reprocessing and recycling and have proliferation vulnerabilities similar to those of plutonium recycling systems. This risk, however, may be reduced in denatured uranium-thorium recycling systems since fresh denatured fuel requires that any uranium extracted from it be further enriched for weapons purposes.[92] By offering the prospect of reduced uranium consumption, power reactor fuel cycles employing thorium may also have the effect of reducing pressures for early commitment to a breeder strategy and a "plutonium economy," with their associated proliferation hazards.

Fast Breeder Systems

Fast breeder fuel cycles are also closed systems in that they entail spent fuel reprocessing and recycling of fissile material. They differ from other recycling systems, however, in the concentrations of plutonium in the fuel system and in the reactors themselves.[93] The reference fast breeder system employing a liquid-metal fast breeder reactor (LMFBR) is illustrated in Figure 3.6.

An important factor affecting the proliferation resistance of fast breeder systems is the very high concentration of plutonium in the MOX fuel materials. The plutonium concentration in the LMFBR MOX, for example, is 15 to 25 percent—a level considered to be usable for weapons. This is in contrast to the 4 to 6 percent concentration in recycle MOX fuel.[94] It is theoretically possible, therefore, that a nuclear explosive could be fashioned directly from fresh LMFBR fuel without resorting to chemical separation. Although most nations would probably still use out-of-system facilities to recover plutonium metal for weapons purposes, the weapons-usable quality of LMFBR MOX increases the vulnerability of the LMFBR system to the threat of subnational proliferation.[95] The proliferation pathways of the reference fast breeder and recycling systems are illustrated in Figure 3.7.

CONCLUSIONS

It should be apparent from the preceding discussion of alternative fuel cycle systems and reactors that significant differences exist with respect to their proliferation resistance and the location of their vulnerabilities to diversion. It is also clear, however, that the number of variables and variants present and the magnitude of uncertainties involved make any effort to quantify these differences extremely hazardous. Not surprisingly, the recently concluded International Nuclear Fuel Cycle Evaluation and the Nonproliferation Alternative Systems Assessment Program refrain from ranking reactors or fuel cycles in terms of a standard proliferation-resistance index. Nevertheless, a number of conclusions can be drawn from our survey and a very tentative nonproliferation report card for alternative reactor systems can be prepared.[96]

1. All nuclear fuel cycles entail some proliferation risks. The once-through fuel cycles for the LWR and CANDU HWR, however, are more proliferation resistant than other fuel cycles in which highly enriched uranium or pure plutonium are more readily available.
2. Although the once-through fuel cycles for the LWR and CANDU HWR presently have relatively high barriers to pro-

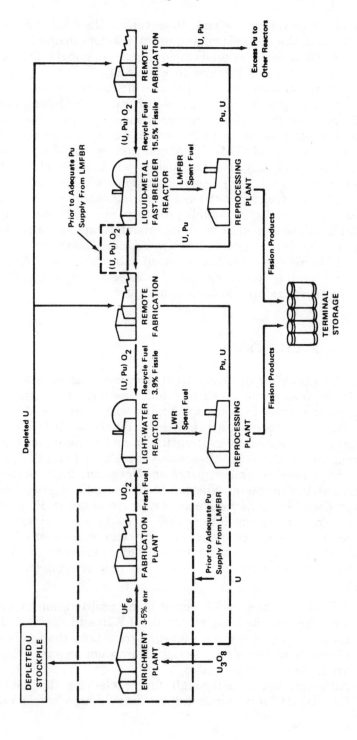

Figure 3.6. Reference fast breeder system. (*Source:* NASAP, vol. 2, p. 2-41.)

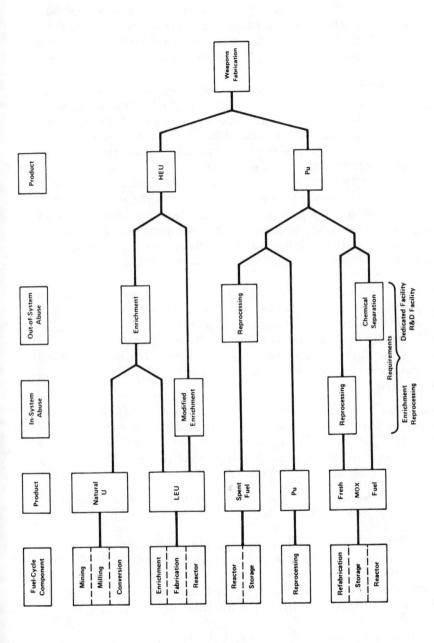

Figure 3.7. Proliferation pathways: reference recycle and fast breeder systems. *(Source:* NASAP, vol. 2, p. 2-23.

liferation, both are susceptible to misuse for weapons purposes if: (a) the potential proliferator has access to a uranium
enrichment plant, or (b) the potential proliferator has access
to a reprocessing facility to recover plutonium from spent
fuel.

3. The isotopic barrier to producing weapons-usable material
from natural or low-enriched uranium fuel currently appears
to be greater than the chemical or radiation barrier to weapons
production from spent fuel, although new enrichment technologies (e.g., the laser) or the spread of existing centrifuge
facilities may alter this assessment.

4. Of currently employed enrichment technologies, the gaseous
diffusion process appears to be the most proliferation resistant.

5. Facilities for closed fuel cycles increase proliferation risks
because plutonium would appear in weapons-usable form and
in forms that are relatively easy to adapt for weapons purposes.
HTGRs which rely on highly enriched U-235 for fuel pose a
similar threat.

6. Reprocessing and recycling increase the opportunities for the
proliferation of national weapons capabilities and the vulnerability to threats by subnational groups.

7. There is little concensus on the nonproliferation utility of
spiking fuel or denaturing fissile thorium. The concept of denaturing Pu-239 with Pu-240, however, is now generally
discredited.[97]

Table 3.4 presents a qualitative comparison of different reactor
systems in terms of their proliferation ranking at different points in
the nuclear fuel cycle. The letter ranks refer to the suitability of the
nuclear material for weapons purposes at each stage of the fuel cycle
according to the following scale:[98]

A—No significant potential for conversion to weapons-usable
form; very sophisticated and costly technical capability
required.

B—Highly dilute and substantially radioactive material.
Diversion possible for national actor but unlikely for subnational group.

C—Concentrated material, but contains sufficient radioactive
isotopes to require heavily shielded processing,
or
highly diluted material so that large quantities must be
diverted. Possible for non-state adversary to steal and convert to weapons material but would be a difficult task.

Table 3.4. Reactor Proliferation-Resistance Report Card

	Fabrication and Transport of Fresh Fuel	Reactor (Including Fuel Storage at the Reactor)	Spent Fuel Transport and Storage	Reprocessing	Reprocessed Fuel Fabrication (Including Transport)
LWR, no reprocessing	A	B	B		
LWR, Pu recycle	C	C (onsite fresh MOX) B (spent fuel)	B	E	E (if fuel not blended at reprocessing plant) C (if fuel blended at reprocessing plant)
HWR (CANDU), no reprocessing	A	B	B		
HTGR	D	D (fresh fuel) C (spent fuel)	C	E	C
LMFBR	E	E (fresh fuel) C (spent fuel)	C	E	E

Source: Derived in large part from the Office of Technology Assessment "Reactor Diversion Report Card" printed in *Nuclear Proliferation and Safeguards,* Office of Technology Assessment Report (New York: Praeger, 1977), p. 165.

D—Substantial chemical and/or mechanical processing required, but possible for nonstate adversary to convert for weapons use. Also can signify material in concentrated form suitable for straightforward conversion to weapons, with modest radioactivity, but needed for continued operation of fuel cycle (i.e., more attractive for overt theft than covert diversion).

E—Material in concentrated form suitable for straightforward conversion to weapons, with modest radioactivity. Easy for nonstate adversary to use as weapons material or to convert for weapons use.

NOTES

1. The principal exceptions are Ted Greenwood, George W. Rathjens, and Jack Ruina, "Nuclear Power and Weapons Proliferation," *Adelphi Paper*, no. 130 (London: International Institute for Strategic Studies, 1976); Albert Wohlstetter et al., *Swords from Plowshares* (Chicago: The University of Chicago Press, 1979); and Office of Technology Assessment, *Nuclear Proliferation and Safeguards* (New York: Praeger Publishers, 1977).
2. This section relies heavily on Greenwood et al.
3. Greenwood et al., p. 3.
4. A material not itself fissionable by slow (thermal) neutrons but that can be converted into a fissile material by irradiation in a reactor is known as *fertile*.
5. Greenwood et al., p. 3.
6. Anthony V. Nero, *A Guidebook to Nuclear Reactors* (Los Angeles: University of California Press, 1979), p. 187. Greenwood et al. (p. 3) cite slightly higher figures.
7. Greenwood et al., p. 6.
8. Ibid., p. 5.
9. Ibid.
10. John E. Gray et al., *International Cooperation on Breeder Reactors* (New York: The Rockefeller Foundation, 1978), p. B-5.
11. A 330 MW high-temperature gas-cooled reactor began service in 1979 in Platteville, Colorado for the Public Service Company of Colorado.
12. For a detailed discussion of both light-water reactors see Nero.
13. Ridgely Evers et al., *Nonproliferation Factbook,* prepared by Reference Research Associates for the U.S. Arms Control and Disarmament Agency (Palo Alto, 1978), p. 47. Refueling does not have to occur quite as often for BWRs. Nero (p. 107) cites 18 months as a recommended refueling sequence for one General Electric BWR.
14. The PWR normally requires one-third of its fuel assembles to be replaced while the BWR requires approximately one-fourth.
15. *Nuclear Proliferation and Safeguards*, p. 152.
16. Ibid., pp. 155-156.
17. Ibid., p. 159.
18. Ibid. The same study estimates that to obtain 10 kg of plutonium at least 5700 kg of low burn-up uranium-oxide fuel would have to be diverted, or about 260 fuel

bundles. For normal burn-up, the fuel requirement is 2800 kg or 130 bundles. As a basis for comparison, in the CANDU-600 model approximately 12 fuel bundles are pushed through the reactor each day.

19. Reported in *Nuclear Proliferation and Civilian Nuclear Power: Report of the Nonproliferation Alternative Systems Assessment Program* (Washington, D.C.: U.S. Department of Energy, June 1980), volume 2, pp. 2-13. In subsequent citations this source will be referred to as NASAP.

20. Ibid., pp. 2-12. Under the London Suppliers Guidelines, the export of heavy water and heavy-water technology is supposed to trigger the application of safeguards.

21. Anthony Nero (p. 228) writes that "the HTGR is in the odd position of no longer being available commercially, but of drawing considerable attention nevertheless." Gulf General Atomic built one 300 MW$_e$ HTGR which is now in operation in Fort St. Vrain, Colorado but in late 1975 cancelled all other orders and suspended sales. Construction of a 300 MW$_e$ German HTGR was listed as 70 percent complete as of December 31, 1980. In Great Britain an "advanced gas reactor" (AGR) utilizing carbon dioxide as a coolant also has been developed. See "Introduction to Nuclear Power," Gray et al., p. B-17.

22. The mix of the fuel changes over the reactor lifetime, the initial loading consisting of highly enriched uranium or Th-232. An alternative fuel cycle employing much lower uranium enrichment is also possible with the HTGR and is discussed below.

23. See Nero, p. 228.

24. NASAP, vol. 2, pp. 2-15.

25. The possibility of breeding fissile fuel from fertile material in a power reactor was first demonstrated in 1951.

26. A description of the LMFBR is provided below and some of the features of the other breeder types are noted in Table 3.1. For a detailed analysis of these other types see Gray et al., vol. II, pp. C-1 to C-124; NASAP, vol. 9, pp. 83-12, 139-158, and 227-240; and Nero, pp. 215-234.

27. Other nations with active programs of research on fast breeders are Belgium, Brazil, Italy, the Netherlands, Spain, and Switzerland. The British, French, and Russians already have prototype LMFBRs in operation with outputs of 250-350 MW$_e$. (Nero, p. 211)

28. See NASAP, vol. 9, pp. 159-160.

29. Ibid., p. 159.

30. Two basic methods may be used to produce Pu fuel: (1) conventional (non-breeding) reactors using U-235/U-238 fuel elements produce Pu material which can be reprocessed; and (2) the first fuel charge for LMFBRs can use U-235/U-238 fuel elements, with the U-235 eventually being replaced in subsequent core reloads by bred Pu. This is described in Gray et al., pp. 1-5.

31. NASAP, Vol. 2, pp. 2-42.

32. The Office of Technology Assessment Study *Nuclear Proliferation and Safeguards*, p. 159, puts the figure at 2-6 times greater concentration for the LMFBR.

33. In the LWR cycle, plutonium of this quality is produced only by operating with frequent and very costly refuelings. (*Nuclear Proliferation and Safeguards*, p. 160.)

34. Thorium-232, a naturally occuring fertile isotope which, by absorbing neutrons, can be converted to the fissile isotope U-233, is a potentially important resource for future reactor fuel cycles. This section, however, focuses primarily on uranium since it is the essential mineral for fuel cycles presently in use.

35. A discussion of uranium availability is provided in Chapter 4, "The Economics of Nuclear Power."

36. At present, there is no industry in the United States for producing thorium as a primary product and no industrial experience in producing throium from thorite vein ores. Recent U.S. production of thorium has been a by-product of monazite recovered in mining titanium. For a description of thorium mining and milling see NASAP, vol. 9, pp. 296–297.
37. Greenwood et al., p. 9.
38. A fifth process, plasma separation, has been under development in the United States since 1976, but is still in the early stages of R&D. The process is based on the frequency differences in ion cyclotron resonance between U-235 and U-238. See *INFCE Summary Volume* (Vienna: IAEA, 1980), p. 96 and NASAP, Vol. 9, pp. 315–316.
39. Nuclear Energy Policy Study Group, *Nuclear Power Issues and Choices* (Cambridge, Massachusetts: Ballinger, 1977), p. 400.
40. Pilot plants employing a gas centrifuge technology are now in operation in Europe by the British-Dutch-West German firm, URENCO. A very large gas centrifuge plant is also scheduled for construction in Portsmouth, Ohio. A discussion of the status of American gas centrifuge development is provided in NASAP, vol. 9, pp. 308–309.
40. For a detailed discussion of the gas centrifuge process see NASAP, vol. 9, pp. 304–308.
42. Ibid., p. 305. Separative work output refers to the work required to separate uranium isotopes in the enrichment process.
43. Greenwood et al., p. 22.
44. See Greenwood et al., pp. 47–48 for a more detailed discussion of this technique.
45. See *INFCE Summary Volume*.
46. This assumes a tails assay of 0.2 percent. See Greenwood et al., p. 47.
47. See Richard K. Lester, "Laser Enrichment of Uranium: Does the Genie Have a Future?" *Technology Review* (August–September 1980), p. 20.
48. For a discussion of the atomic vapor laser isotope separation (AVLIS) and molecular laser isotope separation (MLIS) processes see ibid., pp. 20–22 and NASAP, vol. 9, pp. 312–315.
49. Lester (p. 21) estimates that both AVLIS and MLIS will probably require less than 10 percent of the energy per unit of output than that consumed by the gaseous diffusion process.
50. Such plants typically discharge about a quarter of the original U-235 in a depleted wastes (i.e., "tails") stream. See Lester, p. 21.
51. *Nuclear Power Issues and Choices*, p. 401.
52. Cited in Lester, p. 24. Lester (p. 25) suggests that the MLIS approach may be less challenging technically than the AVLIS process and more attractive to the potential proliferator.
53. Greenwood et al., p. 10.
54. Ibid.
55. Ibid.
56. Ibid.
57. For a description of the PUREX process see Greenwood et al., pp. 35–37.
58. The THOREX process is described in Greenwood et al., pp. 37–38.
59. Greenwood et al., p. 17.
60. Ibid. Reprocessed uranium from HTGRs could be used to produce a low-yield nuclear weapon. As previously noted, the quality of plutonium for weapons purposes would be affected by the reactor in which it was produced and its irradiation time.
61. *Nuclear Power Issues and Choices*, p. 331.

62. See *Nuclear Proliferation and Safeguards,* pp. 200–201. For a more optimistic view of the use of spiking to prevent subnational diversion of plutonium see C. Starr and E. Zebroski, "Nuclear Power and Weapons Proliferation," paper presented at the American Power Conference, April 18-20, 1977, pp. 15–16. A review of alternative technical measures aimed at increasing diversion resistance is provided in *Reprocessing, Plutonium Handling, Recycle,* Report of the INFCE Working Group 4, (Vienna: IAEA, 1980), pp. 144–148.

63. *Reprocessing Plutonium Handling, Recycle,* p. 34. A slightly shorter list of planned commercial reprocessing facilities is provided by Gene I. Rochlin, *Plutonium, Power and Politics* (Berkeley: University of California Press, 1979), pp. 106–108. See also pp. 74–77.

64. On this point see Greenwood et al., p. 18, and *Quick and Secret Construction of Plutonium Reprocessing Plants: A Way to Nuclear Weapons Proliferation?* Report by the Comptroller General of the United States, EMD-78-104 (Washington, D.C.: U.S. General Accounting Office, October 6, 1978).

65. An Oak Ridge National Laboratory memorandum of August 30, 1977 estimated that a small reprocessing facility could be constructed in four to six months. See *Quick and Secret Construction of Plutonium Reprocessing Plants,* p. ii. Greenwood et al. (p. 18) use the much higher figure of three to seven years, the precise time depending on the country. For yet another estimate (one or two years and tens of millions of dollars) see NASAP, vol. 2, p. 2–6.

66. Greenwood et al., p. 18.

67. It is interesting to note that relatively little public concern over nuclear waste has focused on the large volume of highly radioactive mine tailings. One study suggests that this lack of concern may be due to the public's perception of uranium excavation and milling as part of a category of generally accepted mining practices. See Thomas J. Connolly et al., *World Nuclear Energy Paths,* Report of the International Consultative Group on Nuclear Energy (New York: The Rockefeller Foundation/Royal Institute of International Affairs, 1979), p. 116.

68. Rustum Roy, "The Technology of Nuclear-Waste Management," *Technology Review* (April 1981), p. 39.

69. Nero, pp. 173–174.

70. See *Nuclear Power Issues and Choices,* pp. 254–260; NASAP, vol. 9, pp. 379–380; and *Waste Management and Disposal,* Report of INFCE Working Group 7 (Vienna: IAEA, 1980), pp. 52–63.

71. NASAP, vol. 9, p. 380.

72. Ibid., p. 381. Roy (p. 40) reports that "the fundamental strategy for the permanent disposal of radioactive wastes from reactor fuel has recently undergone a significant change. Confidence in geologic isolation has decreased while confidence in the effectiveness of carefully engineered waste packages [consisting of layers of extremely impermeable, chemically resistant solids] has grown." Roy, however, does not cite specific government sources and the "significant change" he refers to is not reflected in the June 1980 NASAP report or in the February 1980 INFCE Report. See *Waste Management and Disposal.*

73. *INFCE Summary Volume,* p. 233.

74. Irwin C. Bupp, "The Actual Growth and Probable Future of the Worldwide Nuclear Industry," *International Organization* (Winter 1981), p. 74. A recent Federal District Court ruling declared that states do not have the right to refuse out-of-state shipments of nuclear waste. See *New York Times,* June 27, 1981, p. 6.

75. Much of the discussion in this section is derived from the nine volume NASAP report, *Nuclear Proliferation and Civilian Nuclear Power.*

76. NASAP, vol. 1, p. 17.
77. Ibid.
78. NASAP, vol. 2, p. 2-4.
79. For a discussion of the technical issues involved see ibid., pp. 2-5 to 2-6.
80. Greenwood et al., p. 25.
81. NASAP, vol. 2, p. 2-6. The report only indicates that the plant would produce enough HEU for tens of weapons per year.
82. On this point see *Advanced Fuel Cycle and Reactor Concepts,* Report of INFCE Working Group 8 (Vienna: IAEA, 1980), p. 74.
83. A total of five HTGRs have been or are being built. See NASAP, vol. 9, p. 123.
84. See *Advanced Fuel Cycle and Reactor Concepts,* p. 81.
85. NASAP, vol. 2, p. 2-20.
86. Ibid., pp. 2-21. For a view that oxides of plutonium are suitable directly for use in weapons see Peter Zimmerman and Forrest Frank "Nuclear Terrorism, Another Look," *Bulletin of the American Physical Society* (April 1979), p. 658.
87. *Nuclear Power Issues and Choices,* p. 331.
88. Ibid.
89. NASAP, vol. 2, p. 2-21.
90. Ibid.
91. Useful discussions of thorium fuel cycles are provided in Anthony V. Nero, "Beyond the Light Water Reactor," *Bulletin of the Atomic Scientists* (February 1980), pp. 31-37; Amory B. Lovins, "Thorium Cycles and Proliferation," *Bulletin of the Atomic Scientists* (February 1979), pp. 16-22; Frank Von Hippel and Robert H. Williams, "On Thorium Cycles and Proliferation," *Bulletin of the Atomic Scientists* (March 1979), pp. 50-52; and *Nuclear Proliferation and Safeguards,* pp. 160-161. See also *Advanced Fuel Cycle and Reactor Concepts,* pp. 86-97 and NASAP, vol. 2, pp. 2-32 to 2-33.
92. The NASAP study, however, points out that "enriching U-233 in denatured fuel requires less separative work to achieve high enrichments than does enriching U-235 in LEU to the same level of enrichment." (See NASAP, vol. 2, p. 2-32). A critical view of the merits of denatured thorium-uranium cycles is provided by Lovins.
93. NASAP, vol. 2, p. 2-40.
94. Ibid., p. 2-43.
95. Ibid.
96. These conclusions are similar to those reached in the NASAP study although NASAP prefers the LWR to the CANDU HWR.
97. For a dissenting view, see Alexander De Volpi, *Proliferation, Plutonium and Policy* (New York: Pergamon Press, 1979).
98. This scale is derived from *Nuclear Proliferation and Safeguards,* p. 163.

Chapter 4

The Economics of
Nuclear Power

In the 1960s and early 1970s the term "nuclear revolution" appeared to aptly characterize the economic as well as military transformation wrought by the splitting of the atom. Major advances in nuclear technology, projections of rapidly expanding global energy demand, and heavy investments by electric utilities in nuclear power contributed to the expectations—widely shared in the United States and abroad—that a nuclear economic era was emerging. This perception was reinforced by the sharp rise in oil prices following the 1973 oil embargo and the corresponding surge in nuclear power plant orders.[1]

Very different expectations prevail in most industrialized countries at the beginning of the 1980s. With the notable exception of France and the Soviet Union, where civilian nuclear power continues to be promoted rigorously, prior faith in nuclear power has been replaced by growing "concern, pessimism and not infrequently hostility."[2] Even before the nuclear accident at Three Mile Island in 1979, U.S. utility companies had virtually ceased to order nuclear-powered generating equipment. Between 1975 and 1980 they purchased fewer than a half-dozen reactors and cancelled approximately fifty previous orders. A similar de facto moratorium on new orders occurred in the Federal Republic of Germany, the Netherlands, Italy, Sweden, and Ireland, and cancellations or indefinite deferrals of reactor orders were commonplace in

Australia, Austria, China, Denmark, Iran, New Zealand, and Norway.[3] In order to explain these developments and to assess their implications for the future of nuclear power and weapons proliferation, it is necessary to examine the recent history of American and global energy demand and supply.

ENERGY DEMAND AND SUPPLY

For approximately a quarter of a century, beginning in the late 1940s, most industrialized states experienced a rapid and steady growth in the demand for electrical energy. This growth rate averaged nearly seven percent per year and, as late as the early 1970s, was regarded as likely to continue at the same pace for at least another quarter of a century.[4] Since 1974, however, projections of future growth rates have been revised downward dramatically to the point where "today the highest official estimates of U.S. energy needs in the year 2000 are below the lowest, most heretical unofficial estimates made in 1972."[5]

A major consequence of the reduced demand for electricity and the failure of utilities in most countries to respond quickly to this development has been the creation of considerable overcapacity in these countries' generating systems. Revised forecasts of electricity demand and the unanticipated development of overcapacity in existing and projected power grids have contributed directly to the plummeting of nuclear power forecasts. Between 1974 and 1979, for example, nuclear power projections for the year 2000 fell by a factor of five for the world, nearly four for West Germany, and eight for the United States.[6] This nuclear power malaise is clearly reflected in reactor-ordering rates. As Table 4.1 indicates, more than six times as many reactors were ordered in the United States between 1970 and 1974 than between 1975 and 1979, with similar if slightly less dramatic drops occurring in other major Western supplier states, except for France.

The economic difficulties responsible for the current recession in nuclear power do not mean that utilities in most countries will abandon nuclear power. One major study on *The Viability of the Civil Nuclear Industry,* for example, maintains that "most utilities still look with favor on nuclear power for the opportunity it provides for diversification of input energy supplies, and for its low running costs."[7] Government policy in many countries also may have the effect of encouraging expanded use of nuclear power for reasons other than strict considerations of economic rationality. These incentives include energy independence, international

Table 4.1. Per Annum Ordering Rates in Domestic and Export Markets, 1970–1974, 1975–1979 (gigawatts per annum)

	Domestic		Export		Total	
	1970–74	*1975–79*	*1970–74*	*1975–79*	*1970–74*	*1975–79*
Canada	0.7	1.2	0.2	0.2	0.9	1.4
France	3.4	3.4	0.4	0.7	3.8	4.1
West Germany	1.8	1.0	0.5	0.7	2.3	1.7
Japan	2.4	0.9	–	–	2.4	0.9
Sweden	0.5	0.2	0.2	–	0.7	0.2
U.K.	0.8	0.0	–	–	0.8	0.0
USA	21.6	2.4	5.7	1.4	27.3	3.8
Other noncommunist countries	6.8	3.0	–	–	–	–
Total	38.0	12.1	7.0	3.0	33.2	12.1

Source: Mans Lönnroth and William Walker, *The Viability of the Civil Nuclear Industry,* Report of the International Consultative Group on Nuclear Energy (New York: The Rockefeller Foundation and the Royal Institute of International Affairs, 1979), p. 28.

prestige, competition for high-technology export markets, and large investments already sunk in partially completed nuclear plant programs. Indeed, much of the variance in the present health of nuclear industries across countries can be explained by the differences in national nuclear energy objectives and the nuclear industries' relationship to government.

CHARACTERISTICS OF THE CIVIL NUCLEAR INDUSTRY[8]

In functional terms, the nuclear industry can be broken down into four segments. Although the characteristics of each segment and the relationship among the parts vary according to reactor and fuel cycle type, the four general segments are: (1) the uranium-mining industry; (2) the fuel cycle industry (front end and back end); (3) the reactor industry; and (4) the fuel cycle equipment supply industry. (See Figure 4.1.) Supporting the development of each of these segments is the nuclear R&D industry. The electricity supply industry, while not actually a part of the nuclear industry, interacts and overlaps with it.[9]

A major feature of the nuclear industry is its concentration on a single market—electricity generation. It consequently lacks significant opportunities to expand its capital base and to spread commercial risks through product diversification. It is also particularly sensitive to conditions within the electrical supply industry, "the pivot around which the nuclear industry rotates and in many respects the key decision-making unit."[10]

Commercial nuclear industries usually have been the recipient of significant government assistance and direction because of their military and energy independence implications, and their enormous, long-term financial requirements. The kind and degree of government influence over the nuclear industry, however, varies considerably across countries and reflects, among other factors, the commitment to a military nuclear program, conditions of energy supply and demand, the period during which the industry was developed, and national traditions of industrial organization. Table 4.2 compares several dimensions of this government involvement in the nuclear industries of eight major nuclear supplier states.

One must be cautious not to equate private ownership with the absence of government control. Nevertheless, one can discern a basic contrast between those states in which ownership and control of the nuclear industry are vested in the central government (for example, France and the USSR) and those countries in which

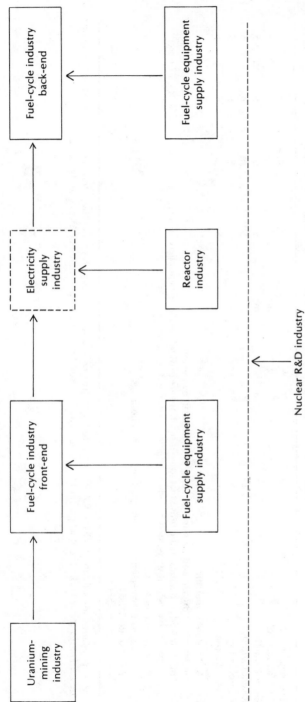

Figure 4.1. Functional breakdown of the nuclear industry. (*Source:* Mans Lönnroth and William Walker, *The Viability of the Civil Nuclear Industry*, Report of the International Consultative Group on Nuclear Energy (New York: The Rockefeller Foundation and The Royal Institute of International Affairs, 1979), p. 8.)

Table 4.2. Patterns of Ownership in the Nuclear and Electric Utility Industries

	USA	Japan	West Germany	Sweden	Canada	France	U.K.	USSR
Enrichment	S	m	P*	—	—	S	S	S
Fuel fabrication	P	P	P	m	P	m	S	S
Electric utilities	m*	m*	m	m*	S	S	S	S
Reactor supply	P	P	P*	m	S	m	m	S
Reprocessing	—	S	P*	—	—	S	S	S
Waste disposal	?	?	S	?	S	S	S	S

Key: S = state ownership
 m = mixed private and state (central and/or provincial) ownership
 m* = mixed ownership, in the sense that some institutions are privately and others publicly owned, e.g., in the United States, 77 percent of electricity is generated by private utilities, 23 percent by public utilities
 P = private ownership
 P* = private ownership with significant utility shareholdings
 ? = undecided
 — = not relevant

Source: Mans Lönnroth and William Walker, *The Viability of the Civil Nuclear Industry*, Report of the International Consultative Group on Nuclear Energy (New York: The Rockefeller Foundation and The Royal Institute of International Affairs, 1979), p. 12.

ownership and coordination are primarily in private hands (most notably the United States). Between these extremes is another category of states in which nuclear decision-making is centralized, "but by joint action within the private sector, with some government involvement" (for example, Sweden and West Germany).[11] A parallel distinction can be made among states in terms of the commercial risks involved in nuclear production borne by the central government.

Although decisions about the ownership and regulation of nuclear industries were, for the most part, taken when market prospects appeared to be favorable, since the mid-1970s deteriorating global economic conditions have clearly favored nuclear industries in countries "in which governments exert strong control over, and share risks with, nuclear industries and, most importantly, electric utilities."[12] Conversely, nuclear power appears to be most vulnerable where there is an absence of centralized planning and control, where risks are borne principally by private concerns, and where the possibilities exist for judicial and political intervention in the decision-making process at local and regional levels.[13]

THE NUCLEAR EXPORT MARKET

The light-water reactor (LWR) developed by the United States has long dominated the international nuclear export market. This dominance was established through the coincidence of a number of factors including: (1) the U.S. headstart in LWR technology due to the American nuclear submarine program; (2) readiness by U.S. manufacturers to license LWR technology to firms overseas; (3) favorable commercial terms attached by the U.S. government to the supply of enriched uranium for LWRs; and (4) U.S. postwar hegemony in political, economic, and military affairs. The latter point was particularly important as it contributed to the perception in the United States that manageable risks were attached to the proliferation of most nuclear technologies (the exception being uranium-enrichment technology, which was closely guarded). Also underlying this perception was the notion of the "nuclear bargain," by which countries were given access to the benefits of nuclear energy in exchange for assurances of the technology's peaceful use.[14] The political economy of Atoms for Peace, in other words, reflected a combination of idealism and self-interest. On the one hand, the promotion of nuclear energy through nuclear exports was regarded as a progressive force which contributed to economic development while deterring nuclear weapons ambitions. On the other hand, "America's leading technological position created the prospect of nurturing and dominating a world nuclear market in a classic model of 'free trade imperialism'."[15]

The optimistic view of U.S. military and economic security underlying the Atoms for Peace approach to nonproliferation gave way by the mid-1970s to a more pessimistic assessment of American power and growing concern over the likelihood and consequences of nuclear weapons proliferation. At the same time as the United States sought to curtail nuclear weapons proliferation by tightening the liberal trading conditions which had characterized the nuclear market in the 1960s and early 1970s, other states began to make aggressive moves into the nuclear export market. France and West Germany promoted for export a complete range of fuel cycle technologies in addition to reactors, and the United Kingdom and the Soviet Union demonstrated a capability to compete with the United States for reprocessing and enrichment customers. A clash, therefore, developed among nuclear supplier countries and between supplier and recipient states over the terms of nuclear trade.[16]

The potential for confrontation among supplier countries over the terms of nuclear trade has been aggravated by the depressed state of most manufacturers' domestic nuclear markets. As one study points out, this risk of confrontation might have been anticipated because exports are apt to be regarded as appropriate means to avoid "necessary but painful adjustments to domestic manufacturing capacities, and of gaining time in which to resolve domestic disputes over nuclear power."[17] Based on domestic nuclear capacity utilization and market prospects, one can usefully distinguish among three groups of nuclear-exporting states.

The first group consists of France and the Soviet Union, countries which remain optimistic about nuclear power, continue to invest heavily in new nuclear programs such as the fast breeder reactor, and have reasonably high nuclear capacity utilization. They consequently face no urgent need to adjust manufacturing capacity and are less dependent on nuclear exports than other supplier states.[18] They have also found that it is more lucrative financially to provide enrichment and reprocessing services from plants located at home than to export small-scale facilities.[19] For the time being, therefore, the economic interests of their nuclear industries would not appear to suffer substantially from a nonproliferation strategy which restricted nuclear exports—something which cannot be said about the other major nuclear exporters. Pierre Lellouche, in fact, goes so far as to assert that "France enjoys a unique position among

Western nations—its nonproliferation policy coincides with the economic interests of its nuclear industry."[20]

The second set of nuclear-exporting states consists of Canada, Japan, and the United Kingdom.[21] These countries remain committed to programs of nuclear power development, although the market prospects for their reactors and associated nuclear services are uncertain. Growth rates for electricity demand are lower than anticipated, and will probably require an adaptation downward in manufacturing capacity for each state's nuclear industry. Economic difficulties, however, do not appear likely to force their withdrawal from the nuclear market.

The United States, West Germany, and Sweden make up the third category of nuclear suppliers and constitute the group whose nuclear industries are most threatened by domestic political opposition, poor fiscal health, substantial overcapacity in their electrical supply systems, and poor short-term market prospects. Given their domestic predicament, the reactor industries of this third group of states are much more dependent than the countries in the first or second groups on nuclear exports. According to one German analyst, for example, "the German reactor industry is condemned to produce for the foreign market even under the most unfavorable conditions, if only to keep its skilled personnel, its production facilities, and R&D capacity together for those halcyon days in the distant future when the present deadlock over domestic reactor construction may have to come to an end."[22] The U.S. industry has been even more constrained than its beleaguered West German counterpart since it could not count on a continuing government commitment to nuclear power and had to contend with strenuous efforts to restrict international transfers of "sensitive" nuclear materials and technologies.[23]

NUCLEAR POWER AND
THE THIRD WORLD

Because the domestic markets of Western supplier states are now virtually closed to international nuclear trade and since Western suppliers have little access to Soviet or East European markets, efforts to expand nuclear exports have increasingly focused on the countries of the Third World. Since a number of these countries are also primary candidates for nuclear weapons status, nuclear trade with them has become highly politicized and the subject of controversy. It has also led to disputes between supplier states over the terms of trade (e.g., between the United States and West Germany over the latter's exports to Brazil) and to conflicts between supplier states and developing countries over the latter's right to acquire certain nuclear technologies (e.g., between Pakistan and France and between South Korea and the United States).

Although the depressed state of Western markets in the late 1970s intensified the search for exports in the Third World, the United States and other nuclear suppliers have long tempted the developing countries with visions of cheap, abundant, and safe nuclear power. As early as 1958, the U.S. Atomic Energy Commission had concluded agreements for nuclear trade and cooperation with over forty states, including many developing nations.[24] Despite this early commitment, however, nuclear power has still made little headway in the Third World, accounting for only 3000 MW$_e$ in 1980 or less than 3 percent of the world nuclear capacity.[25]

The slow pace of nuclear power's introduction into the Third World stems from a number of factors. They include: the incompatibility of the large, standard reactors (600 to 1300 MW$_e$) offered for export by Western suppliers with the small electrical grids in most developing states; the lack of skilled personnel and a technical infrastructure to support nuclear power operation (India is a notable exception in this regard); and the high capital costs usually associated with nuclear power plant construction. Several supplier states recently have developed small, self-contained reactor units of greater potential utility to countries with small electrical systems and frequently have offered large subsidies and other "sweeteners" to potential customers. Despite this, lower-than-anticipated growth rates for energy demand, skyrocketing foreign debts, and an ideological aversion to turn-key imports cloud the future for nuclear development in the Third World.[26] As will be discussed below, non-economic considerations of domestic politics, prestige, and military potential, as well as overall energy supply and dependence pressures and the course of nuclear power development in the industrialized states, probably will ultimately determine the future of nuclear power in developing countries.

PROLIFERATION IMPLICATIONS OF A DEPRESSED NUCLEAR MARKET

Despite the economic difficulties encountered by U.S. reactor manufacturers since the worldwide decline in nuclear power plant orders, the depression in the nuclear market was not altogether unwelcome in Washington. During the outset of the Carter administration, in particular, a view emerged which regarded a de facto moratorium on nuclear power development as a potentially useful instrument of nonproliferation policy.. According to this perspective, since the development of civil nuclear power could facilitate nuclear weapons manufacture (and might be particularly attractive for states that sought to develop a weapons options unobtrusively), a quantitative reduction in nuclear power capability could only assist nonproliferation efforts.[27]

Arguments linking the slowdown in civil nuclear power to a nonproliferation solution, although having a certain intuitive appeal, are subject to a number of criticisms. They pertain to the observed behavior of supplier states and the plausible, if more difficult to substantiate, behavior of recipient countries during the current nuclear power recession.

One demonstrable consequence of the glut in the nuclear market was fierce competition among suppliers in the mid-1970s. This competition led supplier states to offer "sweeteners" (such as high-technology training and fuel cycle facilities) to potential buyers in order to win bids for nuclear projects. Illustrative of this kind of nuclear marketing, where nonproliferation considerations take a back seat to economic interests, were past efforts by French and West German firms to sell fuel cycle facilities to South Korea, Pakistan, and Brazil (either as a possible prelude or supplement to power reactor sales) and more recent West German and Canadian bids to supply Argentina with a heavy-water production plant as a part of a larger package involving one or more heavy-water power reactors.[28]

Competition among nuclear suppliers struggling to obtain customers in a depressed market situation has also discouraged the extension of export controls to new areas. This is illustrated by the recent contract signed with Argentina by the German manufacturer Kraftwerk Union (KWU). As reported in the trade journal *Nucleonics Week,* the winning German bid for the order was higher than that of a competing Canadian firm but, unlike the Canadian one, did not require full-scope safeguards. The KWU contract was also linked to one signed with a Swiss firm providing for the transfer of a heavy-water production plant to Argentina.[29] As Pierre Lellouche points out, the deal with Argentina, although not technically a violation of the London Supplier's Group guidelines, supports "the view that European suppliers are not willing to pay for nonproliferation."[30]

Less demonstrable to date, but plausible, is the argument that a nuclear power slowdown would cause many countries to adopt a holding pattern in which they would defer large-scale commitments to nuclear power, acquiring instead less expensive, small-scale research and training reactors and associated fuel cycle facilities. Such a move, it has been suggested, would be attractive for countries which sought to avoid falling behind technologically in a period of nuclear power uncertainty.[31] The troublesome aspect of this development, from the standpoint of nonproliferation, is that small-scale fuel cycle facilities and research reactors are very useful for the production of weapons-grade material but are extremely difficult to safeguard. A related argument is also sometimes made that a slowdown in civil nuclear power will raise proliferation risks by encouraging highly trained personnel to be rechanneled from civil nuclear power activities to those with a military orientation.[32] Consistent with this perspective is the fear that some of the partially completed nuclear power projects will become bomb projects simply because their project managers see this as "an easy way—the only way—to redeem their investment, to protect their own reputations, or their national interest."[33] Perhaps the most convincing argument is that a recession in nuclear power development cannot counteract international security and political incentives to acquire nuclear weapons. A nuclear energy depression precipitated by global economic difficulties, on the other hand, may well aggravate tensions between North and South and provide additional security incentives for nuclear weapons proliferation.[34]

THE COST OF NUCLEAR POWER

The original justification for nuclear power was that it would produce cheaper electricity than alternative energy sources. Since the 1973 oil embargo the argument also has frequently been made that nuclear power is necessary if the West is to replace its dependence on foreign oil, the worldwide production of which is expected to peak in the 1990s and decline thereafter. The charge is also made, however, that if the costs of nuclear power were adequately accounted for and its subsidies stripped away, it would cease to be competitive with alternative energy sources. To clarify these issues regarding the economics of nuclear power it is useful to review briefly the current economic significance of nuclear power generation and the availability of alternative energy supplies and to estimate the comparative costs of nuclear and other sources of electric power.

Table 4.3.   Power Reactors Currently in Operation, Under Construction, or on Order (as of December 31, 1980)

Country	No. of Units Operating	Total MW$_e$	No. of Units Under Construction or on Order	Total MW$_e$
Argentina	1	335	2	1292
Austria^a	—	—	—	—
Belgium	3	1650	4	3800
Brazil	0	0	3	3116
Bulgaria	2	880	2	880
Canada	10	5226	14	9880
Czechoslovakia	3	990	8	3520
Egypt	0	0	1	622
Finland	3	1500	1	660
France	21	12,818	40	43,350
FRG	11	8576	17	18,982
GDR	4	1390	3	1320
Hungary	0	0	4	1760
India	3	602	5	1082
Italy	4	1387	4	3868
Japan	22	14,552	12	9782
Korea, South	1	564	8	6834
Luxembourg	0	0	1	1250
Mexico	0	0	2	1308
Netherlands	2	495	0	0
Pakistan	1	125	0	0
Philippines	0	0	1	620
Poland	0	0	2	880
Romania	0	0	2	1040
South Africa	0	0	2	1844
Spain	5	1073	14	13,324
Sweden	6	3700	6	5710
Switzerland	4	1940	3	3007
Taiwan	2	1208	4	3716
Turkey	0	0	1	440
U.K.	33	8080	10	6340
USA	72	52,456	100	111,093
USSR	29	15,075	12	9710
Yugoslavia	0	0	1	615

Source: "World List of Nuclear Power Plants," *Nuclear News* (February 1981), pp. 75–94.
^{a}Austria has a 692 MW$_e$ BWR that is completed but has not been approved for operation.

The Current Status of Nuclear Power

The year 1980 ended with 240 nuclear units in commercial operation in 22 nations, representing 134,872 MW$_e$ of capacity. Another 293 units, representing 273,587 MW$_e$ were under construction or on order. The United States at the end of 1980 had 72 units representing 52,456 MW$_e$ in operation and an additional 100 units and 111,093 MW$_e$ under construction or on order.[36] Table 4.3 provides comparable data for other nuclear power users.

Domestic political opposition, rapidly escalating construction costs, and the fragile economic health of civil nuclear industries in most countries make it difficult to estimate when, if ever, nuclear plants under construction or on order will be completed.[36] Projections of U.S. and world nuclear power capacity, as previously indicated, also are very tenuous and, in recent years, have been revised downward dramatically. What can be said with confidence, however, is that at the end of the 1970s the contribution of nuclear power to total energy production was still small, amounting to approximately 2 percent in the United States. Even if one looks only at electric power generation, the sole form of energy that nuclear power can produce on a significant scale in the forseeable future, the contribution of nuclear power is modest, averaging about 12 percent in the United States and other industrialized countries.[37] Electric power generation, in turn, accounts for slightly more than a quarter of the primary energy used in the United States.

Table 4.4 presents a breakdown of the world's primary energy demand by fuel type, assuming economic and electricity growth rates of 3 percent. In this scenario, prepared by the Conservation Commission of the World Energy Conference in 1977,[38] the use of

Table 4.4. World Primary Energy Demand by Fuel Type in the World Energy Conference Scenario

	1972		1985		2000		2020	
Fuel	EJ[a]	%	EJ	%	EJ	%	EJ	%
Coal	66	25	77	22	125	24	276	33
Oil	115	43	147	42	159	31	135	16
Gas	46	17	50	14	67	13	84	10
Nuclear	2	1	22	6	83	16	212	25
Hydro	14	5	23	7	34	7	56	7
Other	26	10	30	9	48	9	70	8
Total	269	100	349	100	516	100	833	100

Source: Thomas J. Connolly et al., *World Nuclear Energy Paths*, Report of the International Consultative Group on Nuclear Energy (New York: The Rockefeller Foundation and The Royal Institute of International Affairs, 1979), p. 24.

[a]Exajoules (10^{18} joules).

electric power is expected to grow more rapidly than overall energy consumption. National and international political impediments to the development of nuclear power are also assumed "to gradually disappear over the next few years."[39] If we make these assumptions, which are favorable to the expansion of nuclear energy, the international economic significance of nuclear power changes from marginal in most states to very substantial in many countries in the next century—coal and nuclear power emerging as the pillars of global energy supply in the year 2000.

This scenario, however, has some major difficulties. It probably exaggerates future electricity demand, inflates projections of nuclear capacity, and entails wishful thinking that public opposition to nuclear power in the United States or abroad will soon disappear as the "true economic and technical facts" become known.[40] The frequent arguments of nuclear advocates that nuclear power is an important substitute for oil and that further increases in oil prices will automatically enhance the economic attractiveness of nuclear power are also less than self-evident. In the first place, only about one-tenth of the world's oil is used for making electricity. The remaining portion serves as fuel for vehicles, direct heating in homes and industry, and petrochemical feedstocks. U.S. nuclear expansion, therefore, has to a large extent served to displace coal, not oil.[41] It is doubtful, moreover, that an escalation of oil prices, if accompanied by general economic inflation and possible recession, will be advantageous to an industry such as nuclear power, which is dependent on highly capital-intensive technology with very long payoff lead times.[42] As one analyst points out, "the most general economic consequences of continued oil price increases seem at least as likely to deter additional investments in nuclear power as to promote them."[43] Although macroeconomic conditions of inflation and recession are apt to be especially burdensome for nuclear industries that cannot resort to government financial and political support, one can now observe a situation in France in which a political change combined with inflation and a slower-than-anticipated growth of demand for electricity may oblige the government to reduce the rate of nuclear power investment.

Alternative Energy Supplies

The cost of energy reflects the availability and cost of fuel supplies. Determining the availability of alternative energy resources, however, is not a simple accounting exercise and is often prejudiced by a bewildering assortment of highly technical methodological assumptions, less-than-reliable data sources, and not-so-subtle policy preferences. As a result, estimates of world energy supply—especially uranium resources—vary widely and are subject to very different interpretations.

Despite these difficulties of analysis, one can identify a convergence of findings in a number of recent, major studies on world energy reserves. They point to the inadequacy of oil and gas to meet future energy demands, the increased importance of coal and nuclear power for electricity generation, and the likelihood that the uranium market will offer supplies in excess of demand at least for the near future.[45]

The Adequacy of Uranium Supply

Most controversial of the energy supply issues and a central item in the debate over nuclear power—with implications for proliferation—is the availability of uranium for future nuclear power needs. If the world's commercially accessible uranium resources are perceived to be large relative to demand, then there is less pressure to move from reliance on natural or slightly enriched uranium reactor fuel to plutonium—"the stuff of nuclear weapons." Alternatively, if uranium resources are believed to be small compared to demand, it is likely that pressure will increase to move to a plutonium economy with reprocessing, recycling, and breeder reactors in order to extract more energy from each pound of uranium.[46]

Although uranium is a limited resource, it is not, as popularly imagined, a rare material in the earth's crust. In fact, it occurs as frequently as tin.[47] Knowledge of world uranium resources, however, is hampered by the relative infancy of uranium exploration and production (going back only forty years) and the extreme secrecy which surrounds the uranium industry.[48]

Although expert opinion varies widely regarding the timing of global uranium depletion, estimates of proven uranium reserves (i.e., the well-identified and commercially extractable resources) have risen steadily over the past fifteen years. The ratio of known uranium reserves and resources to projected nuclear reactor requirements has grown even more rapidly, leading Working Group 1 of the International Nuclear Fuel Cycle Evaluation to conclude that if the necessary exploration and investment were made, "the uranium industry should not experience undue difficulty" during this century in meeting the requirements of the nuclear power industry.[49]

The difficulty with this forecast—as with most other assessments of the uranium supply—is that it attaches little if any importance to geopolitical factors.[50] More specifically, the failure to examine the politicization of natural uranium supplies and the interaction of geological, geographical, economic, political and logistical factors obscure the risks many states associate with dependence on the small number of major uranium exporters (i.e., Australia, Canada, South Africa, Namibia and Niger.)[51]

The uncertain political future of several of the major producers magnifies these supply risks, although the recent discovery of economically recoverable resources in geographically diverse regions may eventually moderate this concern.[52] Those countries that rely heavily on nuclear power, however, are not apt to forget quickly the brief but difficult period in the mid-1970s when uranium production capacity proved inadequate to meet the sudden surge in demand.[53] As a consequence, even though a combination of factors (i.e., expansion of uranium production, large producer and consumer inventories of uranium, and a lack of new demand) would seem to reduce the pressure for prompt development and deployment of proliferation-sensitive, uranium-saving technologies like reprocessing and the breeder reactor, political considerations influenced by past problems of fuel supply may prove to be more consequential.

Uranium Supply and Nonproliferation Leverage

Light-water reactors requiring slightly enriched uranium as fuel account for approximately 90 percent of the world's present nuclear-generating capacity.[54] The assurance of enrichment services as well as a supply of natural uranium is thus crucial for most nations with a major commitment to nuclear power. (The principal present exception is Canada, whose reactors use natural rather than enriched uranium).

The dependence of most reactors on enriched uranium creates a situation in which security and economic issues of nuclear power are easily entangled. As one analyst notes, "if one nation were in a position to dominate the enrichment market, this nation could simultaneously establish a unilateral nonproliferation system and derive considerable commercial profits from the control of its customers' nuclear power programs."[55] This, in fact, was the situation which existed until the mid-1970s, with the United States monopolizing the commercial enrichment market outside the centrally planned economies. Officials associated with the formulation of U.S. nonproliferation policy from 1976 to 1978 appear to have viewed U.S. dominance of uranium enrichment as an important source of leverage.[56] By the end of the 1970s, however, the enrichment services market had changed dramatically due to the revision downward of global nuclear growth projections, an accompanying decline in enrichment contracting demand, and a sharp increase in foreign enrichment services.[57] The resulting surplus of enrichment capabilities presented consumer nations with the opportunity to alter past patterns of enrichment supply and, in some cases, to avoid further dependence on the United States.[58] Perhaps most striking was the rise in Soviet fuel service contracting with non-COMECON parties—estimated to account for between 50 and 80 percent of Western Europe's enriched fuel needs between 1980 and 1984.[59] The second major new source of enrichment supply was the EURODIF gaseous diffusion facility in France, with an annual output approximately half the size of current U.S. capacity.[60]

These changes in the uranium fuel market leave the United States in a weak position to influence markedly the future decisions of the major industrialized states on nuclear technology issues. Indeed, there is much substance to the observation that, "to the extent that there now exists any substantial supplier leverage over major nuclear fuel consumers, it is gradually passing from the United States to the currently largest actual and potential sources of raw uranium, notably Canada and Australia [although] even these two countries may have only transient influence, given the rapid expansion of output in Africa and intensive exploration elsewhere."[61]

The Competitiveness of Nuclear Power

So far our discussion of the cost of nuclear power has focused on the current and projected demand for nuclear-generated electricity and the availability of uranium to support this demand. Although a detailed analysis of the comparative costs of nuclear and alternative energy sources is beyond this study's purview, a brief comparison of coal and nuclear power may illustrate the magnitude of uncertainties which underlie fuel cost comparisons and the difficulty of neatly sorting out economic from political considerations.

Projections about generating costs rely heavily on the assessment of the determinants of past costs and their fluctuations and the judgment of how these factors will operate in the future. As the authors of the Ford/MITRE study *Nuclear Power Issues and Choices* point out, the primary cause for the recent sharp rise in the cost of nuclear power is inflated capital charges related to such factors as the lengthening of construction and licensing time and changes in plant design—factors which can be traced in part to new regulations motivated by safety and environmental concerns.[62] Their forecast, made in 1977, that these kinds of changes would "moderate" in the future and "be offset by other improvements," however, has not been borne out and does not appear likely to be in the near future, if for no other reason than the tightening of government licensing requirements after the accident at Three Mile Island and the lack of progress on radioactive waste disposal. Because the cost of nuclear power is dominated by capital charges,[63] uncertainties in the projection of future nuclear generating costs are enormous. Additional sources of uncertainty in nuclear power cost estimates are uranium price variation,[64] fluctuations in plant capacity factor (i.e., the total amount of electricity actually produced by a unit in a year divided by the amount of electricity the unit could produce running at full capacity), new technology developments, and the dilemma of spent fuel storage, transportation, and disposal.[65] These uncertainties become even greater if one seeks to assess the cost competiveness of nuclear power across countries where vast differences exist in terms of the degree of direct and indirect government subsidies to energy industries and the domestic availability of fuel supply and waste disposal facilities.

Coal-generated electricity is most likely to compete with nuclear power for future electricity generation. Projections of the cost of coal-generated electricity are clouded with uncertainties both similar to and different from those affecting nuclear power. Although capital charges represent a smaller fraction of the total cost of electricity from coal power plants compared to nuclear power plants, these charges are still a major percentage of coal-generated electricity costs and, like costs for nuclear plants, are subject to significant fluctuations due to inflation, variation in labor productivity, and government- and union-imposed environmental and safety regulations. Although greater experience with coal plant construction may account for less variable coal capital costs, the adoption of more stringent safety, health, and environmental standards (or their relaxation) could introduce considerable cost uncertainties. The possibility that new technologies for coal transportation and pollution control will be adopted, fluctuating coal mining costs, as well as variable capacity factors (dependent in part on the economic health of the nuclear industry) make estimates of future coal costs nearly as difficult to make as estimates for nuclear power. Indeed, the major difference in uncertainty appears to be that the topic of coal power plants is not as politicized as that of nuclear power and that the former industry is less likely to suffer major cutbacks due to domestic political opposition. For both industries, however, major sources of cost unpredictability are political variables in the form of government legislation, regulation, safety standards, taxes, and, in the case of many countries, substantial subsidies.

What conclusion can be drawn from this skeleton survey of the economics of coal and nuclear power? Certainly it is not that one should forego the effort to compare the costs of alternative forms of electricity production. It also is not possible on the basis of the material examined to reject out of hand either the claim that nuclear power is a bargain or the charge that it is not commercially viable. What does emerge from the preceding analysis is the extraordinarily complex nature of energy cost comparisons and the multiple sources of uncertainty. Extreme caution, therefore, must be exercised in weighing the evidence that nuclear power is or is not cost competitive. This is especially true for those countries in which governments exert strong control over and share risks with nuclear industries and electric utilities. The most that can be said with confidence in comparing the generating costs of coal and nuclear power is that the uncertainties of projected costs for both fuels are greater than any difference between them.[66]

THE ECONOMICS OF PLUTONIUM

While the dual potential of plutonium to serve as a nuclear explosive and as the key to an enormous source of constructive energy has long been recognized, it is only as commercial reprocessing and recycling have become more viable that major doubts about a "plutonium economy" have surfaced. These doubts pertain to both the economic merits of reprocessing and recycling and the opportunity they may provide for international nuclear weapons proliferation and domestic nuclear terrorism.

Plutonium, it should be recalled, is an element not found in nature but produced in reactors by the transformation of uranium-238 fuel. The spent fuel removed annually from a commercial light-water reactor contains approximately 250 kg of plutonium and 30 tons of uranium.[67] As noted in Chapter 1, it was generally assumed since the beginning of the U.S. nuclear program that spent fuel ultimately would be reprocessed and the recovered uranium and plutonium used to fuel conventional and breeder reactors. The belief also was widely shared that reprocessing was a necessary step in effective nuclear waste disposal[68] and that plutonium fuels would become a standard part of the international fuel cycle.[69] Indeed, it was on the basis of these assumptions that the United States moved between 1955 and 1958 to declassify the technology for the chemical reprocessing of spent fuel.[70]

Confidence in these assumptions, however, began to falter in the United States in the early 1970s for a number of reasons. Technical problems and unanticipated costs forced the permanent shutdown in 1972 of the world's first commercial reprocessing plant (the Nuclear Fuel Services facility in West Valley, New York) and two years later, the second commercial reprocessing facility to be built in the United States (a General Electric plant in Morris, Illinois) also was abandoned. A third commercial reprocessing facility in Barnwell, South Carolina fared little better and, although initially scheduled to begin operation in 1973, remains uncompleted.[71] These technical and economic difficulties, however, were probably less consequential in altering U.S. attitudes toward reprocessing than the 1974 plutonium-based Indian nuclear explosion and the news shortly thereafter that France and West Germany were considering the sale of pilot reprocessing or enrichment facilities to Iran, Pakistan, South Africa, South Korea, and Brazil. These events prompted the United States under President Ford to reexamine the assumption that safeguards were adequate to handle the reprocessing–proliferation connection, and set in motion the Carter administration's efforts to defer the recovery of plutonium from spent fuel and the commercial development of breeder reactors.[72]

Unlike the United States which, at the end of 1980, continued to challenge the wisdom of commercial reprocessing and plutonium recycling on economic and nonproliferation grounds, many other countries (including France, the Soviet Union, the United Kingdom, West Germany, Japan, India, Brazil, and Pakistan) actively pursued a nuclear power strategy of emphasizing fuel reprocessing. France has taken the lead in this area and has the only commercial oxide fuel reprocessing facility now operable.[73] French policy, however, has been to conserve reprocessed plutonium for an ambitious fast breeder reactor program rather than to recycle it for use in light-water reactors.[74]

The commitment many states have made to early commercialization of large-scale reprocessing facilities, however, is difficult to explain purely in terms of plutonium requirements for the fast breeder, since few fast breeders are apt to begin operation before the end of the century. Among the other arguments put forward in support of reprocessing are: (1) its economic advantages, (2) conservation of scarce energy resources, (3) energy independence and/or fuel supply assurance, (4) safe management of nuclear wastes, (5) acquisition of or participation in advanced nuclear technology, and (6) acquisition of the knowledge required for fast breeders.[75]

Economic Advantages

Even a brief survey of the literature on the economics of reprocessing tends to confirm Gene Rochlin's observation that probably no aspect of nuclear technology has inspired so many learned treatises with contradictory results.[76] In part this is probably due to the very different measures of economic advantage employed; the highly politicized nature of the debate; the genuinely complex nature of the issue, about which there can be honest differences of opinion; and the degree of uncertainty which underlies many necessary assumptions. Drawing upon the excellent literature review by Rochlin and the findings of Working Group 4 of INFCE (not available at the time of Rochlin's study), the following conclusions seem reasonable: (1) the economics of reprocessing are very uncertain due to the indeterminate nature of such variables as uranium fuel price, waste management, regulatory criteria, security requirements, maintenance philosophy, and method of financing;[77] (2) the economic advantage of reprocessing and recycling for light-water reactors is not likely to be great;[78] (3) the combination of high capital cost and the reduction of unit costs for large plants in economies of scale makes reprocessing economically unattractive for nations without a very large nuclear power generating capacity;[79] (4) regardless of the net economic benefits or losses of fuel reprocessing, the impact on the cost of nuclear-generated electric power will be small.[80]

Conservation of Scarce Energy Resources

Uranium conservation is often cited as an important reason to develop commercial reprocessing plants. It is estimated, for example, that plutonium recycling can add as much as 18 percent to the energy obtainable from the mining of a given amount of uranium ore.[81] If reprocessed uranium is also recycled, total resource extension can reportedly be as much as 32 percent.[82] These figures, it should be emphasized, pertain to the lifetime maximum savings for a given reactor. The immediate effect that recycling can have on current uranium requirements would be much smaller.

The argument for rapid commercialization of reprocessing and recycling is closely linked to expectations about the uranium resource base and the assurance of future production and enrichment services. The absence of indigenous uranium resources and the belief that shortages may develop in uranium ore and/or enrichment service is consistent with support for pursuing a reprocessing strategy on grounds that are not strictly economic. Alternatively, if uranium resources and enrichment capacity are assumed to be extensive, there is little incentive from the standpoint of resource conservation to move toward reliance on reprocessing and recycling.[83]

Energy Independence

The desire to reduce dependence on outside suppliers for energy needs is another argument often put forward in support of early commercialization of reprocessing. Although this desire is understandable, reduced overall energy dependence on other states through reprocessing and recycling appears to be possible at this time for only a small number of states which possess "the domestic technological base to operate reprocessing and recycle without dependence on foreign sources for components and technical and industrial aid."[84] As Rochlin points out, even for many of the most technologically developed states, such as Japan, the United Kingdom, West Germany, and Sweden, absolute dependence on imported uranium supplies will continue well into the next century, until fast breeder reactors are deployed.[85]

Safe Management of Nuclear Wastes

It is commonly believed, especially abroad, that reprocessing of spent fuel to remove plutonium reduces the long-term hazards of waste. Indeed, most nuclear waste management and disposal plans have been predicated on adequate reprocessing facilities.[86] The "reprocessing for safe waste management" thesis, however, has recently been subjected to sharp attack. On the one hand, it has been criticized by those who maintain that reprocessing "would introduce additional complications and uncertainties in the safe management of radioactive substances contained in spent fuel.[87] These critics emphasize the danger that reprocessing may pose in the form of contamination of large volumes of process chemicals and materials in the reprocessing facility, the release of radioactive gases which would otherwise be contained within the spent fuel rods, and the increased risk of both the illicit diversion of plutonium and of nuclear terrorism.[88] Other critics, while less impressed with the potential hazards of reprocessing, are reluctant for technical reasons to endorse large-scale commercialization before a high probability of success for that approach can be demonstrated.[89]

Unfortunately, the safety and feasibility of alternative management strategies for nuclear waste are also the subject of much debate.[90] The debate, moreover, pits the United States (which since April 1977 has essentially treated spent fuel as a waste to be disposed of) against most other nations (which regard spent fuel as a resource rather than a waste and which embrace reprocessing).[91] Although it is impossible to forecast the ultimate outcome of the reprocessing debate in the United States and abroad, there does appear to be some shift in recent years away from the emphasis on waste management as a primary rationale for reprocessing. This is reflected in INFCE's recognition that "on technical grounds" it can be argued that there is no need to decide at the present between reprocessing and the subsequent disposal of conditioned waste and long-term storage and ultimate disposal of spent fuel.[92] According to the conclusions of INFCE Working Group 7, "taking [into] account not only health and safety and environmental impacts but also the other assessment factors, the difference in the impacts of waste management and disposal among the reference fuel cycles does not constitute a decisive factor in the choice among them."[93] It is also apparent in the American Physical Society study group findings that "the decision to reprocess nuclear fuel does not depend significantly on waste management considerations but rather on resource and economic incentives and on international and domestic safeguards constraints."[94]

Advanced Nuclear Technology

Advanced nuclear technological capability—much like nuclear weapons—is a symbol of scientific expertise and a source of domestic pride and international prestige. This is particularly the case for a developing country like India, which can demonstrate through its nuclear accomplishments that it is poverty and not technical ability that inhibits its emergence as a great power in world politics. For India, as well as Brazil and Argentina, the acquisition of a complete nuclear fuel cycle, including reprocessing facilities, is probably as important in terms of international politics as it is in terms of energy economics or resource conservation. For reasons of North–South politics, it is also unlikely that these countries will forgo the introduction of reprocessing and fast breeder reactors, particularly if industrialized states such as France, West Germany, and Japan continue to support their development. The latter, industrialized countries may also be reluctant to abandon the idea of commercialization of reprocessing if they perceive themselves to be in a favorable international market position in competing for reprocessing services and plant sales.

Learning for the Fast Breeder Reactor

Preparation of the technological and personnel base for the fast breeder is also sometimes set forth as a rationale for early development of commercial reprocessing.[95] According to this view, early installation of reprocessing capacity may be necessary in order not to delay the introduction of fast breeders and to avert the loss of highly skilled personnel to nations where active reprocessing and fast breeder programs are underway.

The counterargument is that the technology of reprocessing is much simpler and better understood than that of the fast breeder and there is no reason to introduce one well before the other. Operation of a commercial-scale reprocessing facility well in advance of fast breeder commercialization, moreover, "would result in excess inventories of plutonium that would have to be recycled in LWRs or otherwise stored and safeguarded."[96] Most critics of early commercialization who do not reject reprocessing out of hand prefer deferral until additional technical and pilot-scale tests have been conducted to determine what can be done to minimize the health, safety, environmental, and proliferation risks of reprocessing and plutonium recycling.[97]

The Future of the Plutonium Economy

Notwithstanding ambiguous economic incentives and the active resistance of the United States, an international plutonium economy appears likely to emerge, even if less rapidly than exponents of commercial reprocessing and fast breeder reactors would have it. The basic technology of reprocessing is well known, several of the major industrialized states have already made extensive commitments to a nuclear energy strategy of fast breeder development,[98] and many developing countries are apt to demand access to if not possession of the full range of nuclear fuel cycle capabilities.

From a technical standpoint, the major delays in expanding the plutonium economy in countries with extensive nuclear programs will probably result from difficulties in resolving waste management, occupational health, and safety issues.[99] The future demand for electrical energy, worldwide uranium prices, and government subsidies also will affect the pace of the expansion of the plutonium economy. The most decisive factor, however, is likely to be political rather than technical or economic and will probably hinge on the extent to which the Reagan administration reverses in practice (as well as in rhetoric) prior U.S. opposition to commercial reprocessing and the domestic and international commerce in plutonium.[100]

Multinational cooperative arrangements for the reprocessing, management, and disposal of spent fuel may ultimately provide a means to resolve contending U.S. and international positions toward a plutonium-based nuclear economy.[101] Increased opportunities for the diversion, theft, and misuse of plutonium, however, are apt to remain an unavoidable consequence and incalculable cost of any movement toward a plutonium economy.[102]

THE CONSTRAINTS ON ECONOMIC RATIONALITY

Underlying most discussions of nuclear power choice is the assumption, frequently implicit, that national decisions to embrace or spurn nuclear power are based on careful calculations of economic costs and benefits. Our survey in this chapter of the economics of nuclear power indeed calls attention to the significant effect a number of economic developments have had on the pace and scope of nuclear power expansion. They include the global economic recession and rise in energy prices since the mid-1970s, reduced electricity growth rates during the same period, major revisions this past decade in uranium resource estimates, recent increases in the number of nuclear reactor exporters and suppliers of fuel cycle services, and the changing terms of nuclear trade in a depressed nuclear market.

It is also apparent from our survey, however, that economic incentives and disincentives for nuclear power represent only one strand of a complex web of determinants, which include political, psychological, and military factors. The finding that nuclear power is alive and well in the Soviet Union, France and India, but is under siege in the United States, West Germany, and Sweden, for example, can be explained to a large extent by the significant degree of government control over and support for nuclear industries and utilities in the first category of states, for reasons which have little to do with narrow considerations of economic costs and benefits. By the same token, the commitment of many developing states to nuclear energy programs (and the specific characteristics of these programs) cannot be understood without reference to international security, prestige, and domestic political incentives. Both with respect to peaceful nuclear energy and nuclear weapons it appears that factors such as the perceived "need" to share advanced nuclear technology, the fear of missing the nuclear revolution, and an unwillingness to accept the position of "have not" in an overtly discriminatory, two-tiered nuclear world order, may take precedence over or at least counteract economic analyses of the costs and benefits of nuclear power.[102] With that in mind, it is appropriate to examine in more detail the politics of nonproliferation.

NOTES

1. See Mans Lönnroth and William Walker, *The Viability of the Civil Nuclear Industry,* Report of the International Consultative Group of Nuclear Energy (New York: The Rockefeller Foundation and the Royal Institute of International Affairs, 1979), p. 1.
2. Ibid. Since the election of Socialist candidate Francois Mitterand as president, the outlook for nuclear power in France has become less certain. See "Uncertain Effects of Mitterand Victory," *Nuclear Engineering International* (June 1981), pp. 3–4.
3. See Irvin C. Bupp, "The Actual Growth and Probable Future of the Worldwide Nuclear Industry," *International Organization* (Winter 1981), pp. 59–60.
4. See Bupp, p. 65, and Lönnroth and Walker, p. 21.
5. Amorty Lovins, L. Hunter Lovins, and Leonard Ross, "Nuclear Power and Nuclear Bombs," *Foreign Affairs* (Summer 1980), p. 1163. For a discussion of the reasons for the decline in energy forecasts, see Lönnroth and Walker, pp. 22–23, and Bupp, pp. 65–67.
6. Lovins et al., p. 1156. See also Lönnroth and Walker, p. 24.
7. Lönnroth and Walker, p. 31.
8. This section relies extensively upon the excellent discussion provided by Lönnroth and Walker, pp. 7–17.
9. See ibid., p. 7.
10. Ibid.
11. Ibid., p. 16. See also Erwin Häckel, Karl Kaiser, and Pierre Lellouche, *Nuclear Policy in Europe* (Bonn: Europa Union Verlag GmbH, 1980).
12. Lönnroth and Walker, p. 17.
13. See ibid., p. 42, and Bupp, p. 70. Lönnroth and Walker, for example, point out that licensing decisions can be challenged in the courts in West Germany and the United States, but not in Canada, Sweden, France, Japan, the United Kingdom, or the Soviet Union. Similarly, they note that nuclear siting decisions are subject to local or provincial government approval in West Germany, Canada, Japan, Sweden, and the United States but not in France, the United Kingdom, and the Soviet Union.

14. See Peter Clausen, "Power, Interdependence and the Nonproliferation Regime" (paper presented at the International Studies Association, March 18, 1981), p. 11.
15. Ibid., p. 3.
16. Lönnroth and Walker, pp. 6–7. See also Henry R. Nau, *National Politics and International Technology: Nuclear Reactor Development in Western Europe* (Baltimore: Johns Hopkins University Press, 1974), and Peter deLeon, *Development and Diffusion of the Nuclear Power Reactor: A Comparative Analysis* (Cambridge, Massachusetts: Ballinger, 1979).
17. Lönnroth and Walker, pp. 94–95.
18. See ibid., p. 74.
19. An excellent discussion of French nuclear export policy is provided by Pierre Lellouche, "French Nuclear Policy: National Progress, European Dimensions, and Nonproliferation," in Erwin Häckel, Karl Kaiser, and Pierre Lellouche (eds.), *Nuclear Policy in Europe*, pp. 31–78. See also Lellouche, "Breaking the Rules without Quite Stopping the Bomb: European Views," *International Organization* (Winter 1981), pp. 39–58. The most comprehensive discussion of Soviet nuclear export policy is provided by Gloria Duffy, *Soviet Nuclear Energy: Domestic and International Policies* (Santa Monica: Rand Report R-2362-DOE, 1979).
20. Lellouche, "Breaking the Rules without Quite Stopping the Bomb," p. 49. This assertion tends to overlook controversial French nuclear export dealings with Iraq, Pakistan, Iran, and South Korea.
21. Lönnroth and Walker, p. 74.
22. Erwin Häckel, "The Domestic and International Context of West Germany's Nuclear Energy Policy," in Häckel et al., p. 110. Häckel reports that Kraftwerk Union (KWU), the German reactor industry, requires an export share of 50 percent for the production capacity of the nuclear power plant industry to break even. In order to attain this goal, KWU operates a production program which includes items that are only in demand abroad, such as heavy-water reactors.
23. Ronald Reagan's election to the presidency and his pro-nuclear power stance has endeared him to the American nuclear industry. It remains to be seen, however, whether he will be able to revise and accelerate the procedures for licensing new plants and completing those already partially constructed. For an industry appraisal of the Reagan administraion's nuclear power stance, see almost any 1981 issue of *Nuclear News* or *Nuclear Engineering International*.
24. See Joseph R. Egan and Shem Arungu-Olende, "Nuclear Power for the World?" *Technology Review* (May 1980), p. 48.
25. Derived from "World List of Nuclear Power Plants," *Nuclear News* (February 1981), pp. 75–198. Only five developing countries had nuclear power plants in operation at the end of 1980.
26. Britain, France, West Germany, and the Soviet Union are all developing small reactors in the 100 to 500 MW$_e$ range. Japan has also expressed an interest in their development. See Egan and Arungu-Olende, pp. 79–80.
27. This attitude on the part of Ford and Carter administration officials is noted by Karl Kaiser, "Nuclear Energy and Nonproliferation in the 1980s," in Häckel et al., p. 6, and by Pierre Lellouche and Richard K. Lester, "The Crisis of Nuclear Energy," *Washington Quartaerly* (Summer 1979), p. 39. A more recent and forceful argument linking nonproliferation with the abandonment of nuclear power is made by Amory Lovins et al., "Nuclear Power and Nuclear Bombs," pp. 1137–1176.
28. See Lellouche and Lester, p. 41. See also Kathleen Bailey, "When and Why Weapons," *Bulletin of the Atomic Scientists* (April 1980), p. 42-43.

29. See *Nucleonics Week* (May 31, 1979 and September 27, 1979) as cited by Lellouche, "Breaking the Rules without Quite Stopping the Bomb," pp. 50–51.

30. See Lellouche, "Breaking the Rules without Quite Stopping the Bomb," p. 50. For a discussion of the emergence of a nuclear "grey market" see Lewis A. Dunn, "Nuclear Grey Marketeering," *International Security* (Winter 1977), pp. 107–118.

31. For this argument see Lellouche and Lester, pp. 39–40, and Kaiser, pp. 6–7.

32. See Lellouche and Lester, pp. 39–40, and Kaiser, p. 7.

33. George Quester, "Introduction: In Defense of Some Optimism," *International Organization* (Winter 1981), p. 5.

34. See Lellouche and Lester, p. 40. A much more optimistic scenario for nonproliferation in a world of nuclear power demise is provided by Lovins et al.

35. Derived from "World List of Nuclear Power Plants," *Nuclear News* (February 1981), pp. 75–94. These figures are for power reactors of 30 MW$_e$ or larger. Slightly higher figures are suggested by the Atomic Industrial Forum, *INFO News Release* (March 13, 1981).

36. See Richark K. Lester, Nuclear Power Plant Lead-Times, Report of the International Consultative Group on Nuclear Energy (New York: The Rockefeller Foundation and The Royal Institute of International Affairs, 1978).

37. Atomic Industrial Forum, *INFO News Release,* March 13, 1981.

38. "World Energy: Looking Ahead to 2020," Report by the Conservation Commission of the World Energy Conference, 1977.

39. Thomas J. Connolly et al., *World Nuclear Energy Paths,* Report of the International Consultative Group on Nuclear Energy (New York: The Rockefeller Foundation and The Royal Institute of International Affairs, 1979), p. 2.

40. See Bupp, p. 64, who maintains that research findings indicate that increased information about nuclear power tends "to mobilize latent fears about perceived nuclear hazards, rather than deepening a consensus in support of nuclear growth."

41. Lovins et al., p. 1149.

42. Bupp, p. 75.

43. Ibid., pp. 75–76. See also Lönnroth and Walker, p. 38.

44. Lönnroth and Walker, p. 37. See also "Uncertain Effects of Mitterand Victory," *Nuclear Engineering International* (June 1981), pp. 3–4. This article points out that a major threat to the smooth development of nuclear power in France could result from the general move to decentralize government. The nuclear industry fear is that antinuclear forces might obtain prominent positions in local and regional councils and obstruct future plant-siting decisions.

45. See, for example, Nuclear Energy Policy Study Group, *Nuclear Power Issues and Choices* (Cambridge, Massachusetts: Ballinger, 1977); Connolly et al.; *INFCE Summary Volume* (Vienna: IAEA, 1980); *Uranium: Resources, Production and Demand,* Joint Report by the OECD Nuclear Energy Agency and the International Atomic Energy Agency (Paris: OECD, 1979); and "World Energy: Looking Ahead to 2020." A strongly dissenting view with respect to the increased importance of nuclear energy is provided by Lovins et al. For a critical analysis of the methodological assumptions of these and other studies see Steven J. Warnecke, *Uranium, Nonproliferation and Energy Security* (Paris: The Atlantic Institute for International Affairs, 1979).

46. See Chapter 3 for a discussion of breeder reactors.

47. Connolly et al., p. 82.

48. Uranium, it should be noted, "was originally a material with a single buyer, the United States government, for a single noncommercial use, weapons-making. Prior to the emergence of commercial customers in the late 1960s, the U.S. govern-

ment set what it judged to be a 'fair' price, and entrepreneurs found material to meet the buyer's terms." *Nuclear Power Issues and Choices,* pp. 74–75.

49. *INFCE Summary Volume,* p. 11.
50. This point is emphasized by Warnecke, pp. 17–18.
51. In 1980 these five countries exported about 16,000 tons of uranium, approximately 80 percent of the uranium produced and used outside the United States. Although U.S. producers sold about 17,000 tons, little entered the world market. See Nancy Stauffer, "Uranium Exporters: Who They Are and How They Work," *Technology Review* (January 1981), pp. 28–29.
52. For a discussion of the increased geographic diversity of uranium production see Thomas I. Neff and Henry D. Jacoby, "World Uranium: Softening Markets and Rising Scarcity," *Technology Review* (January 1981), p. 27.
53. Between 1973 and 1978 the price of uranium oxide (U_3O_8) went from $6 to $40 per pound. It has since dropped to less than $30 per pound. (See Neff and Jacoby, p. 25)
54. *Nuclear Power Issues and Choices,* p. 365.
55. Pierre Lellouche, "Internationalization of the Nuclear Fuel Cycle and Non Proliferation Strategy: Lessons and Prospects" (SJD dissertation, Harvard Law School, November 1979), pp. 321–322.
56. See Thomas Neff and Henry Jacoby, "Nonproliferation Strategy in a Changing Nuclear Fuel Market," *Foreign Affairs* (Summer 1979), pp. 1132–1133.
57. The United States contributed to the rise of non-American enrichment services by its inability in the early 1970s to guarantee a steady supply of fuel at reasonable prices. (See Lellouche, "Internationalization of the Nuclear Fuel Cycle and Non Proliferation Strategy," pp. 326–327.)
58. See Neff and Jacoby, "Nonproliferation Strategy in a Changing Nuclear Fuel Market," p. 1133.
59. Ibid., p. 1134.
60. URENCO, a consortium of the United Kingdom, the Netherlands, and West Germany, also began furnishing enrichment services in 1978 from a centrifuge enrichment facility with a capacity about one-tenth that of the United States. For a discussion of European arrangements in the field of uranium enrichment see Lellouche, "Internationalization of the Nuclear Fuel Cycle and Non Proliferation Strategy," p. 321–365.
61. Neff and Jacoby, "Nonproliferation Strategy in a Changing Nuclear Fuel Market," p. 1136.
62. *Nuclear Power Issues and Choices,* p. 110.
63. More than 70 percent of the cost of electricity from a light-water reactor is attributable to capital charges. These charges per kilowatt-hour are directly proportional to the cost of plant construction and inversely proportional to the plant capacity factor. (See *Nuclear Power Issues and Choices,* pp. 8 and 111.)
64. In contrast to capital charges, fuel costs are minimal and account for approximately five to ten percent of the cost of electricity generation in the United States. (See *Nuclear Power Issues and Choices,* p. 9.)
65. According to Irwin Bupp, the two necessary conditions for keeping the nuclear option to coal open in most countries are (1) unassailable validation of the operational safety of light-water reactors, and (2) unassailable validation of the environmental safety of radioactive waste disposal. He is not optimistic about the prospects of meeting the latter condition, especially in the United States. See Bupp, p. 74.
66. For a similar conclusion, see *Nuclear Power Issues and Choices,* p. 125.
67. Ibid.
68. So widely held was the belief that reprocessing was imminent that, aside from

limited storage pools at reactor sites, no provision was made for the storage of spent fuel in those countries using light-water reactors as their primary nuclear energy source. (See Gene I. Rochlin, *Plutonium, Power and Politics* (Berkeley: University of California Press, 1979), p. 103.

69. See Neff and Jacoby, "Nonproliferation Strategy in a Changing Nuclear Fuel Market," p. 1125.
70. See Vince Taylor, *The Economics of Plutonium and Uranium* (Los Angeles: Pan Heuristics, 1977), p. 23. See also Bertrand Goldschmidt and Myron Kratzer, *Peaceful Nuclear Relations: A Study of the Creation and the Erosion of Confidence*, Report of the International Consulting Group on Nuclear Energy (New York: The Rockefeller Foundation and The Royal Institute of International Affairs, 1978), pp. 23–31.
71. For a discussion of the economic and regulatory problems of the three American facilities see Taylor, pp. 24–32, and Rochlin, pp. 71–72.
72. See Neff and Jacoby, "Nonproliferation Strategy in a Changing Nuclear Fuel Market," p. 1126, and Rochlin, p. 127. As noted in Chapter 2, the change in U.S. policy toward plutonium actually was initiated in October 1976 when President Ford announced that "the reprocessing and recycling of plutonium should not proceed unless there is sound reason to conclude that the world community can effectively overcome the associated risks of nonproliferation." He then concluded that the United States would "no longer regard [re]processing of used nuclear fuel as a necessary and inevitable step in the nuclear fuel cycle . . . ." (Statement by the President on Nuclear Policy, Press Release, Office of the White House Press Secretary, October 28, 1976.) The formal announcement of U.S. plans to defer indefinitely the commercial reprocessing of nuclear fuels and the recycling of plutonium was made by President Carter on April 17, 1977.
73. Rochlin, p. 122.
74. For a review of national perspectives on fuel reprocessing see Rochlin, pp. 120–128.
75. These categories of explanation are identified by Rochlin, p. 109.
76. Ibid., p. 111.
77. See Rochlin, p. 112, and *INFCE Summary Volume*, pp. 18–19. One recent report found that much of the wide variation in prior studies' cost estimates could be accounted for by maintenance philosophy and method of financing. See L. C. Hebel et al., "Report to the American Physical Society by the Study Group on Nuclear Fuel Cycles and Waste Management," *Reviews of Modern Physics* (January 1978), pp. S–1 to S–181. This report is discussed in Rochlin, p. 111.
78. See *INFCE Summary Volume*, p. 18.
79. Rochlin, (p. 104) reports that about fifty 1000-MW$_e$ LWRs can be served by a single 1500 Mg/year reprocessing plant. Richard Betts cites a 20-to-1 ratio between power reactors and reprocessing plants as the minimum for economic operation. See Betts, "Paranoids, Pygmies, Pariahs, and Nonproliferation," *Foreign Policy* (Spring 1977), pp. 159–160.
80. Rochlin (pp. 104 and 112) estimates the impact at no more than several percent. The Ford/MITRE study, *Nuclear Power Issues and Choices* (p. 323) uses a figure of less than 1 percent cost reduction.
81. See Rochlin, p. 109. The precise amdount of savings depends on assumptions about the burn-up of the fuel that was reprocessed and the efficiency of the plutonium recovery and fabrication process.
82. Hebel et al., pp. 558–559, cited by Rochlin, p. 109.
83. See Rochlin, pp. 109–110, and Taylor, pp. 38–43.
84. Rochlin, p. 117. See also *Nuclear Power Issues and Choices*, p. 329.

85. See Rochlin, pp. 116–117.
86. See ibid., p. 112.
87. Taylor, p. 44.
88. See, in particular, Taylor, pp. 44–46; Albert Wohlstetter et al., *Swords from Plowshares* (Chicago: The University of Chicago Press, 1979), pp. 92–94; and *Nuclear Power Issues and Choices*, pp. 331–332.
89. See Rochlin, p. 113.
90. See, for example, Rustom Roy, "The Technology of Nuclear-Waste Management," *Technology Review* (April 1981), pp. 39–49; Connolly et al., pp. 116–127; and *INFCE Summary Volume*, pp. 142–143.
91. Bupp (p. 74) argues that "in spite of official rhetoric about 'indefinite deferals' . . . reprocessing of spent reactor fuel is a dead letter in the United States. There is simply no chance of it happening on any commercially significant scale in this century."
92. *INFCE Summary Volume*, p. 143.
93. Ibid., p. 21. The "reference fuel cycles" assessed were: (1) light-water reactor, once through; (2) light-water reactor with uranium–plutonium cycle; (3) fast breeder reactor with plutonium recycle; (4) heavy-water reactor, once through; (5) heavy-water reactor with uranium–plutonium cycle; (6) heavy-water reactor with uranium–thorium cycle; and (7) high-temperature reactor with uranium–thorium cycle.
94. Hebel et al., p. 56, cited in Rochlin, p. 115.
95. See Rochlin, p. 118.
96. Ibid.
97. These critics tend to discount INFCE's findings about the lack of clear-cut advantages among major fuel cycle alternatives while embracing other INFCE conclusions having to do with uranium availability and the lack of necessity of reprocessing for safe management of nuclear wastes. See, for example, Nye, "Maintaining a Nonproliferation Regime," *International Organization* (Winter 1981), pp. 25–26.
98. For a detailed discussion of national commitments to fast breeders, see John Gray et al., *International Cooperation on Breeder Reactors* (New York: The Rockefeller Foundation, 1978), pp. 2-1 to 2-21.
99. See Bupp, p. 74.
100. In his July 16, 1981 policy statement, President Reagan vowed that the administration would not "inhibit or set back civil reprocessing under breeder reactor development abroad in nations with advanced nuclear power programs *where it does not constitute a proliferation risk*" (my emphasis). See "Reagan Statement on Spread of Atomic Arms," *New York Times* (July 17, 1981).
101. See Lawrence Scheinman, "Multinational Alternatives and Nuclear Nonproliferation," *International Organization* (Winter 1981), pp. 77–102.
102. For a strong dissenting view see C. Starr, and E. Zebroski, "Nuclear Power and Weapons Proliferation" (paper presented to the American Power Conference, April 18–20, 1977).
103. See Lewis Dunn, "The Proliferation Policy Agenda: Taking Stock," Report of the World Peace Foundation Conference on Managing in a Proliferation Prone World, Dedham, Massachusetts, December 9–11, 1977, pp. 6–7. For a discussion of the "diseconomic fallacy" which assumes that nations will have compelling reasons not to acquire nuclear power and/or weapons facilities, see Richard Betts, pp. 160–162.

Chapter 5

The Politics of Nonproliferation

One of the most influential essays on U.S. nuclear proliferation policy adopts as a guiding principle Florence Nightingale's
admonition that "Whatever else hospitals do they should not spread
disease."[1] Retarding the spread of nuclear weapons (or disease),
however, implies having some knowledge of its causes. Although
prescriptions for nonproliferation abound, suprisingly little is
known about the conditions affecting national decisions to "go
nuclear" or decisions to acquire the capabilities to do so.[2] Even more
tenuous is our knowledge of how attempts to fill these prescriptions
by means of exhortation, example, rewards and/or punishment
may affect other significant U.S. foreign policy objectives.

In order better to address the issue of appropriate strategies for
proliferation management and control, an effort is made in this
chapter to assess the relative importance of alternative domestic
and international proliferation incentives and disincentives. This
entails first distilling from the literature on proliferation a list of
plausible factors influencing nuclear decisions, and then examining
the explanatory power of these factors for selected nuclear weapon
states and potential proliferators. Based on this method of focused
comparison,[3] it may be possible to identify a set of broadly applicable
incentives and disincentives, as well as more country-specific
factors. One may also be able to distinguish better between the
necessary and the sufficient conditions for proliferation.

PROLIFERATION DETERMINANTS

The literature on nuclear proliferation presents a wide
assortment of largely speculative and often contradictory insights

Table 5.1. Hypothesized Proliferation Determinants

Determinants	Orientation	Illustrative Sources[a]
I. National prerequisites		
Economic wealth	Internal	Bull (1961)
		Schwab (1969)
Scientific and technological expertise		Barnaby (1969)
II. Underlying Pressures		
Deterrence	External	Beaton and Maddox (1962)
		Dunn and Kahn (1976)
		Epstein (1977)
		Greenwood (1977)
		OTA (1977)
		Quester (1973)
		Rosecrance (1964)
		Schoettle (1976)
Warfare advantage and defense	External	(same as for Deterrence)
Weapon of last resort	External	Dunn and Kahn (1976)
		Haselkorn (1974)
		Harkavy (1977)
		OTA (1977)
Coercion	External	Dunn and Kahn (1976)
International status/prestige	External	(same as for Deterrence)
Assertion of autonomy and influence	External	Beaton and Maddox (1962)
		Epstein (1977)
		Kapur (1979)
		OTA (1977)
		Rosecrance (1964)
		Schoettle (1976)
Economic spillover	Internal	Beaton and Maddox (1962)
		Dunn and Kahn (1976)
		Epstein (1977)
		Greenwood (1977)
		OTA (1977)
		Quester (1973)
		Rosecrance (1964)
Domestic politics	Internal	Dunn and Kahn (1976)
		Kapur (1979)
		OTA (1977)
Technological momentum	Internal	Dunn and Kahn (1976)
		Rosecrance (1977)
		Scheinman (1965)

Table 5.1. *(continued)*

Determinants	Orientation	Illustrative Sources[a]
III. Underlying constraints		
Military reaction by other states	External	Dunn and Kahn (1976)
		Epstein (1977)
		Greenwood (1972)
		OTA (1977)
		Quester (1973)
The strategic credibility gap	External	Dunn and Kahn (1976)
		Epstein (1977)
		Greenwood (1977)
		OTA (1977)
		Quester (1973)
		Rosecrance (1964)
Absence of perceived threat	External	Quester (1973)
		Rosecrance (1964)
International norms	External	Epstein (1977)
		Greenwood (1977)
		Quester (1973)
Economic and political sanctions	External	Dunn and Kahn (1976)
		Epstein (1977)
		Greenwood (1977)
		OTA (1977)
Unauthorized seizure	Internal	Dunn and Kahn (1976)
		Greenwood (1977)
		OTA (1977)
Economic costs	Internal	Dunn and Kahn (1976)
		Greenwood (1977)
		OTA (1977)
		Quester (1973)
Public opinion	Internal	Dunn and Kahn (1976)
		Greenwood (1977)
		OTA (1977)
		Quester (1973)
Bureaucratic politics	Internal	Betts (1980)
		Kapur (1979)
		Rosecrance (1964)
IV. Situational variables		
International crisis	External	Dunn and Kahn (1976)
Weakening of security guarantees	External	Dunn and Kahn (1976)
		Greenwood (1977)
		Lefever (1979)
		OTA (1977)
		Rosecrance (1964)
		Willrich (1976)

Table 5.1. *(continued)*

Determinants	Orientation	Illustrative Sources[a]
Increased accessibility of nuclear materials	Internal/ External	Dunn and Kahn (1976) Ford/Mitre (1977) Wohlstetter et al. (1979)
Vertical proliferation	External	Kapur (1979) Schwab (1969)
Domestic crisis and leadership change	Internal	Dunn and Kahn (1976) Kapur (1979)

Source: This table draws on the categorizations provided by Kegley et al., (1980), p. 235, and Meyer, pp. 64 and 102.

[a]Biographical information on the sources listed in this column follows:

Barnaby, C. F. (1969). "The Development of Nuclear Energy Programs," in Barnaby, ed., *Preventing the Spread of Nuclear Weapons* (London: Souvenir), pp. 16–35.

Beaton, Leonard and John Maddox (1962). *The Spread of Nuclear Weapons* (New York: Praeger).

Betts, Richard K. (1980). "Incentives for Nuclear Weapons," in Joseph A. Yager, ed., *Nonproliferation and U.S. Foreign Policy.* (Washington, D.C.: Brookings Institution), pp. 116–144.

Bull, Hedley (1961). *The Control of the Arms Race* (New York: Praeger).

Dunn, Lewis and Herman Kahn (1976). *Trends in Nuclear Proliferation, 1975-1995* (Croton-on-Hudson, New York: Hudson Institute).

Epstein, William (1977). "Why States Go—and Don't Go—Nuclear," in *The Annals of the American Academy of Political and Social Science* (March), pp. 16–28.

Ford/Mitre Study (1977). *Nuclear Power Issues and Choices* (Cambridge, Massachusetts: Ballinger).

Greenwood, Ted (1977). "Discouraging Proliferation in the Next Decade and Beyond," in Greenwood et al., *Nuclear Proliferation: Motivations, Capabilities, and Strategies for Control* (New York: McGraw-Hill), pp. 25–122.

Harkavy, Robert (1977). *Israel's Nuclear Weapons: Spectre of Holocaust in the Middle East* (Denver: University of Denver Press).

Haselkorn, Avigdor (1974). "Israel—An Option to a Bomb in the Basement," in Robert Lawrence and Joel Larus, eds., *Nuclear Proliferation Phase II* (Lawrence: University Press of Kansas).

Kapur, Ashok (1979). *International Nuclear Proliferation* (New York: Praeger).

Lefever, Ernst (1979). *Nuclear Arms in the Third World* (Washington, D.C.: Brookings Institution).

Office of Technology Assessment (1977). *Nuclear Proliferation and Safeguards* (New York: Praeger).

Quester, George (1973). *The Politics of Nuclear Proliferation* (Baltimore: The Johns Hopkins Press).

Rosecrance, Richard (1964). "International Stability and Nuclear Diffusion," in Rosecrance, ed., *The Dispersion of Nuclear Weapons* (New York: Columbia University Press).

Scheinman, Lawrence (1964). *Atomic Energy Policy in France Under the Fourth Republic* (Princeton: Princeton University Press).

Schoettle, Enid C. B. (1976). "Arms Limitations and Security Policies Required to Minimize the Proliferation of Nuclear Weapons," in David Carlton and Carlo Schaerf, eds., *Arms Control and Technological Innovation* (New York: Halsted Press), pp. 102–131.

Schwab, G. (1969). "Switzerland's Tactical Nuclear Weapon Policy," *Orbis* (Fall), pp. 900–914.

Table 5.1. *(continued)*

Willrich, Mason (1966). "Guarantees to Non-Nuclear Nations," *Foreign Affairs* (July), pp. 683–692.
Wohlstetter, Albert et al. (1979). *Swords from Plowshares* (Chicago: University of Chicago Press, 1979).

on why nations embark or refrain from embarking on paths to acquire nuclear weapons.[2] Table 5.1 provides a list of those factors often cited as proliferation determinants.[5] This list distinguishes among hypothesized national prerequisites (i.e., necessary conditions), underlying pressures and constraints, and more transitory situational variables.

NATIONAL PREREQUISITES

The question of capabilities versus intentions muddies the study of nuclear proliferation just as it does that of Soviet and U.S. strategic policy. Clearly, one cannot infer intent from capability, although one might anticipate a rough correlation between the possession of certain national capabilities and a propensity toward nuclear armament. At a minimum, most observers agree that a nuclear weapons option presupposes a certain level of economic wealth and technological knowhow, although there is little concensus as to what constitutes prohibitive costs and requisite expertise.[6]

The ability to predict national postures toward proliferation based on national economic wealth, scientific expertise, and technological skills has been eroded by the increased accessibility on a global scale of both nuclear technology and fissile material. This trend has led some analysts to abandon altogether the notion of indigenous prerequisites or necessary conditions for weapons proliferation and to posit alternative conceptions of nuclear weapons choice. There is, for example, the school of thought which substitutes the notion of "technological imperative" for that of national technical prerequisites. According to this perspective, once a nation acquires the physical ability to manufacture nuclear weapons it will inevitably proceed to do so.[7] Herbert York's commentary in reference to recent reports of a Japanese atomic weapons program in the Second World War illustrates this viewpoint:

> . . . the Japanese story completes the set, that every nation that might plausibly have started nuclear weapons programs did so: Germany,

Great Britain, the United States, the Soviet Union, France and we now know, Japan. So the case has been weakened for those who have argued that governments, or more precisely, generals, emperors, and presidents can hold back from this decision and say "No." The decision to develop nuclear weapons is but a general technological imperative.[8]

An alternative and less deterministic conception of nuclear weapons choice that directs attention to the impact on 'nuclear weapons proliferation of nuclear technology diffusion can also be identified. This school of thought emphasizes the "synergistic link" between civilian nuclear power and nuclear weapons and assumes that national energy needs, international commerce in nuclear technology, and technology diffusion pressures are critical "contexual variables" which effect the calculus of the nuclear weapons decision.[17] These are also among the factors singled out by advisers to the Ford and Carter administrations as critical elements that could be manipulated to influence the balance of proliferation incentives and constraints abroad and to create a more proliferation-resistant international nuclear regime.[10]

UNDERLYING PRESSURES AND CONSTRAINTS

One method to sort out the different pressures for and constraints on the decision to demonstrate a nuclear explosive capability is to group them according to the relative importance they ascribe to internal or external considerations and military or political-economic objectives. This procedure yields four broad clusters of proliferation incentives and disincentives. They are labelled for the purposes of discussion as factors of international security, international politics, domestic security, and domestic politics. (See Figure 5.1.)

International Security Incentives

Deterrence of Adversaries. A desire to deter external threats is often cited as an underlying international security incentive for proliferation. One finds, for example, arguments that the acquisition of nuclear weapons, even of a rudimentary variety, can afford a measure of deterrence against nuclear attack or blackmail by a superpower, conventional attack by a regional adversary or group of adversaries, and prospective acquisition of nuclear weapons by a

	Domestic	External
Military	Domestic Security	International Security
Political-economic	Domestic Political	International Political

Figure 5.1. Underlying pressures and constraints on proliferation.

regional rival.[11] Implicit in most of these arguments is the notion that nuclear weapons would have the same stabilizing influence on regional balances as they are alleged to have on U.S.–Soviet relations.[12]

Warfare Advantage. Possession of nuclear weapons also may be sought as a means to achieve an advantage in warfare should deterrence of an attack fail. U.S. and British interest in the development of the atomic bomb, for example, can be attributed in large measure to their determination to wage war successfully against the Germans. It has also been suggested that certain small and middle-range powers may seek tactical nuclear weapons in order to defend against nuclear or conventional attack by a superpower or regional adversary, particularly in the absence of credible security guarantees by a superpower.[13] Such a tactical nuclear force, it has been argued, might be particularly attractive to a nation whose adversary possesses superiority in conventional force or to one where natural invasion corridors make defense by battlefield nuclear weapons feasible.[14] It has even been suggested that global proliferation of low-yield tactical nuclear weapons for border defense could be a stabilizing factor which would enable "any nation not now a nuclear power, and not harboring ambitions for territorial aggrandizement, to walk like a porcupine through the forest of international affairs: no threat to its neighbors, too prickly for predators to swallow."[15] Although the international "pariah" states of Taiwan and South Africa are most often thought of as potential proliferators interested in the tactical use of nuclear arms, national debates in Switzerland and Sweden have in the past also centered on the role of battlefield nuclear weapons and their place in a policy of armed neutrality.[16]

Weapon of Last Resort. Related to the "defense against invasion" incentive is the motivation to possess a weapon of last resort—a weapon that would only be used if a nation were on the brink of total destruction and defeat. The rationale for possession of nuclear weapons in this context could be both psychological and punitive ("if we are going to go, we'll take someone with us") and tactical, in the sense of being able to threaten convincingly that the possessor would escalate the conflict to a level in which the benefits to be achieved by the "victor" would be outweighed by the costs of achieving "total victory".

Coercion. Although the international security incentives usually attributed to potential proliferators emphasize deterrence and defense, one should not exclude the existence of incentives oriented more toward compulsion. Nuclear blackmail, intimidation of non-nuclear regional adversaries, and even use of nuclear weapons in "preventive first strikes" may be perceived as desirable policy options for the leaders of certain "crazy states" as well as those facing the prospect of a long-term deterioration of their security vis-à-vis non-nuclear opponents.[17]

International Security Disincentives

Hostile Reactions of a Military Nature by Adversaries and Allies. The anticipation of a hostile response by both adversaries and allies may serve as a disincentive to proliferation. The anticipated response of an adversary might range from the threat of military action to overt military operations designed to destroy an incipient nuclear weapons force and production capability. A country weighing the decision to go nuclear may also be dissuaded by the fear that such action would provoke a neighboring adversary to follow suit, resulting in a costly escalation of the arms race without a commensurate increase in security. Undesirable allied responses of a military nature, on the other hand, might take the form of a reduction or severance of established security guarantees and the disruption of the supply of important conventional armaments.[18]

The Strategic Credibility Gap. The difficulty of obtaining the technical conditions usually associated with a credible nuclear deterrent (e.g., secure second strike forces, effective systems of command and control, and reliable delivery vehicles) may diminish the attraction of nuclear weapons for potential proliferators. An embryonic and poorly defended nuclear force, it can be argued, serves as an incentive for a preemptive strike and as a source of crisis instability.[19] Although this line of logic is compelling in the abstract, it remains to be demonstrated whether or not the subtleties of Western strategic analysis are relevant to the process of nuclear decision-making in many near-nuclear countries.[20]

Absence of Perceived Security Threat. If the existence of acute external threats provides an argument for the acquisition of nuclear weapons, it is plausible to assume that the absence of a hostile international environment, or more precisely, the perception of such a condition by a nation's leadership, would serve as a disincentive to acquire nuclear arms. Even in a more threatening international milieu, confidence in the security guarantees of a militarily powerful ally might be expected to reduce the pressure to develop an independent nuclear deterrent.

International Political Incentives

Increased International Status. Nuclear weapons are a symbol of scientific expertise and technological development. They are almost synonymous with great power status (although arguably not the primary cause for a great power's international standing) and are viewed by many states as a source of international prestige and autonomy. Aside from bolstering a nation's self-confidence, an important consideration for many "have-not" nations and others who perceive a disparity between their actual and "rightful" place in the international pecking order, nuclear weapons capability may engender both fear and respect from one's neighbors and adversaries.

A number of studies indicate that considerations of international prestige and influence are particularly important incentives for potential Third World proliferators who despair over gross inequities in the global distribution of wealth and power.[21] From their vantage point, nuclear weapons may appear as a useful lever in North–South politics and as a means to reshape the structure of the contemporary international order. More specifically, demonstration of a nuclear weapons capability or even the credible threat to proliferate might be regarded as a way to command the attention of the industrialized states and to prompt greater economic assistance and political support. As one study notes, for example, "the developing states probably did not overlook the fact that India's economic aid from the Western industrial states was increased by some $200 million less than a month after its nuclear explosion."[22]

Increased Autonomy. Aside from its symbolic importance and relevance for North–South politics, a nuclear weapons capability may be sought to enhance intra-alliance influence and international freedom of action. A nation considering a proliferation option, it has been suggested, may expect that possession of nuclear weapons would enable it to exert greater influence on regional security arrangements and international political forums (e.g., the U.N. Security Council, General Assembly, and its specialized agencies).[23] Development of the French *force de frappe*, for example, has been explained in part as a French attempt to gain a greater voice in NATO affairs and as an assertion of national autonomy.[24]

International Political Disincentives

International Norms. Although the month-long, second Non-Proliferation Treaty Review Conference in 1980 failed to produce even a bland document supporting the principles of the NPT, no country indicated that it was reviewing its adherence to the treaty (unlike the situation in 1975 at the first NPT Review Conference).[25] Moreover, 113 nations remain parties to the Non-Proliferation Treaty (NPT) which explicitly states that proliferation of nuclear weapons would seriously increase the danger of nuclear war. This norm is also embodied in the Treaty of Tlatelolco[26] and the safeguard statutes of the International Atomic Energy Agency, and is reflected in the efforts taken by such politically diverse states as the Soviet Union and the United States to restrict the export of sensitive nuclear technology and fuel cycle components.[27] Although some countries may assume treaty membership and a public nonproliferation stance to conceal their real nuclear weapons ambitions, most international treaty commitments are not undertaken lightly or easily repudiated. It may even be the case, as one analyst suggests, that "the political commitments involved in the acceptance of the NPT and IAEA safeguards are as important as the accompanying physical constraints."[28]

Economic and Political Sanctions by Other States. The fear of political and economic reprisals may serve as another disincentive for potential proliferators. This concern is apt to be greatest among those nations which depend heavily on the superpowers for economic assistance and technological aid. Would-be proliferators also run the risk of censure and sanctions by international organizations, although no international agreement exists which would mandate such action.

Domestic Security Incentives and Disincentives

The literature on nuclear proliferation does not indicate any domestic security incentives for acquiring a nuclear weapons capability. The risk of unauthorized seizure of nuclear weapons, however, may be a domestic security disincentive, especially for countries subject to frequent political upheavals and domestic turmoil.[29]

Several scenarios involving unauthorized acquisition of nuclear weapons have been suggested. One involves the possible seizure of all or part of a nation's nuclear weapons stockpile by revolutionary groups or terrorists for purpose of political blackmail.[30] Another identifies the military as a possible threat in a "nuclear coup d'état."[31]

Domestic Political Incentives

Economic Spillover. The economic potential of peaceful nuclear explosions (PNEs) was heralded by the United States in the 1950s as part of President Eisenhower's "Atoms for Peace" program. Over $200 million was spent by the U.S. government and industry to explore such economic applications of nuclear explosions as excavations of canals and harbors, production of oil from shale, and gas and oil stimulation.[32]

Although most U.S. analysts became convinced in the 1970s that PNEs were not cost-effective and/or posed significant environmental hazards, many potential proliferators at least profess to retain the view, intially fostered by the United States, that PNEs have substantial economic promise. The desire to obtain economic benefits, therefore, is sometimes cited as an incentive to develop a nuclear explosive capability, despite the guarantee in the NPT that "potential benefits from any peaceful applications of nuclear explosions will be made available to non-nuclear weapon States party to the Treaty on a nondiscriminatory basis. . . ."[33]

Aside from the attraction of direct economic benefits from possession of a nuclear weapons capability, reference is also occasionally made to the utility a nuclear weapons program may afford in retaining highly skilled scientists and technicians who might otherwise emigrate to nations with more sophisticated nuclear research establishments.[34] The magnitude of this potential "brain drain" is suggested by the fact that over 10,500 scientists from countries outside the Soviet–European bloc participated in U.S. Atomic Energy Commission research between 1955 and 1976.[35]

Bureaucratic and Domestic Politics. There is a tendency in the literature on nuclear proliferation to emphasize a model of rational decision-making and the maximization of national interests. One can discover, however, a number of domestically oriented pressures to go nuclear which may be difficult to justify either militarily or economically from a national perspective. These include pressures from various industrial, scientific, and military groups that would stand to benefit from an expensive nuclear program; broad-based public support for an independent nuclear force; and pressure from politicians anxious to divert attention from other domestic and foreign policy failures.[36]

Technological Momentum. Development of nuclear weapons, it has been suggested, may also result from technological momentum in which the technological feasibility of the project takes precedence over the military or political necessity of the task and in which a formal decision to go ahead may in fact be lacking. The phenomenon of "technological creep" may also be in effect, in which significant progress toward a nuclear weapons capability is achieved by incremental advances in different fields of nuclear engineering without a formal decision being taken to develop a nuclear explosive. It is reported, for example, that lower-level French scientists and bureaucrats took major steps toward developing a nuclear weapon capability before they were specifically directed to do so by the national leadership.[37]

Domestic Political Disincentives

Cost. The economic cost of developing and maintaining a nuclear weapons program may be prohibitive for certain countries. The cost disincentive, it has been suggested, is apt to involve not only the absolute level of expenditures, but also the opportunity costs of diverting monetary and manpower resources from economic and social projects to a nuclear weapons program.[38] These perceived costs, however, may be diminishing with a growth of civilian nuclear power industries in many countries and "the concurrent decline in the incremental cost associated with a weapons program."[39]

Public Opinion. Adverse domestic opinion may also serve as a constraint on the acquisition of nuclear weapons by some nations. Japan, West Germany, Sweden, and Canada are examples of democracies where public opposition could have a decided effect on nuclear weapon decisions. Recent antinuclear energy campaigns in West Germany and Sweden are consistent with this interpretation. The fear of adverse public opinion, on the other hand, might be expected to be marginal for many developing nations without a strong democratic tradition.

Bureaucratic Politics. The play of bureaucratic politics may be expected to work as a disincentive as well as an incentive to development of nuclear weapons. Competition for scarce resources, in particular, could produce an alignment of bureaucratic actors who, for parochial organizational reasons, opposed the creation of new institutional actors and potential competitors. The military, or at least certain branches of it, for example, might oppose a nuclear weapons program if it were perceived as likely to interfere with the funding of preferred weapons systems or to shift the distribution of the military service fiscal pie. One can also include in this category of domestic political disincentives opposition to the acquisition of nuclear weapons by key individuals in the decision-making process whose stance is determined by personal philosophical convictions (Nehru is the most frequently cited example) or by calculations of self-interest.

SITUATIONAL VARIABLES

Regardless of the role they attribute to national prerequisites for proliferation (i.e., *necessary conditions*), most analyses of nuclear weapons choice imply the operation of two sets of *sufficient conditions*: (1) the balance between underlying proliferation incentives and disincentives and (2) the presence of one or several situational factors that might precipitate a decision to go nuclear whenever incentives outweigh constraints.[40] The most widely cited potential "trigger events" are summarized below:

International Crisis. A variety of international crisis situations have been identified as possible precipitants of a nation's decision to acquire nuclear weapons. The one most commonly mentioned is the nuclearization of another state, particularly a neighboring state or a regional rival. In this scenario an action-reaction dynamic is assumed to operate in which one nation's decision to go nuclear intensifies an adversary's sense of insecurity and simultaneously reduces some of the psychological and political barriers to proliferation. A widely shared nuclear taboo, for example, might be weakened, which, in turn, could alter the balance in the domestic debate over the desirability of possessing nuclear weapons.[41] More generally, it has been suggested that a foreign crisis may provide the opportunity for forging a new bureaucratic consensus in support of a decision to go nuclear.[42]

Weakening of Security Guarantees. The bipolarity of strategic competition and credible alliance guarantees by the two superpowers are often credited with reducing proliferation incentives.[43] Conversely, any diminution of superpower alliance guarantees, or the perceived collapse of their nuclear umbrellas, might lead to a revision of national security calculations and a decision to acquire nuclear weapons for deterrence purposes.

Increased Accessibility of Necessary Technology and Material. A necessary but not sufficient condition for proliferation is access to nuclear technology and material. For some would-be proliferators, the increased availability of these resources might trigger a decision to initiate a nuclear weapons program.

Vertical Proliferation. The failure of the superpowers to implement their promise in Article VI of the NPT to undertake effective measures to halt the nuclear arms race (i.e., vertical proliferation) has been a major complaint of non-nuclear parties to the NPT. An abandonment of the SALT process may further widen the gap perceived by many non-nuclear states to exist between the words and actions of the nuclear powers. This could bolster the case of *N*th country advocates of an independent nuclear force option. As one exponent of this perspective put it, "until the existing five nuclear-weapons states are able to . . . reduce their nuclear arsenals in a manner that reflects a process of making *real sacrifices,* the in-house bureaucratic debates in Third World societies are not likely to be impressed with, say, President Carter's 'open-mouth' antiproliferation speechmaking."[44]

Domestic Crisis and Leadership Change. It is sometimes suggested that a decision to go nuclear might also be triggered by a number of domestic events. These include political crises in which the leadership might attempt to capitalize on a nuclear weapons decision to divert domestic attention and restore popular confidence in the government, and a change in political leadership involving the elevation to power of individuals committed to a nuclear weapons program.[45]

COMPARISON AND SYNTHESIS

The literature on the determinants of nuclear proliferation consists primarily of case studies which emphasize the country-specific attributes of past and potential proliferators.[46] A review of this literature yields an extensive list of variables which may influence a nation's nuclear weapons posture but provides little insight into the relative explanatory power of these variables across nations.

It is beyond the scope of this study to employ the method of focused comparison rigorously in analyzing decision-making regarding nuclear weapons. An effort is made below, however, to examine the applicability of our list of potential determinants for select past and potential proliferators and to synthesize, where possible, the findings of previous research. The countries examined include all of the states that had demonstrated a nuclear explosive capability by the end of 1980, regional representatives from most lists of critical potential proliferators, and a state which has consistently pursued a policy of nuclear weapons abstinence although having long had the capability to join the nuclear weapons club.

The Case of the United States

Almost immediately after the discovery of nuclear fission by Otto Hahn and Fritz Strassman in Germany in late 1938, there was widespread speculation in the international scientific community about the prospects for utilizing the discovery to produce chain reactions that would generate large amounts of energy and possibly enormous explosions.[47] Initially, experiments in the United States to probe the process of nuclear fission were conducted by individual scientists without governmental support or supervision. In August 1939, however, an important appeal for a systematic American research program was made in a letter to President Roosevelt by Albert Einstein at the instigation of Leo Szilard. The letter revealed the military potential of nuclear energy, warned of German interest in the subject, and urged an accelerated U.S. research program.[48] As the result of this and other appeals, a small amount of federal support for nuclear research was initiated in February 1940, but a decision to reorganize and conduct a full-scale American effort to produce an atomic bomb was not made until December 1941, the month Japan attacked Pearl Harbor.[49]

Although initially U.S. government interest in atomic fission focused as much on controlled chain reactions as a source of submarine propulsion as on fission for an atomic bomb, the incentive to build a bomb was unambiguous.[50] That incentive was to defeat Nazi Germany. This motivation was spurred by the knowledge that Hitler's scientists were also pursuing nuclear weapons research and by the need to develop a bomb before it was built and used by the Nazis.[51] The strength of this security incentive is reflected in the contrast between the urgency and specificity of focus of the early British program of nuclear research and the more theoretical, conservative, and uncoordinated approach pursued at the same time in the United States.[52] The difference in approaches to a large extent was due to the fact that the British were at war and the United States was not. As Richard Hewlett and Oscar Anderson point out:

> Too many scientists, like Americans in other walks of life, found it unpleasant to turn their thoughts to weapons of mass destruction. They were aware of the possibilities, surely, but they had not placed them in sharp focus. The senior scientists and engineers who prepared the reports that served as the basis for policy decisions either did not learn the essential facts or did not grasp their significance. The American program came to grief on two reefs—a failure of the physicists interested in uranium to point their research toward war and a failure of communication.[53]

Only when the threat of U.S. involvement in the war became acute did American research on the military uses of nuclear energy accelerate.[54]

Just as the fear of German development and use of atomic weaponry was the primary motivation for the U.S. atomic bomb program, the end of the war with Germany removed a major incentive for the bomb's development. Many of the scientists in the U.S. nuclear program, in particular, felt that the bomb was no longer necessary militarily.[55] Ironically, Leo Szilard, who had instigated the letter from Einstein to Roosevelt in 1939 calling for an American atomic bomb program, took the lead in 1945 in opposing the use of the yet-untested atomic weapon. In early July Szilard argued, in a petition to the President signed by 69 of his colleagues, that the nations which set the precedent for the bomb's use would have "to bear the responsiblity of opening the door to an era of devastation on an unimaginable scale."[56] If the United States were to use the bomb, Szilard asserted, it would so weaken America's moral position that it would be hard for the United States ever to bring the new forces of destruction under control.[57] Despite this sentiment in 1945, it appears that since August 1942, when the Manhattan Energy District was established under the War Department to develop an atomic bomb, most of the small group of government officials aware of the bomb's development assumed that the bomb would be used as soon as it became available.[58] As Secretary of War Stimson put it:

> The possible atomic bomb was considered to be a new and tremendously powerful explosive, as legitimate as any other of the deadly explosive weapons of modern war. The entire purpose was the production of a military weapon; on no other ground could the wartime expenditure of so much money have been justified.[59]

In a memorandum for President Truman in April 1945, Stimson prophetically noted that although the United States would in all probability soon be the sole possessor of atomic weaponry, it could not occupy this exclusive position indefinitely. It was extremely probable, he argued, that "much easier and cheaper methods of production would be discovered by scientists in the future, together with the use of materials of much wider distribution." The result, he concluded, was that "the future will make it possible for atomic bombs to be constructed by smaller nations or even groups, or at least by a larger nation in a much shorter time."[60] This prognosis was proved correct when the Soviet Union exploded its first atomic bomb on August 29, 1949.

The Case of the Soviet Union

"The Soviet decision" to develop an atomic bomb is better viewed as a sequence of three decisions taken by a number of individual and institutional actors in 1940, 1942, and 1945. Each of these decisions were influenced by different incentives and constraints.[61] The first decision, taken by the Soviet Academy of Science in 1940, was a judgment not to request additional funds from the government for nuclear research. This decision appears to have been the product of a clash between younger scientists without institutional power who sought to make their reputation in a yet uncharted but promising field and a group of senior scientists with powerful positions in the academy who were reluctant to take risks which might jeopardize their positions.[62] The more well-established scientists prevailed in this instance, despite the fact that some Soviet physicists were then aware of the military potential of atomic energy.[63] Although there is no evidence that Stalin knew of the possibility of an atomic bomb at that time, there is little reason to believe that such knowledge would have led to additional support. As David Holloway points out, this is because the leadership's efforts to strengthen the Soviet Union's defense "made them take a shorter-term view than even those scientists who were most optimistic about harnessing atomic energy."[64] External threats and bureaucratic politics in this case thus served as constraints on, rather than incentives for, the development of an atomic bomb.

The German invasion of June 1941 brought nuclear research in the Soviet Union to a virtual halt.[65] Scientific interest in (as opposed to active research on) atomic energy, however, was not completely stifled, and in 1942 a combination of circumstances finally led the political leadership to initiate a small-scale atomic weapons project. The major factors in this decision appear to have been the persistent pleas by a young Soviet physicist, Flyorov, who took his case directly to Stalin, and knowledge that the United States and Germany were already working on the bomb.[66] One can infer from the slow pace at which the project was undertaken that the Soviets did not anticipate having the bomb ready for use in the war.[67] Stalin envisaged the bomb as a hedge against uncertainty in a postwar world in which the Soviet Union might have to face an adversary armed with atomic weapons.

The potential of atomic energy was uncertain when Soviet nuclear decisions were made in 1940 and 1942. There was no uncertainty about its prospects in August 1945 when the final Soviet decision was made to launch a full-scale atomic weapons project. This decision appears to have been a clear reaction to the United States' demonstration of its atomic military might. From the Soviet perspective, international security and political considerations must have dictated that the Soviet Union build the bomb too if it were to protect its recent military achievements and deter the United States from offensive military or political action.[68]

As Holloway notes, the Soviet decision to build an atomic bomb in many respects resembles the classic pattern of technological innovations:

> As in every innovation, technological opportunity had to be fused with a demand for the application of the new technology. In this instance the fusion was brought about largely by events outside the Soviet Union. The key factor in the 1942 decision . . . was the awareness of German and American work. The final demand for applications of the new technology was created by American possession and use of the bomb.[69]

The Case of Great Britain

Great Britain was the first nation to initiate a high-priority program of nuclear weapons research.[70] The wartime British program, like that of the United States, was motivated primarily by international security considerations or, more specifically, the need to develop a weapon with which to wage war successfully against Germany.[71] There is evidence, however, that even during the war, this incentive was supplemented by an interest in the postwar security assets of possessing nuclear weaponry and the commercial energy potential that might be an outgrowth of nuclear weapons research.[72]

After the war, Britain was again faced with a decision on whether or not to develop an atomic bomb, having largely dropped an independent nuclear weapons research program in 1943 when its scientists went to work in the United States.[73] The postwar incentives, however, were quite different than those during the war and probably entailed more international political than military–security incentives. Considerations of international prestige and intra-alliance influence appear to have been particularly important and were probably reinforced by U.S. restrictions on sharing nuclear information with its British ally.[74] As Prime Minister Attlee explained:

> We had to hold up our positions *vis à vis* the Americans. We couldn't allow ourselves to be wholly in their hands, and their position wasn't awfully clear always . . . . At that time we had to bear in mind that there was always the possibility of their withdrawing and becoming isolationist once again. The manufacture of a British atomic bomb was therefore at that stage essential to our defense.[75]

In certain respects the British postwar decision to develop an atomic bomb also appears to have been simply a continuation of the decision and momentum established during the war. As one observer put it, "Work on the bomb had already been initiated; the technical problems were well understood. All that remained was a decision actually to build the factories, separation plants, and reactors necessary for the job."[76] The technological momentum, in other words, had already been set in motion, great scientific effort had been expended, and large numbers of military and scientific personnel were committed to completion of the task.[77]

Little attention appears to have been given by the British to possible liabilities of nuclear weapons possession. Although the argument was raised by a prominent physicist, P. M. S. Blackett, that a British decision to manufacture atomic bombs might provide a stimulus for other countries to follow suit,[78] many of the factors which today are regarded as likely disincentives were then not apparent. Perhaps most conspicuous by its absence was a theory of deterrence which emphasized the need for invulnerable retaliatory forces. Also absent was the threat of a nuclear armed adversary.[79] The British decision to develop an atomic bomb after the war, therefore, did not pose the kind of vulnerability problem—particularly the danger of preemptive nuclear attack before deployment of a reliable second strike force—which confronts today's would-be proliferators. Although the postwar British decision to develop an atomic bomb apparently was not stimulated by immediate or specific international security threats, the pace of the British program accelerated with the deterioration in East–West relations and the intensification of the Cold War.[80] The situational variable, international crisis (specifically the Communist coup in Czechoslovakia, the Berlin Blockade, and the North Korean attack on South Korea), therefore, may account in part for the timing of the first British atomic explosion in 1952.

The Case of France

The public justification for development of the French *force de frappe* (or *force de dissuasion*, as it is now known) is closely associated with Charles De Gaulle and emphasizes international security considerations. The "decision" to develop a French nuclear force, however, was made under the Fourth Republic and was as much the product of political circumstances and technological momentum as military security.[81]

At the end of the Second World War, France ranked behind the United States, the Soviet Union, Great Britain, and probably Canada in atomic energy knowhow.[82] In contrast to the postwar position of the United States and Great Britain, France initially forswore a major military program of nuclear research and instead concentrated on its industrial applications.[83]

According to the official White Paper report on the first French nuclear explosion of 1960, France's defense decision-makers first seriously studied the possibility of a nuclear option in 1951.[84] Although one can date the origin of the trend toward a French atomic bomb at about this time, the manner in which a nuclear weapons program evolved during most of the Fouth Republic, without major guidance or decisions by the political leadership, supports Lawrence Scheinman's observation that "the question is not so much what induced France to take the nuclear plunge as it is a question of whether the eventual outcome could have been otherwise."[85] As Scheinman points out, because no government in the

Fourth Republic before 1958 was strong enough politically to take the risk of making a definite decision one way or another on a military atomic program, steps leading toward the atomic bomb were taken by a small number of secondary government officials under the principal administration of the Commissariat à l' Energie Atomique.[86]

Scheinman makes a strong case for the force of technological and bureaucratic momentum as a determinant of France's nuclear weapons program. The direction of French policy, however, was also reinforced by a number of international developments, especially the French defeat in Indochina in 1954 and the retreat at Suez in 1956. These foreign policy defeats contributed to the perception among the nuclear protagonists in the Fourth Republic that nuclear weapons could endow France with increased international status and enable her to exert greater influence over her NATO allies, particularly the United States. Although military arguments for a nuclear force were also made, it appears that prior to the formal government decision to build the atomic bomb in April 1958,[87] international political considerations of prestige and influence, rather than military incentives, predominated. Moreover, little attention seems to have been given to the difficulties of establishing a credible nuclear deterrent or the economic burden or relief a nuclear force might provide.[88]

The proliferation incentives of increased prestige and national autonomy were accentuated with the advent of the Fifth Republic and the concentrated pursuit of French grandeur by Charles De Gaulle. The Gaullist nuclear force, however, was primarily justified as an instrument of nuclear deterrence. As articulated most clearly by Pierre Gallois, the French force was designed to deter a superpower attack by making credible the threat to "tear off an arm" and to achieve what was referred to as "proportional deterrence." This public justification of nuclear weapons in terms of international security needs was developed well after the decision had already been made to acquire nuclear weapons.

The Case of China

Much less is known about the Chinese atomic bomb decision than about decision-making for the other nuclear powers. Available evidence, however, indicates that the primary incentive for the development of Chinese nuclear weapons was a perceived need to deter external military threats.[89]

The United States was initially depicted as the major external danger, and in the 1950s the Chinese had occasion to experience firsthand U.S. efforts at atomic diplomacy. They were the target of nuclear threats during the Korean War in 1953, again in 1954 when Secretary of State Dulles raised the prospect of massive retaliation against both the Vietminh and the PRC in response to the French predicament in Indochina, and in 1957, when the United States deployed on Taiwan a 600-mile-range missile designed to deliver tactical nuclear warheads.[90] As Jonathan Pollock points out, although "the impact of these actions on Chinese behavior is still disputed, they undoubtedly made the conscious decision to proceed with the development of nuclear weapons far more compelling."[91] This point was made explicitly by the Chinese following their first nuclear weapons test in May 1964:

It was the nuclear blackmail and nuclear threat of U.S. imperialism that compelled the Chinese people to rely on themselves and work hard to turn their country into a mighty power... now they have finally gained the means of resisting the U.S. nuclear threat.[92]

Disclosures during the Sino-Soviet polemics indicate that the actual decision to develop an atomic bomb was taken sometime in 1957.[93] The timing of this decision is interesting as it seems to precede the major deterioration in Sino-Soviet relations and the Chinese realization that the Soviets were unwilling to risk confrontation with the United States over the pursuit of Chinese objectives.[94] Indeed, there is evidence that the Soviet Union provided the Chinese with considerable technology regarding basic atomic research in the 1950s, although the Soviets apparently refused a Chinese request for a sample atomic bomb and technical data concerning its manufacture.[95] The extent of the Soviet contribution to the Chinese atomic weapons program is unclear, but the withdrawal of Soviet technicians and advisors in August 1960 undoubtedly slowed the pace of its development.

Two additional factors that may have affected the rate of development of China's atomic bomb, and can be regarded as possible disincentives, were the deterioration in China's economic situation after 1959[96] and Mao's consistent deprecation of the utility of nuclear weapons as an instrument of warfare. There is practically no evidence available regarding the impact of economic strains on Chinese defense planning, other than an occasional statement that "the development of nuclear weapons was not being given a high priority since there was so much else to do."[97] Considerable data, however, exist to support the contention that Mao consistently doubted the military utility of nuclear weapons.[98] This perception, reflected in his characterization of the atom bomb as a "paper tiger," however, never interfered with China's major economic and technological effort to acquire nuclear weapons.[98] One explanation for the apparent discrepancy between public pronouncements and behavior is calculated strategic deception on the part of a militarily inferior party. More compelling, however, is the interpretation that despite a sincere belief in the American and Soviet overestimation of the military significance of nuclear weapons, Mao regarded an indigenous atomic weapons program as necessary to assure Chinese autonomy, independence, and claim to major power standing.[99] This point is underscored in the statement made by the Chinese in 1964:

> The atom bomb is a paper tiger. This famous saying by Chairman Mao Tse-tung is known to all. This was our view in the past and this is still our view at the present. China is developing nuclear weapons not because we believe in the omnipotence of nuclear weapons .... The truth is exactly the contrary. In developing nuclear weapons, China's aim is to break the nuclear monopoly of the nuclear powers and to eliminate nuclear weapons.[100]

Chinese competition for influence within the international communist movement appears to have been an additional incentive for its developing an independent nuclear weapons force. Although the "Detonation Statement" and other public commentary at that time made only veiled reference to this incentive, Chinese public support for the independent French nuclear force and criticism of U.S. attempts to dominate the Western alliance may be interpreted, by anology, as arguments for a Chinese nuclear capability.[101] This is also suggested by the arguments raised by the Chinese in rejecting (as did the French) the 1963 Test Ban Treaty against Soviet wishes:

> For the Soviet statement to describe all the socialist countries as depending on the nuclear weapons of the Soviet Union for their survival is to strike an out-and-out great chauvinistic note and to fly in the face of facts.[102]

> It is absolutely impermissible for two or three countries to brandish their nuclear weapons at will, issue orders and commands, and lord it

over in the world as self-ordained nuclear overlords, while the over-whelming majority of countries are expected to kneel and obey orders meekly, as if they were nuclear slaves.[103]

As Morton Halperin notes, Soviet and U.S. pressures to halt the diffusion of nuclear weapons within the socialist and capitalist camps raised the value of nuclear weapons as a source of intra-alliance power in the minds of the Chinese and convinced the Peking regime to develop its own nuclear capability.[104]

Chinese aspirations for national autonomy, major power standing, intra-alliance influence, and nuclear weapons suggest interesting parallels with the psychological and political motivations underlying the French nuclear weapons program.[105] The major differences appear to have been the more concrete external threats which China faced, greater isolation, and the greater risk of preemptive military action.[106]

The Case of India

On May 18, 1974, India detonated an underground nuclear explosion in the Rajastan desert. This test of a plutonium explosive, supplied by a 40 MW research reactor, ended the decade-old moratorium on nuclear proliferation.

Since the explosion, Indian officials have repeatedly declared that the detonation was a peaceful nuclear experiment motivated by economic incentives and disavowed the notion that India had any intentions of developing nuclear weapons. Although the absence of subsequent Indian nuclear detonations is consistent with the official government position, other evidence suggests that the 1974 test was the product of a long-fought and high-level domestic debate affected by often conflicting international and domestic security and political considerations.[107]

Unlike most developing states, India has long had a large cadre of skilled workers and scientists.[108] Research on atomic energy, in fact, began in India in 1944, and in 1956 the first experimental research reactor, designed and constructed by Indians, went critical. Indigenous expertise and substantial atomic energy assistance from the West (especially Canada), therefore, provided India with the technological base and an institutional lobby for a nuclear weapons program well before a decision to detonate an atomic explosion was made.[109]

Although India has not detonated a second nuclear explosion, it has continued to develop a self-sufficient nuclear industry capable of fabricating "all sensitive nuclear instrumentations, fueling assemblies, special alloys and materials, heavy water coolants, plutonium and thorium from its own separation plants, and—according to speculation—thermonuclear substances."[110] Because the Indian program has been so comprehensive, there is little doubt that it could support military and civilian atomic energy projects simultaneously. Indeed, many reports suggest that India already has stockpiled a large amount of fissile material suitable for weapons use—perhaps enough plutonium for nearly two hundred "minimum bombs, or a still appreciable number of larger devices."[111]

India's decision to proceed with a nuclear explosion was most likely made in 1972.[112] Although it is difficult to sort out the relative significance of the determinants of the decision, considerations of domestic politics, international prestige, and regional politics were all probably instrumental.

The case for a domestic politics explanation rests primarily on strong public opposition to the NPT and support for an Indian nuclear option,[113] and the fact that the explosion came at a time when Prime Minister Gandhi's popularity had sunk precipitously. Domestic weakness and internal crisis, it can be argued, created pressures for a nuclear test in order to divert public attention from Mrs. Gandhi's domestic woes. According to one Indian analyst, circumstantial evidence suggests that not only the actual detonation decision but each major decision since 1964 leading toward the bomb had been taken by prime ministers at times of political weakness.[114]

If Mrs. Gandhi's first audience in May 1974 was a domestic one, a second intended audience was probably the superpowers. According to this interpretation, the message of the nuclear test was that India was an emerging global as well as regional power and could no longer be taken for granted by the superpowers in international affairs.[115] As articulated by K. Subrahmanyam, "In a world organized about the acquisition of power, the nation which does not acquire power to deter power being used against itself is at a substantial disadvantage."[116]

Two events in 1971 seem to have triggered or at least reinforced this perspective. The first was the dramatic rapprochement between the United States and China, interpreted by many Indians as an effort by the Americans to contain both Indian and Soviet influence in the region.[117] The second was the "American tilt" toward Pakistan during the Indian military conquest of East Pakistan and increasing Indian dependence upon the Soviet Union. Deployment of the U.S. carrier *Enterprise* in the Bay of Bengal during the 1971 Indo-Pakistan conflict, in particular, could be regarded by the Indians as an attempt at coercive diplomacy.[117] Although the Indian victory demonstrated New Delhi's regional dominance, it did not appreciably change the manner in which India was treated by the superpowers. The Indians may well have perceived the demonstration of a nuclear capability as the most effective way of altering this condition and acquiring wider respect. More specifically, the ambiguity inherent in a single nuclear test may have been expected not only to gain the attention of the superpowers without inviting punishment, but to improve the basic position of the Indians, particularly in international nuclear negotiations.[118] As noted by one Indian politician in 1973:

> The strongest case for going nuclear now rests not on "domestic political reasons" ... but on the foreign policy consideration that only a nuclear India can extract political, military, and economic advantages from the two Super-powers. The essential line of development of Indian thinking is now to downgrade in the policy area the leverage of the Super-powers in the form of withdrawal of economic aid or outright military threats.[119]

The prestige incentive also can be viewed as compensatory. As Richard Betts points out, "the 1974 explosion showed that, despite the modesty of industrial and economic progress, in the nuclear field India is first class."[120]

The third audience for whom the Indian nuclear explosion was probably intended was China. According to Ashok Kapur, the explosion signaled "India's intention to take the nuclear route unless the PRC was more accommodating in Indian–PRC and subcontinental relations."[121] A related argument emphasizes the growing Chinese military and political influence in Southeast Asia, U.S. withdrawal from the region, and the uncertainty about the future relationship between India and China, especially in the event of Sino–Soviet rapprochement.[122] From this perspective, a major incentive for development of an Indian nuclear option was to establish a strategic hedge against military and political uncertainty in the region.

As long as Jawaharlal Nehru was Prime Minister (1947–1964), the major constraint on the technological momentum toward an Indian nuclear explosion was probably Nehru's own antinuclear weapon philosophy.[123] After Nehru's death, opposition to a nuclear weapons option centered on the financial burden such a venture would pose and, to a lesser extent, on the difficulty of developing a credible nuclear deterrent posture.[124] Fear of tarnishing India's pacifist image, the possible loss of superpower support, and the risk of stimulating Pakistan's nuclear program appear to have been much less significant disincentives.

Given India's state of economic underdevelopment and widespread poverty, one might have expected arguments about cost to have been a decisive factor in the debate over a nuclear weapons option. In fact, however, although the "guns versus butter" proposition served as the principal bulwark for those opposing Indian nuclear weapons between 1964 and 1974, it is a mistake to exaggerate the force of the cost/benefit economic rationality argument. In part, this is because Indian decision-makers have perceived high investments in nuclear research as a means to generate significant long-term industrial spin-off benefits in electronics, mining, metallurgy, and other non-nuclear sectors of the economy. Perhaps more importantly, the Indian leadership, like that of other developing states, may attach importance to such objectives as scientific equality and modernity, which may compensate for many of the uneconomical aspects of nuclear programs often cited by Western critics.[125] This perspective is illustrated by Indian statements in support of full-cycle nuclear energy capabilities and breeder reactors, which argue, in effect, "that the third world missed the industrial revolution and will not make the same mistake by missing the nuclear revolution."[126]

The detonation of a single nuclear device is estimated to have added little to India's budget for nuclear energy development.[127] More likely to act as constraints on India's nuclear weapons program are the much larger costs associated with moving from a single fission test to a large and sophisticated nuclear force. Ironically, the major source of opposition to pursuit of a full-fledged nuclear weapons program may well be the military establishment, which in the past has shown little enthusiasm for a nuclear weapons program because of the fear that it would mushroom into a costly enterprise and drain funds from conventional weapons.[128]

The Case of Pakistan

Pakistan, like India, is not a party to the NPT. Although it has submitted its currently operating nuclear research and power reactors to IAEA safeguards and publicly has disavowed an intention to acquire nuclear weapons, it has also expressed anxiety over India's nuclear capability and has taken steps since the Indian explosion to acquire the nuclear fuel cycle facilities necessary to develop its own atomic bomb. At the same time, Pakistan has acknowledged the hazards to economic development posed by diverting resources to a nuclear program, has sought security guarantees from the United States and China, has initiated proposals to restrict nuclear arms in the region, and has acted to bolster its conventional military force. In short, Pakistan's nuclear posture, like that of many Third World potential proliferators, is an ambiguous one that reflects competing proliferation incentives and disincentives.[129]

The Pakistani nuclear program began in the mid-1950s at the time of the United States Atoms for Peace initiative. Pakistan set up an institute for atomic research in 1955, and ten years later began operating an enriched uranium fueled research reactor supplied by the United States. Since 1971 a CANDU heavy-water 125-MW power reactor has also been in operation near Karachi. It has been estimated that the latter reactor may be capable of producing up to 137 kg of plutonium a year and that "if supply and maintenance obstacles can be overcome, Pakistan may soon have enough separable plutonium for up to fifty small bombs."[130] The relevance of this plutonium stockpile to nuclear weapons proliferation, however, depends on the acquisition of separation facilities. It was Pakistan's nearly successful efforts to acquire such equipment from France in 1976 which provoked international concern over Pakistan's nuclear intentions. Although the deal for the nuclear reprocessing plant was effectively cancelled in 1978 due to French insistence on contractual amendments to make military use of the plant's end product more difficult, Pakistan's continued interest in a weapons option is apparent in its efforts to construct—at first clandestinely—a uranium-enrichment plant.[131]

The most widely accepted reason for Pakistani interest in a nuclear weapons option is international security considerations, especially the perceived nuclear threat from India.[132] Former Prime Minister Bhutto's vow as foreign minister in 1966 that Pakistan would eat grass rather than forgo a bomb if India produced one is often cited as indicative of the strength of this security incentive.[133] The recent history of warfare and religious strife between the two countries and India's annexation of Sikkim since the 1971 war also suggest that Pakistan's international security fears are not unfounded.[134] A case, therefore, can be made that Pakistan's nuclear incentives correspond to the original deterrence rationales behind Western nuclear armament and that "Pakistan has as much legitimate need for a nuclear deterrent as the United States did in the late 1940s, or as the United States, Britain, France, and China do today."[135] Pakistan may also regard nuclear weapons as useful for tactical defense should nuclear deterrence fail, as a political bargaining chip in negotiating mutual restraints with India, and as a deterrent for Indian nuclear blackmail.

Underlying all of the forementioned incentives is Pakistan's fundamental security dilemma—the absence of a reliable and able nuclear protector.[136] This absence was magnified by the loss of the eastern wing of the country in 1971, the U.S. failure to take harsh measures against India after the 1974 nuclear explosion, the Carter administration's decision to deny the sale of A-7 attack jets to Islamabad, U.S. pressure on France to cancel the French reprocessing plant sale, and the American offer of 400 million dollars in aid following the Soviet invasion of Afghanistan—an offer characterized as "peanuts" by President Zia. Particularly galling from Pakistan's vantage point was the Carter administration's decision to supply nuclear fuel to India after its atomic detonation at the same time that the United States terminated arms and economic aid to Pakistan.[137] These actions were seen as an American effort to frustrate Pakistan's desire to achieve at least a symbol of national autonomy and status as a regional power. This resentment is reflected in the complaint of one Pakistani official: "The Iranians have oil, Indians have Carter as well as the Device—it's only fair that Pakistan should have at least the Bomb."[138] Indeed, based on the Indian experience, the Pakistan leadership may have concluded that the only way to overcome superpower indifference to Pakistan's vulnerability was to move toward an atomic bomb option.

Although Pakistan's considerations of international security appear to be the most compelling incentives for nuclear weapons, a case can also be made for the significance of domestic political incentives. This is done persuasively by Ashok Kapur, who emphasizes the difference between public Pakistani pronouncements about the Indian threat and Pakistan's "real assessment" (inferred from private conversations) which is "not of overconcern."[139] The pronuclear pronouncements, he argues, can be explained to a large extent in terms of the "power struggle of Pakistani domestic politics." Nuclear nationalism, according to this view, is (1) good national politics; (2) consistent with public support for a Pakistani nuclear option; and (3) reflects "empire building by Pakistan's nuclear atomic scientists."[140] The real surprise, Kapur argues, is the slow pace of Pakistan's nuclear decision-making. The primary explanation for this, he suggests, is that, at least until the current regime, Pakistan's leaders (including Bhutto) had given economic development and military modernization higher claim to resources than atomic power.[141]

Despite the strength of incentives for Pakistan to acquire nuclear weapons, one cannot dismiss the disincentives as inconsequential. They pertain primarily to the danger of provoking India to exercise its so-called nuclear option, possible Indian preemption before the Pakistan nuclear force is fully developed, and the loss of bargaining leverage with the United States for conventional arms assistance.[142]

There is little doubt, as Zalmay Khalilzad points out, that "Pakistan's acquisition of nuclear weapons would . . . provide India with the rationale for an overt and more extensive nuclear weapons program."[143] Representatives of the Indian government have expressed the same point, warning that if Pakistan assembled an atomic bomb, India would be forced to amass its own nuclear arsenal.[144] The danger of an arms race escalating into a nuclear war is also apt to be strategically distressing for Pakistan given its smaller area and centralized population and industry. As Khalilzad notes, "Pakistan is very vulnerable to nuclear destruction even if a limited number of bombs are used."[145] Pakistan thus has particular reason to fear a preemptive Indian attack. A more remote but nevertheless real concern may also exist about preemptive action by the United States which, according to a *New York Times* account, considered covert operations against Pakistan's uranium-enrichment facility at Kahuta.[146] To the extent that Pakistan's nuclear ambitions are perceived abroad as leading toward an "Islamic bomb,"[147] Islamabad may also be concerned that an Israeli airstrike, like the one which destroyed the French-built nuclear reactor in Iraq in June 1981, may be repeated in Pakistan. Although these fears are likely to be subordinate to the perception of existing strategic vulnerability, they may well encourage the maintenance of maximum ambiguity in the Pakistani nuclear program and the emulation of the Indian "nuclear device" or Israeli "bomb in the basement" as opposed to overtly deployed nuclear weapons.

Fear over the loss of bargaining leverage with the United States may at one time have been a significant disincentive to developing nuclear weapons. There are indications, for example, that the Pakistani military was concerned about the effect of the French reprocessing plant deal on U.S. conventional arms sales. In August 1976 the Pakistani military favored acceptance of Kissinger's offer of 100 A-7s in exchange for foregoing the reprocessing plant.[148] It is likely, however, that the inconsistency of recent U.S. foreign policy in general, and nuclear proliferation policy toward India and Pakistan since 1974 in particular, has undermined the Pakistani leadership's confidence in its ability to manipulate (or even predict) Washington's behavior. If this interpretation is correct, a perceived weakening of U.S. interest in and security guarantees for Pakistan may have reinforced its interest in nuclear weapons. Pakistan may have drawn the correct conclusion that the superpowers only pay attention to other nuclear powers and that Pakistan has no choice but to pursue a nuclear option.[149]

The Case of Argentina and Brazil

Argentina and Brazil are the two South American countries most frequently mentioned as proliferation candidates.[150] Although both countries' official policy has been that they do not seek to acquire nuclear weapons, they meet two conditions often attributed to a proliferation-prone nation—opposition to the NPT and a quest to acquire complete nuclear fuel cycle facilities. They also have consistently maintained the right to conduct peaceful nuclear explosions.

The present nuclear rivalry between Argentina and Brazil can be traced to the early postwar period and has periodically included flirtations with nuclear weapons manufacture. The first episode occurred in 1951 shortly after President Juan Peron appointed Ronald Richer, an Austrian physicist who had worked on nuclear fusion in Nazi Germany, to head a new nuclear research facility. In March 1951, twenty months before the first U.S. thermonuclear (hydrogen) explosion, President Peron announced the discovery of a simple method to control thermonuclear reactions and Richer proclaimed that Argentina had discovered the H-bomb.[151] Although Richer was fired the following year and subsequently jailed following disclosure of his nuclear bluff, his widely publicized claims may have led to a more serious effort by Brazil to obtain technology developed in the unsuccessful Nazi atomic bomb project. This effort involved a secret deal in 1953 to import three gas centrifuges for uranium enrichment from Germany. The clandestine operation reportedly was discovered just before the centrifuges were to be shipped and the equipment was seized on order of the U.S. high commissioner to Germany.[152]

The atomic energy programs of Argentina and Brazil accelerated in the mid-1950s with the assistance of the U.S. Atoms for Peace program. The paths to nuclear development that the two countries pursued, however, differed substantially. Argentina opted for an indigenous nuclear development policy based on a natural uranium fuel cycle, while Brazil chose to develop a light-water reactor program dependent on enriched uranium from the United States.

Argentina is generally regarded as having a more advanced civilian nuclear program than Brazil in terms of experience, technology, and scientific expertise. This is reflected in the fact that since 1975 it has operated the only power reactor in South America.[153] The gap, however, appears to be narrowing as a consequence of Argentina's financial difficulties, the flight of many of its nuclear scientists abroad (to Brazil, among other states), and the major nuclear effort undertaken by Brazil in the mid-1970s, highlighted by the 1975 multibillion-dollar deal with West Germany to acquire a complete nuclear fuel cycle.[154] Although rising costs and technical problems have undermined some of the enthusiasm for nuclear power that existed in Brazil in the 1970s, it remains the case in 1980 that both Argentina and Brazil can legitimately boast of advanced civilian nuclear programs with significant military potential.

Unlike many *N*th country candidates whose proliferation posture reflects objective military challenges from abroad, neither Brazil nor Argentina is beset with serious external threats to their national existence. There is a tendency, nevertheless, in most analyses of Argentine and Brazilian nuclear policies to emphasize the historical rivalries between the two countries and the importance of international security deterrence incentives to proliferation.[155] This is despite the fact that, as William Courtney points out, "the current level of military rivalry between the two countries is low and that in recent decades Brazil and Argentina have been more preoccupied with perceived internal threats to national security than with external threats."[156]

In part this concentration on deterrence incentives, especially for Argentina, may be a function of the analyses' vintage. Clearly, mutual suspicion was intensified in the 1975 period by Brazil's ambitious program to acquire uranium-enrichment facilities. Brazil's nuclear ambitions, in turn, may have been intensified by the nuclear information exchange pact signed by Argentina and India shortly after the Indian explosion in 1974 and by news that Argentina planned to acquire a French plutonium production plant.[157] It was also at this time when a legislator allied with the Peronist majority introduced a bill in Argentina's Congress calling for government manufacture of a nuclear bomb for national defense.[158]

Although one should not dismiss international security incentives as inconsequential—particularly for Argentina, which is at a disadvantage vis-à-vis Brazil in most indices of national power—Kapur and Courtney's deemphasis of extreme threat incentives seems vindicated by the concrete steps taken to improve mutual confidence about nuclear intentions during the May 1980 visit of the Brazilian President to Argentina.[159]

An alternative nuclear weapons incentive—international (as opposed to regional) prestige and influence—is more consistent with the apparent rapprochement between the Argentine and Brazilian governments and their mutual assertion of independence vis-à-vis the superpowers. This interpretation is also reinforced by the consistent opposition of both countries to the provisions of the NPT that enshrine the special status of the nuclear powers. As emphasized by Argentina's Minister of Foreign Affairs at the 1978 U.N. Special Session on Disarmament, the NPT seeks to freeze existing disparities among states and "is tantamount to an attempt to perpetuate the scientific and technological oligopoly established by a handful of industrialized states which is to [the] direct detriment of the interests of the developing countries."[160] This view is echoed by the Brazilian leadership, which has sought to achieve a greater role for itself in the international system consistent with its growing economic power. The prestige incentive of maintaining a nuclear weapons option through the pursuit of sophisticated and sensitive technologies is not identical, however, for Brazil and Argentina. As one observer puts it, "For Argentina it is a strong point that compensates for other weaknesses in national power and image . . . . For Brazil it is both an instrument and a sign of rapidly growing national power."[161]

The strength of plausible domestic incentives to acquire nuclear weapons is different for Argentina and Brazil, although public support for pursuing a nuclear option has been high in both cases, especially after the Carter administration's attempts to restrict European exports of sensitive nuclear technologies.[162] The principal difference in domestic incentives would seem to be the greater instability of the Argentine government, its financial difficulties, and its possible temptation to develop a weapons program in order to enhance the legitimacy of the regime and foster domestic cohesion by increasing the level of regional tension. The difficulty with this interpretation, although it cannot be altogether discounted, is that it is at odds with the history of Argentine foreign policy, which has been basically nonadventurist despite fifty years of political instability.[163]

The very instability which theoretically might induce a regime to utilize a nuclear weapons program for domestic purposes may, simultaneously, serve as a significant nuclear disincentive. The military in both Brazil and Argentina appear to be in complete control at the moment. In 1973, however, a terrorist organization tried, unsuccessfully, to seize an atomic plant under construction.

This raised the terrorist disincentive to more than an academic possibility.[164] At a minimum, it seems correct to say that internal sources of insecurity for Argentina and Brazil outweigh external ones.[165]

Given the demonstrated commitment by Argentina and Brazil to acquire full nuclear fuel cycle facilities capable of yielding weapons-grade plutonium and uranium, it is unlikely that either country would be dissuaded by economic considerations from acquiring the additional manufacturing and testing equipment necessary for a nuclear explosion. This is clearly implied in the claim made by the head of Argentina's National Atomic Energy Commission in 1975 that within four years his country could build a bomb "at a very reasonable cost—say $250 million, which is 10 months of deficit on the Argentina State Railways."[166] Brazil also clearly has the resources to finance the expense of adding military applications to its extensive nuclear energy program.[167] Unlike Argentina, however, domestic criticism of the costs of Brazil's nuclear program has mounted in recent years, particularly among leading members of the scientific community. They have questioned both the choice of nuclear as opposed to hydro-electric plant development and the option of an enriched-uranium fuel cycle.[168]

Having emphasized the absence of immediate international security threats to both Argentina and Brazil, it is important to note that acquisition of nuclear weapons by either country would be perceived as a major provocation by the other and would likely trigger a nuclear arms race that neither nation would welcome. Although it is difficult to gauge the strength of this disincentive for the two countries, the risks appear greater for Argentina given its smaller conventional forces and economic resources and its geographical disadvantage in terms of the location of most strategic targets in Argentina near the Brazilian border.

The leaders of Argentina and Brazil are strongly committed to acquiring independent nuclear fuel cycles. They also appear to be aware of the international security risks that demonstration of a nuclear capability might generate in a region that, in 1980, was relatively free of direct Soviet–American military competition. The international security incentives to pursue the Indian path of nuclear demonstration would therefore appear to be less attractive to Argentina and Brazil than, for example, to Pakistan. More likely, both South American nations will continue to keep their nuclear options open, while abstaining from overt nuclear weapons tests. The decisions to abstain, however, are unlikely to result from external pressures, which both countries fervently reject, but from "national sovereign decisions" and self-restraint.[169]

The Case of Israel

Israel's nuclear weapons posture may be described as one of "cultivated ambiguity."[170] It consists of opposing NPT membership, insisting that it will not be the first party to introduce nuclear weapons into the region, creating all the material prerequisites for the production of nuclear weapons (and perhaps even assembling and testing them), and not acknowledging that it has a demonstrated weapons capability, but encouraging, or at least not discouraging, speculation about its existence. The Israeli posture thus represents an intermediate position between the Indian strategy of demonstrating a nuclear capability but denying its military use and the South African strategy of retaining an undemonstrated nuclear option but discouraging speculation about it.[171]

According to some accounts, Israel, and not India, was the sixth nuclear weapons state.[172] Although this contention is difficult either to refute or document, there is no question about Israel's long-time interest in a nuclear weapons option. Indeed, like India, Israel has displayed a commitment to nuclear research and development since it became a state in 1948. A Research and Planning Branch in the Israeli Defense Ministry was set up that year to survey possible uranium resources in the Negev desert, and in 1952 the Israeli Atomic Energy Commission was established under the jurisdiction of the Defense Ministry.[173]

Both the United States and France have contributed to Israel's nuclear development. In terms of military significance, French assistance was particularly important. Although the terms of Israeli-French cooperation between 1953 and 1967 have never been fully disclosed, it appears that Israel offered France information on the production of heavy water and the extraction of uranium from low-grade ore in return for access by Israeli scientists to French nuclear technology and training and, quite likely, provision of technical data from early French atomic tests in the Sahara.[174] It has also been suggested, although not substantiated, that a nuclear bomb of French–Israeli design may have been tested by the French in the early 1960s.[175]

The major product of French-Israeli nuclear collaboration was the construction of a nuclear reactor at Dimona beginning in the late 1950s. After initially contending that the facility was a textile plant, Israel and France finally acknowledged in December 1960 the existence of the joint venture to build a natural uranium reactor. The reactor is reported to have become operational by 1964. It is estimated to have a power output of at least 24 MW.[176] As a by-product, a reactor of this size could produce approximately 6 kg of plutonium a year, enough for a little more than one Nagasaki-size bomb annually.[177]

Although there have been reports of Israeli nuclear arms since the 1960s,[178] the most detailed and serious charges were made in early 1976 when Israel's possession of between 10 and 20 deployed nuclear weapons was first asserted by a CIA official at a "semipublic" meeting, then reported in the *Washington Post* and *New York Times,* and finally featured in a *Time* special report which affirmed the CIA disclosure and elaborated on it.[179]

Most sensational and detailed was the *Time* account which reported that Israel not only had 13 atomic bombs ready for use on Kfir and Phantom jets and Jericho missiles, but had actually been prepared to use them during a 78-hour period at the start of the October War in 1973.[180] According to the *Time* report:

> At 10 p.m. on October 8, the Israeli commander on the northern front
> . . . told his superior: "I am not sure we can hold out much longer."
> After midnight Defense Minister Moshe Dayan solemnly warned
> Premier Golda Meir: "This is the end of the third temple." Mrs. Meir
> thereupon gave Dayan permission to activate Israel's Doomsday
> weapons . . . . Before any triggers were set, however, the battle on both
> fronts turned in Israel's favor. The 13 bombs were sent to desert
> arsenals, where they remain today. . . .[181]

Analysts remain divided on the extent to which the *Time* story represents speculation or revelation. Despite subsequent disclosure of a CIA memorandum indicating its conclusion that in 1974 Israel had produced nuclear weapons, the United States has never officially announced the existence of an Israeli nuclear weapons capability, and the subject remains, as the Israelis probably prefer, ambiguous.[182]

As a state which owes its existence largely to its mastery of the art of war, it is perhaps to be expected that many of Israel's proliferation incentives are reducible to international security considerations. Foremost among these security rationales for possession of nuclear weapons or a weapons option are deterrence of regional and global adversaries and the ability to inflict massive punishment as a last resort should deterrence fail.

The potential contribution of nuclear weapons or a weapons option to Israeli deterrence policy has been formulated in many ways. It has been advocated, for example, that an overt nuclear weapon capability would promote regional stability in a fashion approximating the superpower "balance of terror," or, at a minimum, provide a credible deterrent against an all-out Arab offensive.[183] A sophisticated version of this open nuclear weapons strategy is the proposed substitution of the threat of nuclear retaliation should agreed upon borders be violated for the present policy of territorial security (i.e., occupation of Arab populated territory).[184]

Alternatively, it has been argued that the best means to intimidate and deter the Arabs and perhaps the Russians is to have a ready but unannounced nuclear capability.[185] The case for the Soviet Union as a plausible target of Israeli deterrence policy is made most persuasively by Avigdor Haselkorn, who argues that "if Israel in fact moved from an *option* to build nuclear weapons to a decision to do so, the initial judgment was made in [the] mid-1970s" when it appeared to Israeli leaders that "Moscow might play an active *offensive* role against Israel."[186] As Haselkorn points out, the targets of an Israeli nuclear strike at that time could have been Soviet forces in Egypt, the Soviet Mediterranean fleet, or even Soviet territory itself. All were within Israel's reach "and the Soviets could not know for sure what Israeli action might be if the Israeli's perceived themselves to be in a last resort circumstance where courting suicide would be preferable to doing nothing again (as was the case when the Jews were marched off to the German death camps)."[187]

It is difficult for a foreigner to gauge the depth of the average Israeli's reaction to and preoccupation with his or her nation's security dilemma and the prospect of total annihilation.[188] This fear, sometimes referred to as the "holocaust syndrome," provides an additional, plausible rationale for development of a nuclear weapon of last resort. Psychologically, it may be argued, possession of nuclear weapons may be necessary to provide an alternative "final solution" in which the historical example is one of Samson, whose suicide brought about the destruction of his enemies, rather than Masada, where the Jewish Zealots of the first century killed only themselves.[189] A nuclear weapon of last resort, in other words, may well be viewed in Israel as a rational alternative in a context in which the only choice is perceived to be between annihilation by conventional or by nuclear means. This is a very different nuclear scenario, as Robert Harkavy points out, from that facing the United States where, if deterrence should fail, the "rational" alternative to a nuclear holocaust may be "better red than dead."[190]

Most accounts suggest that an Israeli threat to use nuclear weapons would be credible only in "last resort" circumstances.[191] George Quester, however, suggests that use of tactical nuclear weapons might be militarily advantageous as a defense against a large concentration of armor in the Sinai desert or against a Russian amphibious fleet.[192] Israel's highly concentrated population and small territory would nevertheless seem to make fighting with nuclear weapons extremely unattractive to Israeli leaders, assuming that others could or would respond in kind.[193]

Although military considerations appear to provide the primary incentives for Israel's development of a nuclear weapons capability, one can also identify international and domestic political rationales. Most frequently cited in the literature on Israel's nuclear decision-making are the incentives of achieving increased international autonomy and the acquisition of "more bang for the buck."

Arguments for increased Israeli autonomy through possession of an overt or ambiguous nuclear weapons capability take a variety of forms, although most can be reduced to proposals either for reduced dependency on the United States[194] or various bargaining chip rationales. The latter category includes the routine *N*th country option of threatening to develop nuclear weapons to elicit conventional arms and diplomatic support. Former Defense Minister Moshe Dayan's efforts to publicize the Israeli nuclear potential in 1975 and 1976 may well have been calculated with this form of leverage in mind, although the disclosures also may have been designed to assist the Israeli government in rationalizing the territorial concessions sought by the United States.[195] Other nuclear aspirants such as South Africa, Taiwan, and South Korea might also be attractive targets for Israeli use of diplomatic bargaining chips. These states, rather than trading conventional arms for Israeli nuclear restraint, may be tempted themselves to barter diplomatic support, uranium reserves, and capital assets for Israeli nuclear technical expertise.[196] In addition, although there is little evidence that the policy has been pursued, Israel might attempt to use its nuclear weapons potential as a bargaining chip against the Arabs to promote a political settlement. Variants of this approach have been proposed by Paul Jabber, Shlomo Aronson, and Robert W. Tucker.

It is very difficult to assess the economic incentives for Israeli development of nuclear weapons. On the one hand, there are those who maintain that Israel is at a serious disadvantage with the Arabs in a long-term non-nuclear competition. Moshe Dayan, has at times, explicitly made this argument for nuclear weapons.

Israel has no choice. With our manpower we cannot physically, financially or economically go on acquiring more and more tanks and more and more planes. Before long you will have all of us maintaining and oiling the tanks.[197]

For a nation with a current annual defense budget of approximately $5.2 billion, the costs of a modest plutonium bomb program is probably tolerable, although it is not clear that nuclear force production would reduce the burden of conventional force expenditures as Dayan suggested.[198] Indeed, one could argue that possession of nuclear weapons would increase rather than decrease Israel's economic defense burden since maintenance of conventional force superiority might be required to deter and/or defend against Arab military operations below the level of a massive attack.

One political incentive important in the case of France, India, Argentina, and Brazil—national prestige—does not appear to have played a significant role in Israel's nuclear decision-making. Interestingly, it has even been suggested that an "anti-technological military *machismo* which has underplayed and underused high technology" may actually have postponed Israel's nuclear development, or caused lingering resistance among some military and civilian elites.[199]

Most proliferation disincentives in the Israeli case apply to overt possession of nuclear weapons rather than to an ambiguous nuclear option. Principal among these are the risks of stimulating regional adversaries to develop their own nuclear forces and the likelihood of seriously damaging U.S.–Israeli relations.[200]

A major advantage of the ambiguous character of Israel's nuclear policy has been its compatibility with the efforts of both superpowers to preserve the non-nuclear status of the Arab states.[201] A switch to an unambiguous nuclear strategy would clearly undermine superpower nonproliferation efforts, perhaps bring about nuclear guarantees to the Arabs by the Soviet Union, and make it difficult politically for Arab leaders to resist the development or acceleration of nuclear weapons programs, even if they were unconvinced of the military dividends of going nuclear.

Adoption of an open nuclear weapons strategy could also be extremely costly to the Israelis in international political terms. Not only would they lose whatever bargaining leverage that may accrue from the threat of exercising a nuclear option, but they would risk further diplomatic isolation and the alienation of their most valuable ally, the United States. As George Quester points out, it is "one thing for Israel to refuse to sign the NPT, another to go ahead and violate it. Such a move would shock and perhaps even immobilize the American Jewish community and would generally antagonize much other pro–Israel opinion in America, as well as in Great Britain and Europe."[202] The Israeli leadership would even have to calculate that an American administration might seize upon the policy shift as a pretext to disengage from an uneasy relationship. The paucity of solid evidence about the history of Israel's nuclear decision-making makes it very difficult and hazardous to associate specific military and political rationales and domestic and international events with major decisions along the path to actual development and deployment of nuclear weapons. If Israel, in fact, has moved from a nuclear option to a decision to build nuclear weapons, circumstantial evidence points to the fear of Soviet intervention in the region in 1970 and the prospect of the loss of Israeli superiority in conventional weapons as the primary catalysts. The nuclearization of any regional adversary, the loss of U.S. diplomatic and military support, or the perception of an impending Arab attack might have the similar effect of moving Israel from a policy of calculated nuclear ambiguity to one of demonstrated capability. It is also possible, however, that nuclear decisions have been made and will continue to be made less in response to specific and immediate security threats and more as a consequence of the incremental actions of a small number of individuals pursuing solutions to technical rather than political problems. At least one analyst maintains that Israeli nuclear decisions, more than likely, "were made gradually, even haphazardly, . . . in response to an ineluctable momentum, against a background of uncertainty and the fear of 'last resort' scenarios . . . ."[203]

The Case of South Korea and Taiwan

South Korea (The Republic of Korea) and Taiwan (the Republic of China) often are discussed together on issues of nuclear proliferation.[204] Although both nations are now parties to the NPT and formally disavow any nuclear weapons intentions, they share a number of characteristics which contribute to their inclusion on most lists of prime proliferation candidates. Among these characteristics are occupation of territory in Northeast Asia claimed by militarily powerful Communist adversaries, heavy reliance on and recent concern over U.S. security guarantees, and a strong commitment to the development of nuclear energy.

South Korea and Taiwan are both heavily dependent on imported energy and have invested extensively in civil nuclear energy programs, especially since the 1973 oil embargo. Taiwan's nuclear program generally is considered to be more advanced than South Korea's, although neither state has nuclear fuel cycle facilities beyond laboratory scale other than power and research reactors and a small fuel fabrication plant. An Energy Research and Development

Agency report of potential *N*th countries in 1977 includes Taiwan among the ten states most able technically to detonate a nuclear device within the "short term" (within less than one and up to three years of a decision to do so) and lists South Korea in the second tier of states capable of detonating a device within the "intermediate term" (within four to six years of a decision to do so).[205]

A major feature of Taiwan's short-term nuclear weapons potential is its operation since 1973 of a 40 MW Canadian research reactor of the type India used for production of its nuclear explosive material. It is estimated to have a maximum capacity to produce twenty-two pounds of plutonium a year.[206] In contrast, South Korea's two research reactors of 2 MW and .25 MW capacity are not capable of producing significant quantities of plutonium.[207]

Despite Taiwan's apparent edge in nuclear technology and scientific infrastructure, South Korea's reluctance to ratify the NPT until April 1975, and its none-too-subtle efforts in the same year to obtain a plutonium-reprocessing plant, have made its nuclear intentions as suspect if not more so than those of Taiwan.[206] Taiwan, in contrast to South Korea, was one of the first states to ratify the NPT and, while advocating reprocessing as the proper solution to the problem of spent fuel management, has publicly strongly supported the concept of regional as opposed to national reprocessing and fuel storage centers.[209]

The primary incentives for South Korea and Taiwan to acquire nuclear weapons are considerations of international security. The strength of these incentives, however, appears to be conditioned as much by the Taiwan and South Korean leadership's perceptions of U.S. security guarantees as by the behavior of their heavily armed regional adversaries.

In the case of Taiwan, the primary military threat for which nuclear weapons appear to be viewed as a significant deterrent is the invasion of Taiwan by the People's Republic of China's conventional forces.[210] George Quester, for example, argues that even crude plutonium bombs would be tactically useful against an amphibious invasion "since amphibious forces classically have had to be concentrated to fight their way ashore. If a nuclear device promised to be effective in defending against such an attack, it might *ipso facto* deter such an attack."[211] Movement toward a nuclear weapons posture sufficient to make credible a deterrent threat, however, would be extremely risky for Taiwan, as it might provoke preemption from the mainland. The value of the deterrent would also appear to hinge on Taiwan's ability to project an image of desperation and perhaps even irrationality, given the overwhelming military superiority of the People's Republic of China.[212] For Taiwan the last resort circumstance which might drive it to adopt so risky a policy is the perception that it has been abandoned by the United States, a perspective closely linked to the pace and direction of U.S.-PRC relations.[213]

Like Taiwan and Israel, the Republic of Korea (ROK) confronts a well defined and serious external military threat to its existence. Indeed, the immediate threat to its security is probably greater than that faced by Taiwan, despite the non-nuclear status of its major adversary, North Korea. The geography of North and South Korea, moreover, prompts the consideration by the ROK of a nuclear weapons deterrent and/or warfare posture. This international security incentive is clearly spelled out by William Overholt. He contends that "Korean geography channels troup formations through a few valleys flanked by mountain chains and the sea, and therefore makes such concentrations unusually vulnerable to nuclear attack."[214] The proximity of the South Korean capital to North Korea, although a serious strategic disadvantage, may also serve as an incentive for the South Koreans to acquire nuclear weapons since these may be regarded as the best means to deter a surprise attack on Seoul or to repulse an attack if deterrence fails.

This deterrent incentive for an independent nuclear weapons program was probably minimal as long as a major U.S. military presence in South Korea, including nuclear weapons, remained unquestioned.[215] The failure of U.S. policy in Vietnam, followed by President Carter's announcement in 1977 of plans to withdraw U.S. ground combat troops from South Korea undermined this attitude and, by eroding South Korean confidence in an American security guarantee, probably strengthened the position of proponents of an independent South Korean nuclear weapons program.[216] There are also signs that even before the clear, if unintended, signal of U.S. security policy reformulation in 1977, South Korea was uneasy about U.S. military guarantees. One indication is a statement by President Park Chung Hee, reportedly made in 1975, that "If the U.S. nuclear umbrella were to be removed, South Korea would have to start developing a nuclear capability to save [itself]."[217]

Nuclear weapons decisions in both Taiwan and South Korea are likely to be influenced primarily by international security considerations.[218] There are circumstances, however, where the leadership of Taiwan (and to a much lesser extent of South Korea) might also regard nuclear weapons as useful for international and domestic political purposes.

The difference in the political utility of nuclear weapons for

Taiwan and South Korea derives from the former state's greater diplomatic isolation and uncertain future. Taiwan's leadership may see nuclear weapons as a means to heighten domestic morale and gain international recognition of its viability. Although movement toward a "Taiwan bomb" would entail grave risks, it might also be deemed necessary by Taiwan's leadership "to reassure the public and demonstrate that they had indeed been doing something to ensure the island's future."[219]

Anticipation of a hostile reaction by adversaries and allies serves as the primary constraint on the nuclear weapon ambitions of Taiwan and South Korea. For Taiwan, already diplomatically isolated and confronted with a nuclear armed adversary, fear of mainland Chinese preemption is probably the foremost disincentive to pursuing a nuclear weapons program. For South Korea, the fear of hostile reaction is more likely felt in regards to its military allies and major trading partners, particularly Japan and the United States.[220]

It is reported that some Korean scholars have suggested a policy of nuclear ambiguity—after the Israeli model—as a means to achieve some of the alleged deterrent benefits of nuclear weapons without assuming the political and military costs.[221] The Israeli model of creating the widespread impression that it possesses nuclear weapons—without overtly confirming it—may also be attractive to Taiwan. It can even be argued that Washington might favor emergence of a Taiwan "bomb in the basement" as a means to ensure two Chinas while continuing the process of normalizing relations with the PRC.[222] South Korea and Taiwan, however, would confront significant problems if they chose to emulate the Israeli posture. Both adhere to the NPT and do not have the luxury of Israel's large, unsafeguarded research reactor.[223] South Korea and Taiwan also do not enjoy the clear conventional military superiority over their regional adversaries Israel possessed during its development of a nuclear weapons option. The risk of preemptive attack for South Korea and Taiwan is therefore much greater. Finally, it is not clear how much deterrent value is derived from a bomb in the basement.

At present neither Taiwan nor South Korea appear to be committed to the acquisition of nuclear weapons, although both sides in the past probably have considered moving closer to a nuclear weapons capability.[224] Should either state decide to pursue an overt nuclear capability in the future, it is likely to do so only as a last resort, precipitated by the perception that it no longer can rely upon an American security guarantee.

The Case of Canada

Canada is a prime example of a nation with an undoubted capability to produce nuclear weapons that has consciously and explicitly chosen not to do so.[225] Its consistent policy of nuclear weapons restraint, coupled with its long-standing place in the forefront of nuclear energy research, serves as an important reminder of how misleading it is to conceptualize proliferation primarily in terms of technological causes, and cautions against accepting the notion that no country able to produce nuclear weapons will be able to resist the temptation.

Canada, like Britain, was involved in the U.S.-orchestrated Manhattan Project, which produced the first atomic bombs, and emerged from the Second World War with a functioning atomic reactor, the world's second largest reserves of uranium ore, and a cadre of scientists and engineers trained in atomic energy research.[226] Indeed, at the end of the war, Canada ranked among the top four nations in nuclear knowhow, ahead of France. It has been estimated that, had it desired to do so, Canada could have produced nuclear weapons as early as 1955.[227] There is no public evidence, however, that Canada, at any time since 1945, seriously contemplated building an atomic bomb or pursuing a policy of nuclear ambiguity.

The overriding incentive for the Canadian wartime nuclear program, like that of the United States and Great Britain, was to develop an atomic bomb with which to defeat Nazi Germany. By late 1945, however, having contributed to the successful development of a U.S. atomic weapon, the Canadian government rejected an independent atomic weapons program. This rejection appears to have been a very "conscious decision made after an extensive discussion of the issue at the Cabinet meeting of 17 November 1945."[228] The factors primarily responsible for this initial policy of nuclear restraint were: (1) confidence in the American security guarantee and nuclear umbrella; and (2) a self-image as a relatively small nation without great power aspirations but with an opportunity to promote international arms control.

Canada's geographic and political closeness to the United States and the resultant indivisibility of Canadian and U.S. security was probably the single most important disincentive to a Canadian nuclear weapons program in 1945 and one which continues to be significant today. The special security relatioship which derives from Canada's geographic proximity to the United States and which enables Canada to forgo an independent nuclear strategy is emphasized by one of Canada's leading military specialists:

The construction of our own nuclear weapons system, costly and difficult as it would be, is not beyond our financial and technological capacity ... But, altogether fortunately, our occupancy of the northern half of the North American continent makes such expense and effort wholly unnecessary. Any atomic attack upon North America would bring about United States retaliation. The Soviet Union, therefore, cannot under imaginable circumstances contemplate a nuclear strike directed specifically against Canada. The American apparatus for massive retaliation seems to deter attack on Canada precisely to the same extent that it serves to deter attack on the United States itself. We are the sole ally of the United States of which this can be said.[229]

Although, as Arthur Steiner points out, the American nuclear umbrella may have been perceived by Canadians as less leaky than it in fact was, the credibility of the American commitment to Canada has remained high.[230] As a consequence, there are few Gallois-type scenarios which would argue convincingly for an indigenous Canadian nuclear deterrent.[231].

The Canadian decision to forgo nuclear weapons, while heavily influenced by the perception of U.S. security guarantees, also appears to be the result of the absence of great power aspirations and an aversion to acting in a fashion which might undermine the prospects for the international control of atomic energy. Records of the Cabinet War Committee meetings in 1945, for example, suggest that the Canadian leadership had a realistic appraisal of Canada's middle power status and perceived its primary international influence to derive from a close relationship with the United States and a foreign policy emphasizing international cooperation. As one historian has pointed out, "Ottawa wanted to set an example ... of a small nation which had a nuclear capability but which voluntarily foreswore the possession or manufacture of nuclear weapons."[232] One can argue further that, to the extent Canadian nuclear policy has been driven by considerations of international prestige, it has held a conviction that its nuclear abstinence is a source of prestige and influence.

Arthur Steiner suggests as an additional reason for Canada's decision to forgo a nuclear weapons program in 1945 the simultaneous overestimation of the cost of manufacturing atomic bombs and the underestimation of the difficulty of building them.[233] Although such miscalculations may explain the reluctance of the Canadian leadership to assume the burden of a nuclear weapons program in the immediate postwar period of relative optimism regarding the prospects for international control of nuclear energy, other factors have assumed greater importance as proliferation disincentives for Canada in the more recent past.

One disincentive not suggested in the general proliferation literature is the Canadian government's apparent appreciation, at least since the late 1950s, that a policy of nuclear weapons abstinence is a sign of national independence vis-à-vis the United States and is a domestic political asset. As the political debates in the late 1950s and early 1960s indicate, Canadians tend to see nuclear weapons thrust upon them by the Americans, and perceive a compatibility rather than a conflict between renouncing nuclear weapons and staying independent of the United States.[234] In other words, while the French and Indians attempt to show their political independence by demonstrating a nuclear weapons capability, the Canadians show theirs by renouncing that option.[235]

An important nonproliferation disincentive also continues to be Canada's unwavering support for international arms control in general, and the control of the spread of nuclear weapons in particular. The strength of this commitment is suggested by Canada's stringent nuclear export policy since 1974, its refusal to recognize any distinction between nuclear explosives for peaceful and military purposes, and its consistent and vigorous support of the NPT.[236] In short, as Beaton and Maddox noted almost two decades ago, Canada may be regarded as an odd case in the universe of countries able to or on the verge of building nuclear weapons. "She does not think her presence in the highest counsels is indispensable to peace; she does not fear desertions by her allies; and she cherishes no tradition of military grandeur."[237]

THE TYPICAL PROLIFERATOR

Table 5.2 summarizes the major findings from the preceding survey of nuclear decision-making in thirteen past and potential proliferators. Although the limited number of countries examined and the lack of in-depth analyses make efforts at generalization hazardous, several hypotheses on proliferation are suggested.

One hypothesis supported by the survey is the predominance of international over domestic pressures for, as well as constraints on, proliferation. Indeed, only in the case of France was a domestic factor, bureaucratic momentum, identified as a primary underlying pressure for acquisition of nuclear weapons. The role of domestic factors as primary disincentives also is rare in our sample. The only

Table 5.2. Summary of Proliferation Determinants

Country	Underlying Pressures		Underlying Constraints		Most Likely Precipitants
	Primary Determinant	Secondary Factor	Primary Determinant	Secondary Factor	
Argentina	5,6	8	10,12,14	13,15	19
Brazil	5,6		10,12,14	13,15	19
Canada[a]	2		12,13	6,16,17	
France	5,6,9			16	
India	5,6	1,8,9	19	10,11,13,14,16	19,20,24
Israel	1,3	2,6	10,14	17	19,20,24
PRC	1,5,6			10,16,18	
Pakistan	1,2,6	8	10,14	11	19,21,22
South Korea[a]	1,2	6	10,14	15	21
Taiwan[a]	1,2,3,6	5	10,14	11	21,24
U.K.[a] (WW II)	2	7			20
(postwar)	5,6	9			20
USA[a]	2	9			20
USSR[a]	1		18[b]		19

[a]NPT party
[b]For 1940 decision

Key:

1 Deterrence	15 Unauthorized seizure
2 Warfare advantage and defense	16 Economic costs
3 Weapon of last resort	17 Public opinion
4 Coercion	18 Bureaucratic politics
5 Status/prestige	19 Nuclearization of other states
6 Autonomy/influence	20 International crisis
7 Economic spillover	21 Weakening of security guarantees
8 Domestic politics	22 Increased accessibility of know-
9 Technological momentum	how/material
10 Military reaction by other states	23 Vertical proliferation
11 Strategic credibility gap	24 Domestic crisis/leadership change
12 Absence of perceived threat	
13 International norms	
14 Economic and political sanctions	

cases are India before Nehru's death (his personal philosophical opposition) and the Soviet Union in 1940 (bureaucratic politics in the form of opposition by entrenched senior scientists to the nuclear research proposals of younger colleagues with less institutional power). International factors, in contrast, appear as primary pressures in every case and as primary constraints in seven of the nine cases of countries for which major underlying constraints were discerned.

Our proliferation profiles also indicate that the primary incentives to acquire nuclear weapons have remained relatively unchanged over time—at least in terms of broad categories of determinants such as deterrence, warfare advantage, and international prestige and influence.[238] This finding suggests that future studies of the proliferation incentives for "near nuclear" states might profit from a closer examination of the historical examples provided by the United States, the Soviet Union, Great Britain, France, and Mainland China.

Although proliferation disincentives also have remained fairly constant—by far the most significant one being the anticipated reaction of other states—the absence of major or persisting political or security disincentives for the first five nuclear weapons states is highlighted by our comparative survey. Stated somewhat differently, the major potential proliferators today, in contrast to the first members of the nuclear weapons club, appear to attach more importance to the anticipated political and military reactions of other states. Their greater sensitivity to external factors is not surprising given their lower ranking on most indices of international power relative to the first nuclear weapons states—all of whom were generally regarded as greatpowers or superpowers prior to their acquisition of nuclear weapons.

Were it not for the case of France and, to a much lesser degree, India, one would be tempted to emphasize the existence of an acute security threat as the major factor that discriminates between necessary conditions (e.g., technical knowhow and availability of fissile material and weapon fabrication facilities) and the determining or sufficient condition to "go nuclear." The perception of an acute security threat and the desire to achieve deterrence and/or warfare advantages were the major underlying pressures to acquire nuclear weapons for the United States, the Soviet Union, Great Britain (through 1945) Mainland China, and also Israel (if one includes it in the category of nuclear weapon states). The change in threat perception (from a situation of international crisis and severe military danger to one of relative security) also largely accounts for the reversal in Canadian interest in nuclear weapons. One can even argue that although the postwar British decision to develop nuclear weapons was not directly stimulated by international security concerns, the atomic explosion in 1952 was simply the fulfillment of a task whose decision and momentum were established during the war.[239]

One might infer from these historical cases that "near nuclear" states like Brazil and Argentina, which are relatively free from international security challenges, will be less inclined to opt for nuclear weapons than more security-conscious and threatened states such as Pakistan, South Korea, and Taiwan. A difficulty with this interpretation—although on balance it is still probably correct—is that it discounts the example of France, for whom international security considerations were of secondary importance, and perhaps also the case of India, depending on when one dates the Indian decision to develop a nuclear option. It also probably does not attach sufficient importance to psychological and nonrational bureaucratic political determinants—dimensions which our proliferation profiles inadequately tap, as do most other studies of nuclear proliferation. It is probably not coincidental, for example, that the two studies which stand out as exceptions to this rule in terms of their efforts to focus on the bureaucratic politics of decision-making—books by Kapur and Scheinman—also find considerations other than those of international security to be important in Indian and French nuclear decisions.[240]

It is possible to interpret our comparative survey as consistent with the perspective that no *typical* Nth country exists in terms of the mix of underlying pressures, constraints, and precipitating factors. This interpretation, however, obscures the fact that a small number of variables appear to be of primary importance in the nuclear weapon decisions for most of the thirteen states examined. What appears to vary most is not the proliferation motivations or constraints, but the sequence in which political decisions to "go nuclear" precede, follow, or coincide with technological developments. In the French and Indian cases, technological developments preceded and paved the way for political decisions to produce nuclear explosives. The reverse sequence appears to have occurred in the Soviet Union and the People's Republic of China (PRC), where political decisions to acquire nuclear arms were made in advance of major technological developments or the commitments of substantial resources to nuclear weapons projects. Illustrative of a third pattern of nuclear decision-making, in which technology and politics go hand in hand, are the cases of the United States and Great Britain during World War II.[241]

These different patterns of interaction between technology and politics and the very different levels of nuclear weapons capability sought and achieved by the nations in our survey highlight the need to specify with more precision what is meant by "going nuclear." In particular, it may be useful analytically to define this concept in a fashion which facilitates the observation and measurement of potentially meaningful differences in nuclear weapons behavior. In other words, before we can better explain or influence a nation's nuclear weapons posture, it may be necessasry to devote more attention to the description of the dependent variable.[242]

Traditionally in the proliferation literature, the acid test for going nuclear has been the detonation of a single atomic explosion. The emphasis has been on the divide between nuclear and non-nuclear status rather than on the disparity among proliferators (those who have crossed the divide) in terms of the number of subsequent detonations, the size of the nuclear weapons arsenal, the availability of invulnerable and reliable delivery systems, and the articulation of a strategic doctrine.

An alternative means to conceptualize "going nuclear" is to think in terms of a range of nuclear decisions (related to increasing levels of nuclear capability) rather than in terms of a discrete event.[244] Figure 5.2 provides such a conception of going nuclear for the thirteen states in our survey. At one end of the continuum, or ladder, of nuclear capability are the two superpowers in possession of vast arsenals of thermonuclear weapons, reliable second strike delivery vehicles, and sophisticated command, control, and communication (C^3) systems. At the other end of the continuum, near the bottom of our ladder of nuclear capability, are those states, such as South Korea, which probably have the technical knowhow and industrial infrastructure to build and to detonate a nuclear device, although they may lack ready access to fissionable material useful for weapons purposes. Between these end rungs of the ladder one finds the bulk of the states in our survey, some resting at readily identifiable heights such as India, others, like Israel, more difficult to locate precisely.

A ladder of nuclear capability, similar to the one depicted in Figure 5.2, may be of assistance in associating consequences of proliferation with specific stages of vertical proliferation. It may also direct attention to points along the vertical proliferation continuum which are most subject to external influence.[245] A more adequate graphic representation of the process of going nuclear, however, should also depict the manner in which technical capabilities intersect with military and political pressures. An admittedly crude effort to depict the juxtaposition of technical capabilities and military–political pressures with reference to our case studies is presented in Figure 5.3, which superimposes an axis measuring the balance of proliferation incentives and constraints upon the nuclear capability axis. Although one can quarrel with the precise location on the two axes of some of the states in our survey, the graph calls attention to the two dimensions of going nuclear—technical capabilities (which do not end the detonation of a single atomic ex-

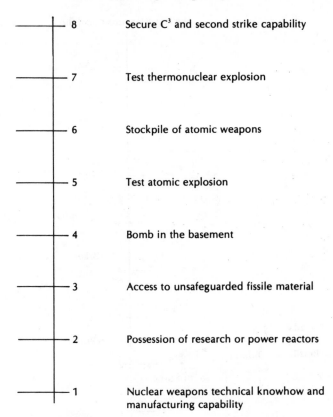

8	Secure C³ and second strike capability
7	Test thermonuclear explosion
6	Stockpile of atomic weapons
5	Test atomic explosion
4	Bomb in the basement
3	Access to unsafeguarded fissile material
2	Possession of research or power reactors
1	Nuclear weapons technical knowhow and manufacturing capability

Although not included in the ladder because of difficulty in locating its hierarchical position, possession of a nuclear weapons delivery system is a critical component of a state's nuclear capability.

For alternative nuclear capability ladders, see Lewis A. Dunn and William H. Overholt, "The Next Phase in Nuclear Proliferation Research," in William H. Overholt, ed., *Asia's Nuclear Future* (Boulder: Westview Press, 1977), p. 4, and Kathleen Bailey, "When and Why Weapons," *Bulletin of the Atomic Scientists* (April 1980), p. 43.

Figure 5.2. Ladder of nuclear weapons capability.

plosion) and the balance of military, political, and economic pressures and constraints. By compiling similar plots for different points in time, one can also capture the dynamic nature of the proliferation process. In addition, one may be able to discern some clues as to the impact of one nation's proliferation posture on the scope and pace of other nations' nuclear programs.

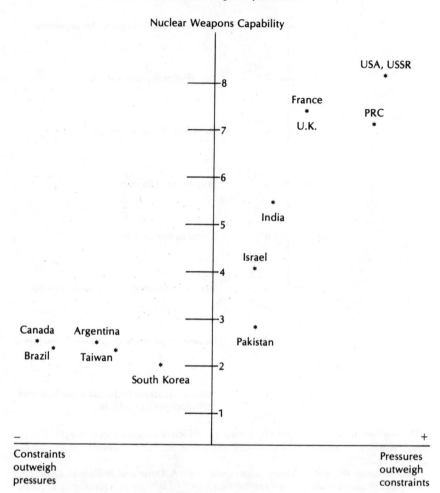

Figure 5.3. Dual dimensions of proliferation for 1981.

NOTES

1. Albert Wohlstetter et al., *Moving Toward Life in a Nuclear Armed Crowd?* Report to the U.S. Arms Control and Disarmament Agency (Los Angeles: Pan Heuristics, 1976), p. 1. A revised version of this study is published under the title *Swords from Plowshares* (Chicago: University of Chicago Press, 1979).
2. "To go nuclear" is an imprecise phrase that may indicate a variety of nuclear decisions and military capabilities. It is used here to mean the demonstration of

a nuclear explosive capability. An alternative way to conceptualize the meaning of this phrase is discussed at the end of this chapter.

3. The method of focused comparison is described by Alexander George, "Case Studies and Theory Development: The Method of Structured, Focused Comparison," in Paul Gordon Lauren, ed., *Diplomacy* (New York: The Free Press, 1979), pp. 43–68.

4. The most rigorous efforts to establish the correlates of nuclear proliferation have been made by Stephen M. Meyer, "Probing the Causes of Nuclear Proliferation: An Empirical Analysis, 1940–1973" (Ph.D. dissertation, University of Michigan, 1978) and Charles Kegley, Gregory Raymond, and Richard Skinner, "A Comparative Analysis of Nuclear Armament," in Patrick McGowan and Charles Kegley, eds., *Threats, Weapons, and Foreign Policy*, Sage International Yearbook of Foreign Policy Studies, vol. 5 (Beverly Hills, 1980), pp. 231–255. See also Charles Kegley, "International and Domestic Correlates of Nuclear Proliferation: A Comparative Analysis," *Korea and World Affairs* (1980), pp. 5–37.

5. The organization of the table draws heavily on Table 7.1 in Kegley et al., pp. 235–236.

6. Charles Kegley reports a moderate correspondence between level of military expenditures and propensity toward nuclear proliferation but no significant relationship between either national levels of economic wealth and scientific capacity and nuclear proliferation behavior. See Kegley, "International and Domestic Correlates," pp. 20–22. Operational indicators for the variables are discussed by Kegley, pp. 12–20.

7. See Meyer for a discussion of this school of thought and a sophisticated effort to test its explanatory power empirically.

8. Reported in Deborah Shapely, "Nuclear Weapons History: Japan's Wartime Bomb Prospects Revealed," *Science* (January 13, 1978), p. 155. Meyer cites this quotation, p. 28.

9. Kegley et al., pp. 38–40.

10. See, for example, Wohlstetter et al., *Moving Toward Life in a Nuclear Armed Crowd?;* Nuclear Energy Policy Study Group, *Nuclear Power Issues and Choices* (Cambridge, Massachusetts: Ballinger, 1977); Joseph S. Nye, "Nonproliferation: A Long-Term Strategy," *Foreign Affairs* (April 1978), pp. 601–623.

11. See, for example, Lewis A. Dunn and Herman Kahn, *Trends in Nuclear Proliferation, 1975–1995* (Croton-on-Hudson, New York: Hudson Institute, 1976), pp. 2–3; Enid C. B. Schoettle, "Arms Limitation and Security Policies Required to Minimize the Proliferation of Nuclear Weapons," in David Carlton and Carlo Schaerf, eds., *Arms Control and Technological Innovation* (New York: Halsted Press, 1976), p. 107–111; William Epstein, "Why States Go—and Don't Go—Nuclear," *The Annals of the American Academy of Political and Social Science* (March 1977), pp. 18–21; Office of Technology Assessment, *Nuclear Proliferation and Safeguards* (New York: Praeger, 1977), pp. 94–95; Ernest W. Lefever, *Nuclear Arms in the Third World* (Washington, D.C.: The Brookings Institution, 1979), pp. 19–20; Ted Greenwood, Harold Feiveson, and Theodore Taylor, *Nuclear Proliferation: Motivations, Capabilities, and Strategies for Control* (New York: McGraw-Hill, 1977), pp. 38–41.

12. See Chapter 1 for a discussion of the fallacies of the regional adversary–superpower analogy. A useful primer on the hazards of making inferences about the nuclear policy of small powers on the basis of the experience of the superpowers is Yehezkel Dror, "Small Powers' Nuclear Policy: Research Methodology and Exploratory Analysis," *The Jerusalem Journal of International Relations* (Fall 1975), pp. 29–49.

13. See, for example, Schoettle, p. 108, and Dunn and Kahn, p. 96. See also Geoffrey Kemp, *Nuclear Forces for Medium Powers,* Parts 1-3, Adelphi Papers 106 and 107 (London: International Institute for Strategic Studies, 1974).

14. Dunn and Kahn, p. 96.

15. R. Robert Sandoval, "Consider the Case of the Porcupine: Another View of Nuclear Proliferation," *Bulletin of the Atomic Scientists* (May 1976), p. 19.

16. See Dunn and Kahn, p. 3.

17. See Yehezkel Dror, *Crazy States* (Lexington, Massachusetts: Lexington Books, 1971).

18. For a discussion of this point, see Dunn and Kahn, p. 14, and *Nuclear Proliferation and Safeguards,* p. 97.

19. This traditional perspective is challenged by Dror (p. 38), "Small Powers' Nuclear Policy," who maintains that for Third World countries "protection through hiding and hardening of a few nuclear bombs against a conventional first-strike and even against a very limited first nuclear strike, is easy or, at least quite feasible." He further asserts that as "strategic alternatives are limited and simple, command and control . . . present no unsurmountable problem."

20. On this point, see Greenwood et al., p. 46.

21. See, for example, Ashok Kapur, *International Nuclear Proliferation* (New York: Praeger, 1979) and T. T. Poulose, "Nuclear Proliferation: A Third World Perspective," *The Round Table* (April 1979).

22. Greenwood et al., p. 51.

23. *Nuclear Proliferation and Safeguards,* p. 94, and Greenwood et al., pp. 48-49.

24. Dunn and Kahn, pp. 3-4, and *Nuclear Proliferation and Safeguards,* p. 100.

25. See Marsha M. McGraw, "The NPT Review Conference," *Arms Control Today* (February 1981), p. 3.

26. For an analysis of the Treaty of Tlatelolco, formally called the Treaty for the Prohibition of Nuclear Weapons in Latin America, see John R. Redick, "The Tlatelolco Regime and Nonproliferation in Latin America," *International Organization* (Winter 1981), pp. 103-134.

27. For a discussion of the way U.S. and Soviet policy toward nuclear exports converge in important regards, see Gloria Duffy, "Soviet Nuclear Exports," *International Security* (Summer 1978), pp. 83-111.

28. Greenwood et al., p. 52.

29. One analyst has hypothesized, for example, that the "fear of losing civilian control over the military aspect of nuclear energy is a brake against nuclear weapons proliferation in third world countries where nuclear power struggles are unsettled and the authority structure is not completely legitimate and popular." See Ashok Kapur, "A Nuclearizing Pakistan: Some Hypotheses," *Asian Survey* (May 1980), p. 551.

30. *Nuclear Proliferation and Safeguards,* p. 98.

31. Lewis Dunn, "Military Politics, Nuclear Proliferation, and the 'Nuclear Coup d' État'," *The Journal of Strategic Studies* (May 1978), pp. 31-50.

32. A useful review of the economics of PNEs is provided by Henry Rowen, "The Economics of Peaceful Nuclear Explosions" (report prepared for International Energy Atomic Authority, 1976).

33. Article V, Treaty on the Nonproliferation of Nuclear Weapons. See *Nuclear Proliferation and Safeguards,* p. 96.

34. *Nuclear Proliferation and Safeguards,* p. 94.

35. Henry Rowen and Richard Brody, "Nuclear Potential and Possible Contingencies," in Joseph A. Yager, ed., *Nonproliferation and U.S. Foreign Policy* (Washington, D.C.: The Brookings Institution, 1980), p. 216.

36. This point is discussed by Dunn and Kahn, p. 5.
37. *Nuclear Proliferation and Safeguards*, p. 100.
38. Dunn and Kahn, p. 10.
39. *Nuclear Proliferation and Safeguards*, p. 96.
40. A similar formulation is suggested by Kegley et al., p. 234.
41. See Wohlstetter et al., *Swords from Plowshares*, pp. 138–139, and Dunn and Kahn, p. 8.
42. Lewis A. Dunn and William H. Overholt, "The Next Phase in Nuclear Proliferation Research," in Overholt, ed., *Asia's Nuclear Future* (Boulder, Colorado: Westview Press, 1977), p. 11.
43. See, for example, Richard K. Betts, "Incentives for Nuclear Weapons," in Yager, p. 117.
44. Kapur, *International Nuclear Proliferation*, p. 167. Kapur follows the official Indian position of treating India's nuclear explosive capability as distinct from a weapons capability.
45. See Dunn and Kahn, pp. 8–9.
46. Major exceptions are Richard Rosecrance, "International Stability and Nuclear Diffusion," in Rosecrance, ed., *The Dispersion of Nuclear Weapons* (New York: Columbia University Press, 1964), pp. 299–314; Leonard Beaton and John Maddox, *The Spread of Nuclear Weapons* (London: Chatto and Windus, 1962), pp. 185–200; Dunn and Kahn; and Meyer. Useful collections of case studies which, however, do not attempt to provide a synthesis of the findings across nations include Onkar Marwah and Ann Schulz, eds., *Nuclear Proliferation and the Near-Nuclear Countries* (Cambridge, Massachusetts: Ballinger, 1975); Robert M. Lawrence and Joel Larus, eds., *Nuclear Proliferation Phase II* (Lawrence: University Press of Kansas, 1974); and George Quester, *The Politics of Nuclear Proliferation* (Baltimore: The Johns Hopkins University Press, 1973).
47. See Herbert York, "Introduction" to *Readings from Scientific American* (San Francisco: W. H. Freeman, 1973), pp. 3–7.
48. See York, p. 4, and Richard G. Hewlett and Oscar E. Anderson, Jr., *The New World, 1939–1946* (University Park: Pennsylvania State University Press, 1962), pp. 16–17.
49. See York, p. 4, and Hewlett and Anderson, pp. 44–52.
50. The May 17, 1941, report of the Committee on Uranium regarding the military applications of nuclear fission listed an atomic bomb as the last of three possibilities, after radioactive fission products which could be dropped over enemy territory and an atomic pile for submarine propulsion. See Hewlett and Anderson, pp. 37–38.
51. See ibid., pp. 15–17 and p. 21, and Henry C. Stimson, "The Decision to Use the Atomic Bomb," in Paul R. Baker, ed., *The Atomic Bomb* (Hinsdale, Illinois: Dryden Press, 1968), p. 10.
52. Rosecrance, p. 50.
53. Hewlett and Anderson, p. 43.
54. Hewlett and Anderson make a strong case that "only British confidence that fission could influence the war and [Vannevar] Bush's skillful leadership [of the National Defense Research Committee] gave the United States the beginnings of an atomic energy program by the eve of Pearl Harbor" (p. 5).
55. A poll conducted in July 1945 among a sample of 150 scientists involved in the Manhattan Project indicated that 15 percent "favored using atomic weapons in whatever would be most effective militarily in bringing prompt Japanese surrender at the minimum cost to American armed forces," 46 percent "held for a military demonstration in Japan followed by a renewed opportunity to surrender

before full use of the weapons," 26 percent "advocated an experimental demonstration in the United States before Japanese representatives as a warning," 11 percent "preferred a public demonstration and nothing more," and 2 percent "believed the United States should forego combat use and keep the entire development as secret as possible." (Hewlett and Anderson, pp. 399-400).

56. Cited in ibid., p. 399.
57. Ibid.
58. Stimson, p. 10
59. Ibid.
60. Ibid., p. 12.
61. The most valuable reference works on Soviet decision-making for the atomic bomb are David Holloway, "Entering the Nuclear Arms Race: The Soviet Decision to Build the Atomic Bomb, 1938-1945," Working Paper No. 9, The Wilson Center International Security Studies Program (Washington, D.C., 1979), and Arnold Kramish, *Atomic Energy in the Soviet Union* (Stanford: Stanford University Press), 1959. Also useful are Arthur Steiner, *The USSR's Road to the Atomic Bomb*, Monograph No. 6, Report prepared for the Energy Research and Development Agency (Los Angeles: Pan Heuristics, 1977) and I. N. Golovin, *I. V. Kurchatov: A Socialist Realist Biography of the Soviet Nuclear Scientist*, translated by H. Dougherty (Bloomington, Indiana: The Selbstverlag Press, 1969). The following account draws extensively on Holloway's excellent study.
62. Holloway, pp. 19-20, 48.
63. This point is well documented by Holloway, p. 18.;
64. Ibid., p. 19.
65. Kramish, p. 31.
66. Holloway, pp. 25-29.
67. Holloway (pp. 27-28) emphasizes that even a small atomic weapon project probably met fierce resistance in 1942 from scientists and defense officials who saw it as a waste of resources at a time when the Soviet Union was in desperate military straits.
68. Holloway, pp. 51-52. Interestingly, and contrary to conventional wisdom about Soviet decision-making for defense, the decision to develop the atomic bomb appears not to have been guided by military doctrine or influenced by military actors.
69. Ibid., p. 52.
70. Arthur Steiner, *Great Britain and France: Two Other Roads to the Atomic Bomb*, Monograph No. 7, Report prepared for the Energy Research and Development Agency (Los Angeles: Pan Heuristics, 1977), p. 2. Useful background information on the British nuclear weapons program is provided by Margaret Gowing, *Britain and Atomic Energy* (New York: St. Martin's Press, 1964); Margaret Gowing, *Independence and Deterrence: Britain and Atomic Energy, 1945-1952, I Policy Making and II Policy Execution* (New York: St. Martin's Press, 1974); Andrew J. Pierre, *Nuclear Politics* (London: Oxford University Press, 1972); and two chapters by Richard Rosecrance in Rosecrance, ed., *The Dispersion of Nuclear Weapons*, pp. 48-65 and 66-86.
71. See Pierre, p. 1, Rosecrance, pp. 50-51, and *Nuclear Proliferation and Safeguards*, p. 99.
72. Rosecrance, pp. 51-53. The British interest in the security benefits of the bomb is explicit in the July 1941 report of the MAUD Committee, a group organized to study the possibility of making an atomic bomb during the war. According to the report, "Even if the war should end before the bombs are ready, the effort would not be wasted . . . since no nation would care to risk being caught without a weapon of such decisive possibilities." (Cited by Steiner, *Great Britain and France*

p. 6.)

73. See H. A. DeWeerd, "British–American Collaboration on the A-Bomb in World War II," in Rosecrance, pp. 35–43.

74. Rosecrance, p. 55.

75. Cited by Steiner, *Great Britain and France,* p. 10.

76. Rosecrance, p. 55.

77. See Alfred Goldberg, "The Atomic Origins of the British Nuclear Deterrent," *International Affairs* (July 1964), pp. 409–429.

78. See Steiner, *Great Britain and France,* pp. 12–13, for a discussion of Blackett's views.

79. Rosecrance, p. 60. The postwar British decision to acquire atomic weapons was made in January 1947. The decision was made public in the House of Commons in May 1948.

80. See ibid., pp. 62–64.

81. Important sources on French nuclear decision-making are Bertrand Goldschmidt, *The Atomic Adventure,* translated by Peter Beer (New York: Macmillan, 1964); Lawrence Scheinman, *Atomic Energy Policy in France Under the Fourth Republic* (Princeton, New Jersey: Princeton University Press, 1965); Wilfred L. Kohl, *French Nuclear Diplomacy* (Princeton, New Jersey: Princeton University Press, 1971); George A. Kelley, "The Political Background of the French A-Bomb," *Orbis* (Fall 1960), pp. 284–306; and Ciro Zoppo, "France as a Nuclear Power," in Rosecrance, pp. 113–156.

82. Steiner, *Great Britain and France,* p. 18. Steiner points out that each of the other four countries had nuclear reactors in operation before the French.

83. See Goldschmidt, p. 63; Steiner, *Great Britain and France,* pp. 18–19; and Zoppo, p. 117.

84. Zoppo, p. 117.

85. Scheinman, pp. 215–216.

86. Ibid., pp. 208–210.

87. Ibid., p. 183.

88. Ibid., pp. 218–219. George Kelly (p. 292) identifies four public arguments that were made by late 1955 in support of the French bomb. They were: "1) the bomb as a symbol of national rank and prestige; 2) the bomb as a justification for demanding considerably more voice in Western strategy; 3) the bomb as an element of political bargaining power; and 4) the bomb as a threat of retaliatory capacity at a time and place of France's own choosing."

89. Valuable sources on Chinese nuclear decision-making are Morton Halperin, *China and the Bomb* (New York: Frederick A. Praeger, 1965); Alice L. Hsieh, "Communist China and Nuclear Force," in Rosecrance, pp. 157–185; Jonathan Pollock, "Chinese Attitudes toward Nuclear Weapons, 1964–1969," *The China Quarterly* (April–June 1972), pp. 244–271; and Pollock, "China as a Nuclear Power," in Overholt, pp. 35–65.

90. See Pollock in Overholt, p. 38.

91. Ibid.

92. "Break Nuclear Monopoly, Destroy Nuclear Weapons," *Peoples Daily* (October 22, 1964), cited by Pollock in Overholt, p. 38.

93. See Pollock in Overholt, p. 36, and Halperin, p. 72.

94. See Donald Zagoria, *The Sino-Soviet Conflict* (Princeton, New Jersey: Princeton University Press, 1962). This recognition was driven home during the 1958 Quemoy Crisis.

95. See Pollock in Overholt, p. 39, and Halperin, p. 79. A much more modest Soviet contribution is suggested by Hsieh, p. 177. See also David Inglis, "The Chinese

Bombshell," *Bulletin of the Atomic Scientists* (February 1965), pp. 19-21, and Arnold Kramish, "The Great Chinese Bomb Puzzle—and a Solution," *Fortune* (June 1966), pp. 157-158 and 246-250.

96. See Michael Minor, "China's Nuclear Development Program," *Asian Survey* (June 1976), p. 572.

97. Chou En-lai is reported to have made this comment to Lord Montgomery in October 1961. Cited by Hsieh, p. 158. See also Halperin, pp. 73-74, for an estimate of the Chinese nuclear weapons program.

98. See Pollock in Overholt, pp. 36-37.

99. See ibid., p. 27, and Halperin, pp. 49-52. Pollock suggests that a dual perspective on nuclear weapons may also have stemmed from the fear that they posed a threat to long dominant Chinese organizational values and military traditions (p. 61.).

100. Cited in Halperin, p. 85.

101. Ibid., pp. 49-51.

102. "Statement by the Spokesman of the Chinese Government—A Comment on the Soviet Government's Statement of August 3," cited by Halperin, p. 47.

103. "People of the World Unite! Strive for the Complete Prohibition and Thorough Destruction of Nuclear Weapons!" *Peoples Daily*, August 2, 1963, cited by Halperin, p. 52.

104. Halperin, pp. 52-53.

105. These parallels are explored in B. W. Augenstein, "The Chinese and French Programs for the Development of National Nuclear Forces," *Orbis* (Fall 1967), pp. 846-863.

106. Chinese perceptions of the dangers of their nuclear test are discussed by Halperin, pp. 90-92.

107. Among the major sources of information on Indian nuclear decision-making are Ashok Kapur, *India's Nuclear Option: Atomic Diplomacy & Decision-Making* (New York: Praeger, 1976); K. Subrahmanyam, "India: Keeping the Option Open," in Lawrence and Larus, pp. 112-148; Quester, pp. 56-81; Betts, Chapters 5, 6, and 7 in Yager, pp. 85-176; Beaton and Maddox, pp. 136-150; J. P. Jain, *Nuclear India*, Vols. 1 and 2 (New Delhi: Radian Publishers, 1974); T. T. Poulose, ed., *Perspectives of India's Nuclear Policy* (New Delhi: Young Asia Publications, 1978); and Shelton Williams, *The U.S., India and the Bomb* (Baltimore: The Johns Hopkins University Press, 1969).

108. Richard Betts notes that the overall level of India's scientific and technical manpower ranks behind only the United States and the Soviet Union (p. 97). See also Onkar Marwah, "India's Nuclear and Space Programs: Intent and Policy," *International Security* (Fall 1977), pp. 96-121.

109. India may have had the capability to build an atomic bomb since the early 1960s. See Beaton and Maddox, p. 141. Onkar Marwah reports that in 1958 Dr. Homi Bhabha, the Chairman of athe Indian Atomic Energy Commission, "made the first public but muted claim of Indian ability to construct nuclear explosive devices within eighteen months of the decision" (p. 98).

110. Marwah, p. 99.

111. Betts, p. 99. See also Marwah, p. 102, and Tyler Marshall, "India's Do-It-Yourself Nuclear Industry Becomes Fully Self-Sufficient," *Los Angeles Times* (February 18, 1981).

112. Marwah, p. 99.

113. See Kapur, *International Nuclear Proliferation*, p. 196; Poulose, *Perspectives of India's Nuclear Policy*, p. 105; and Quester, p. 71. A major source of opposition to

the NPT and support for an Indian option was the perceived double standard on the part of the superpowers who were anxious to deny nuclear weapons to India but not to themselves.

114. Dr. Bhabani Sen Gupta, "Dilemma without Anguish: India, Morarji, and the Bomb," in Poulose, pp. 224–239.
115. Kapur, *International Nucelar Proliferation*, p. 173.
116. Subrahmanyam, p. 134.
117. I am grateful to Thomas Graham for alerting me to the importance of the Enterprise's deployment. See also Betts, p. 119. Indian fears of the emergence of a United States-China-Pakistan axis were stimulated by the significant role played by Pakistani President Yahya Khan in arranging Kissinger's visit to Peking in 1971.
118. Kapur, *International Nuclear Proliferation*, p. 48.
119. M. L. Sondhi quoted by Lefever, p. 34.
120. Betts, p. 119.
121. Kapur, *International Nuclear Proliferation*, p. 173.
122. See K. Subrahmanyam, "Indian Nuclear Force in the Eighties?" in *The Institute for Defense Studies and Analyses Journal* (New Delhi), 1973 and John Maddox, *Prospects for Nuclear Proliferation*, Adelphi Papers, No. 113 (London: International Institute for Strategic Studies, 1975), p. 18.
123. See Subrahmanyam, "India: Keeping the Option Open," pp. 114–115.
124. For a discussion of the credibility gap disincentive, see Williams, p. 71–75.
125. This point is well argued by Betts, p. 88.
126. Ibid, p. 89.
127. Subrahmanyam, "India: Keeping the Option Open," p. 130.
128. See Quester, p. 69, and Betts, p. 140.
129. Useful background information on Pakistan's nuclear weapons posture is provided by Zalmay Khalilzad, *Pakistan: The Nuclear Option,* Monograph No. 10, Report prepared for the Energy Research and Development Agency (Los Angeles: Pan Heuristics, 1977); Khalilzad, "Pakistan: The Making of a Nuclear Power," *Asian Survey* (June 1976), pp. 580–592; Ashok Kapur, "A Nuclearizing Pakistan," pp. 495–516; Shirin Tahir-Kheli, "Pakistan's Nuclear Option and U.S. Policy," *Orbis* (Summer 1978), pp. 357–374; and Lefever, pp. 25–46.
130. Betts, pp. 100–101. Khalilzad suggests the figure may be closer to 100 bombs (in *Asian Survey,* p. 587).
131. Pakistan acknowledged the project only after the United States publicly charged Pakistan with covert efforts to construct the facility and threatened to cut off foreign aid. Pakistan continues to maintain, however, that the facility will not produce weapons-grade uranium. (See Betts, pp. 102–103.) For accounts of Pakistani efforts to build the plant clandestinely, see David Binder, "How Pakistan Ran the Nuke Round the End," *New York Times* (April 19, 1979); Colin Smith and Shyam Bhatia, "Stealing the Bomb for Pakistan," *World Press Review* (March 1980), pp. 26–28; and "A Clue to the Bomb Mystery," *The Economist* (July 14, 1979), pp. 60–61. It has also been reported that Saudi Arabia has agreed to sign an $800 million pact to assist Pakistani development of an atomic bomb in order to prevent Pakistan from turning to Iraq or China for financing the project. According to a *London Sunday Times* report, Libya's Moammar Kadafi had offered funds and uranium to Pakistan Prime Minister Ali Bhutto but after Bhutto's execution in 1979 Pakistan refused the aid because Kadafi insisted that his own nuclear experts have access to the project *(The Los Angeles Times,* January 19, 1981).

132. The most sophisticated argument challenging an Indian threat explanation is provided by Kapur in *International Nuclear Proliferation,* pp. 189–190, 205–206, and in "A Nuclearized Pakistan," pp. 495–516.
133. See Betts, p. 113, and Khalilzad, "Pakistan: The Making of a Nuclear Power," p. 588.
134. See Betts, p. 126. Alternatively, as Betts notes, the greatest threat to Pakistan's territorial integrity may be internal (e.g., Baluchi secession) and not very susceptible to nuclear deterrence.
135. Betts, p. 128.
136. This point is emphasized by Neil Joeck, "The Dilemma of Nuclear Proliferation," (unpublished manuscript, University of California, Los Angeles, 1980), pp. 38–39.
137. See Betts, p. 130.
138. Cited by Tahir-Kheli, p. 367.
139. Kapur, *International Nuclear Proliferation,* p. 205.
140. Ibid.
141. Ibid., pp. 205–209. Kapur also identifies a clash between "the diplomatic elite which produced the anti-India speeches, and the economic and military modernization elite which produced decisions to support economic and military modernization rather than atomic energy development" (p. 221). Other sources also indicate that even after the removal of Bhutto from office and the takeover by the military, some senior officers were wary that Pakistan's development of a nuclear option would jeopardize American arms sales. See Tahir-Kheli, pp. 368–369.
142. The international political disincentives of violating international norms and alienating world opinion were apt to be negligible in Pakistan's case, given its existing opposition to the Partial Test Ban Treaty and the NPT. The Pakistan leadership may even perceive an international Islamic consensus in favor of a Pakistan bomb. (See Joeck, p. 51.)
143. Khalilzad, "Pakistan and the Bomb," *Survival* (November/December 1979). p. 248.
144. *New York Times* (August 16, 1979).
145. Khalilzad, "Pakistan: The Making of a Nuclear Power," p. 592.
146. *New York Times* (August 12, 1979). See also Joeck, p. 50. Prompt denials by Washington did not prevent Pakistan from immediately emplacing anti-aircraft batteries at the site.
147. The following statement, reportedly written by Bhutto from his death cell, suggests this perception is not off the mark: "We know that Israel and South Africa have full nuclear capability. The Christian, Jewish and Hindu civilizations have this capability. The dominant powers also have it. Only the Islamic civilization is without it, but that position was about to change." Cited by Major General K. K. Palit and R. K. S. Namboordiri, *Pakistan's Islam Bomb* (New Delhi: Vikas, 1979), p. v.
148. See Tahir-Kheli, pp. 368–369.
149. See ibid., p. 362.
150. See, for example, H. Jon Rosenbaum, "Brazil's Nuclear Aspirations," in Marwar and Shulz, pp. 255–277; C. H. Waisman, "Incentives for Proliferation: The Case of Argentina," in Marwah and Shulz, pp. 279–293; William H. Courtney, "Nuclear Choices for Friendly Rivals," in Yager, pp. 244–279; Edward Wonder, "Nuclear Commerce and Nuclear Proliferation: Germany and Brazil, 1975," *Orbis* (Summer 1977), pp. 277–306; Ernest Lefever, pp. 100–117; John Redick, *Military Potential of Latin American Nuclear Energy Programs,* (Beverly Hills: Sage Publications, 1972); Kapur, *International Nuclear Proliferation,* pp. 330–355.

151. See *La Nacion* (March 25, 1951), p. 1, cited by Normar Gall, "Atoms for Brazil, Dangers for All," *Foreign Policy* (Summer 1976), pp. 180–181. See also Waisman, pp. 282–283.
152. See Gall, p. 181, and Wonder, p. 287.
153. It is estimated that the 335-MW power reactor has produced the equivalent of several hundred kilograms of plutonium. (See Redick, "The Tlatelolco Regime," p. 118.) A second 600-MW CANDU power reactor is scheduled for completion in 1982. Brazil's first power reactor, a 626-MW PWR, is scheduled to begin operation by the end of 1981.
154. The key provisions in the agreement called for West Germany to provide: (1) the construction of up to eight light-water power reactors; (2) the transfer of technology and equipment to Brazil for uranium enrichment, fuel fabrication, and the reprocessing of spent fuel; and (3) joint ventures in uranium exploration and mining. In return for its estimated investment of $10 billion, Brazil hoped to produce 10,000 MW of nuclear power by 1990. (See Gall, p. 160.)
155. See, for example, Rosenbaum, pp. 261 and 267; *Nuclear Proliferation and Safeguards,* p. 104; Lefever, p. 116; and Waisman, p. 292. Kapur, again, is an exception and tends to minimize the regional rivalry explanation (see *International Nuclear Proliferation,* pp. 330–355).
156. Courtney, p. 264.
157. See Rosenbaum, p. 261.
158. See Etel Goldman, "Atoms and Generals: The Argentine and Brazilian Nuclear Programs" (unpublished manuscript, University of California, 1980), p. 23, and Rosenbaum, p. 261. Goldman reports that the Argentine National Atomic Energy Commission severly criticized the proposal calling it "risky and taboo."
159. For a discussion of this agreement for nuclear cooperation signed in May 1980, see Redick, "The Tlatelolco Regime," pp. 129–133.
160. Cited by Kapur, *International Nuclear Proliferation,* p. 348.
161. Courtney, p. 254.
162. See Courtney, "Brazil and Argentina's Strategies for American Diplomacy," in Yager, p. 379.
163. This point is developed by Waisman, p. 291.
164. See Goldman on the terrorist attack (p. 32).
165. In the case of Brazil this is due in large part to the absence of any plausible military challenge from abroad. See Courtney on this point ("Nuclear Choices for Friendly Rivals," p. 261).
166. Dr. Jorge Sabato quoted in Lefever, p. 111.
167. See Lefever, p. 113.
168. See *Journal de Brasil* (May 12, 1978), p. 8, and *O Estado de São Paulo* (December 22, 1978), p. 6. See also Goldman, pp. 7–8 and 15; Courtney, "Nuclear Choices for Friendly Rivals," pp. 246–247; and George Quester, *Brazil and Latin American Nuclear Proliferation: An Optimistic View* (ACIS Working Paper No. 17, UCLA Center for International and Strategic Affairs, 1979), p. 28.
169. This point is made explicitly in a recent Argentine news commentary: "What should be made clear is that if Argentina wants to, it could produce nuclear weapons and, if she does not do so, it is not because she has been pressured—she has already rejected these—but because our officials have made a sovereign decision" (*Clarin,* February 18, 1979, p. 4).
170. Useful background information on Israeli nuclear decision-making is provided by Beaton and Maddox, pp. 168–184; Fuad Jabber, *Israel and Nuclear Weapons* (London: Chatto and Windus, 1971); Robert E. Harkavy, *Spectre of a Middle Eastern Holocaust: The Strategic and Diplomatic Implications of the Israeli*

Nuclear Weapons Program, University of Denver, Monograph Series in World Affairs, Volume 14, book 4 (1977); Avigdor Haselkorn, "Israel: From an Option to a Bomb in the Basement," in Lawrence and Larus, pp. 149–182; Efraim Inbar, *Israel's Nuclear Policy After 1973,* Monograph No. 12 (Pan Heuristics Report to the Energy Research and Development Administration, 1977); Lefever, pp. 64–81; Quester, *The Politics of Nuclear Proliferation,* pp. 82–102.

171. Useful discussions of alternative proliferation postures are provided by Kapur, *International Nuclear Proliferation,* p. 330, and Waisman, pp. 284–286.
172. See, for example, Lefever, p. 165, and "How Israel Got the Bomb," *Time* (April 12, 1976), pp. 39–40.
173. The best account of the origins of the Israeli atomic energy program is provided by Jabber, pp. 15–24.
174. See ibid., pp. 20–24.
175. Lefever, p. 68, and "How Israel Got the Bomb," pp. 39–40.
176. See Jabber, p. 37; Harkavy, p. 6; and Inbar, p. 5.
177. Relevant calculations are provided by Jabber, p. 88. Slightly different figures are reported by Inbar, p. 5.
178. See, for example, *New York Times* (July 18, 1980), p. 1 and *New York Times* (October 5, 1971).
179. See *Washington Post* (March 15, 1976), p. A2; *New York Times* (March 16, 1976), and "How Israel Got the Bomb."
180. "How Israel Got the Bomb," p. 39. See also Shlomo Aronson, *Israel's Nuclear Option,* ACIS Working Paper, No. 7 (UCLA Center for Arms Control and International Security, 1977), p. 14.
181. "How Israel Got the Bomb," p. 39.
182. For an account of the CIA memorandum released on January 26, 1978, see *New York Times* (January 27, 1978) and Lefever, p. 65. A major source of disagreement among analysts is the existence of Israeli facilities for separating weapons-grade plutonium. Cf. Lefever, p. 70; Inbar, p. 5; and Harkavy, pp. 8–10. Speculation regarding Israeli nuclear capabilities was intensified again after two mysterious light flashes in September 1979 and December 1980 in the South Atlantic. For a discussion of these events, see Philip J. Klass, "Clandestine Nuclear Test Doubted," *Aviation Week and Space Technology* (August 11, 1980), pp. 62–72, and Arnold Kramish, "Nuclear Flashes in the Night," *The Washington Quarterly* (Summer 1980), pp. 3–11.
183. See Steven Rosen, "Nuclearization and Stability in the Middle East," *Jerusalem Journal of International Affairs* (Spring 1978), pp. 1–32, and Rosen, "A Stable System of Mutual Nuclear Deterrence in the Arab-Israeli Conflict," *American Political Science Review* (December 1977), pp. 1367–1383; Paul Jabber, *A Nuclear Middle East: Infrastructure, Likely Military Postures and Prospects for Strategic Stability,* ACIS Working Paper No. 6 (UCLA Center for Arms Control and International Security, 1977), p. 39.
184. See Aronson.
185. See Quester, *The Politics of Nuclear Proliferation,* p. 99.
186. Haselkorn, p. 168.
187. Ibid., p. 170.
188. See Harkavy on this point, pp. 1–2.
189. This distinction is made by Norman Podhortz in "The Abandonment of Israel," *Commentary* (July 1976), p. 31, and is cited by Harkavy, p. 115.
190. Harkavy, p. 111.
191. See Haselkorn for a discussion of four alternative futures which might create last-resort circumstances (p. 151).

192. Quester, *The Politics of Nuclear Proliferation*, p. 99.
193. Harkavy goes so far as to state that "there are no conceivable nuclear defense considerations" (p. 86).
194. See Robert W. Tucker, "Israel and the United States: From Dependence to Nuclear Weapons," *Commentary* (November 1975), pp. 29–43.
195. See Harkavy, p. 17. Israeli efforts to bargain for conventional arms clearly would be undermined by an overt as opposed to an ambiguous nuclear weapons capability.
196. See Robert Harkavy, "Pariah States and Nuclear Proliferation," *International Organization* (Winter 1981), pp. 135–164.
197. Dayan in an interview with Marlin Levin, reported in "How Israel Got the Bomb," p. 39.
198. Alternative estimates of the financial cost of an Israeli nuclear weapons program are provided by Quester, *The Politics of Nuclear Proliferation*, p. 90 and Harkavy, *Spectre of a Middle Eastern Holocaust*, p. 31.
199. Harkavy, *Spectre of a Middle Eastern Holocaust*, p. 83.
200. Domestic opposition command and control problems, and the risk of Soviet preemption appear to be subordinate disincentives. For a discussion of these points, respectively, see Inbar, p. 11; Henry S. Rowen and Richard Brody, "Regional Instabilities," in Yager, p. 199; and Rowen and Brody, "Nuclear Potential," p. 190.
201. Although Soviet efforts in the field of nuclear nonproliferation have received little scholarly attention, there is evidence that the Soviets pressured Egypt to sign the NPT and rejected Egyptian requests for nuclear weapons assistance (see Quester, *The Politics of Nuclear Proliferation*, p. 94).
202. Quester, *The Politics of Nuclear Proliferation*, p. 96. Quester (p. 99) suggests that periodic Israeli commentary on and leaks of its nuclear intentions and capabilities are designed to test Washington and the world's reaction to a more overt Israeli policy.
203. Harkavy, *Spectre of a Middle Eastern Holocaust*, p. 84.
204. Useful background information on the nuclear weapon postures of these two countries is provided by Lefever, pp. 82–99; Joseph Yager, "The Republic of Korea" and "Taiwan," in Yager, pp. 47–75 and 66–84; George Quester, "Taiwan and Nuclear Proliferation," *Orbis* (Spring 1974), pp. 140–150; David McGarvey, Brian C. Jack, and David Snyder, *South Korea and Nuclear Weapons*, Monograph No. 5, Report prepared for the Energy Research and Development Administration (Los Angeles: Pan Heuristics, 1977); and Young-Sun Ha, "Nuclear Future of Korea and World Order," paper presented at the Annual Meeting of the International Studies Association, 1979.
205. *Nuclear Proliferation Factbook* (House Committee on International Relations and Senate Committee on Governmental Affairs, 95th Congress, 1st Session, 1977), p. 334.
206. Lefever, p. 89.
207. McGarvey et al., p. 54.
208. American pressure on South Korea to ratify the NPT is discussed by Lefever, p. 86. For a discussion of the cancellation of a pilot reprocessing plant from France in 1976 after intense pressure from the United States see McGarvey et al., pp. 14–15.
209. Taiwan's public commitment to regional fuel reprocessing, however, is not perfectly consistent with her reported construction of a small reprocessing laboratory that was disassembled after protests by the United States. See Lefever, p. 89; Yager, pp. 79–80; and *Nuclear Proliferation and Safeguards*, p. 110. Yager (p. 68) also reports that Taiwan's discussions with a British firm concerning

reprocessing services were halted only after U.S. opposition became clear.

210. The factors inhibiting a nuclear attack by the PRC on Taiwan are discussed by Yager, p. 72–73.

211. Quester, "Taiwan and Nuclear Proliferation," pp. 145–146.

212. See Yager, pp. 75–76.

213. For a discussion of this incentive see Lefever, p. 92, and Yager, p. 78.

214. William Overholt, "Nuclear Proliferation in Eastern Asia," in Overholt, p. 146.

215. The presence of U.S. nuclear weapons in South Korea was acknowledged by Secretary of Defense James Schlesinger at a press conference on June 20, 1975.

216. Some measure of confidence in the U.S. guarantee most likely was restored by President Carter's decision in July 1979 to defer further troop reductions until after 1981.

217. Rowland Evans and Robert Novak, *Washington Post* (June 12, 1975).

218. Overholt (p. 52) goes so far as to say that the case for nuclear weapons in South Korea rests entirely on considerations of national security.

219. Yager, p. 78. See also Overholt, p. 143, and Quester, "Taiwan and Nuclear Proliferation," p. 144.

220. The prospect of a nuclear-armed South Korea would be viewed with great alarm by the Japanese and would probably precipitate severe economic reprisals. A decision by Seoul to acquire nuclear weapons would also probably lead to major U.S. economic and military sanctions, including termination of supplies of nuclear fuel and equipment. A breach in U.S.-South Korean relations also might prompt the North Korean leadership to calculate that it could attack the South with a reduced risk of U.S. intervention (see Yager, p. 61).

221. Reported by Yager, p. 64.

222. For a related argument see Quester, "Taiwan and Nuclear Proliferation," p. 148.

223. Although ousted from the IAEA in 1972, Taiwan has continued to accept the full range of IAEA safeguards, including on-site inspection of all its nuclear facilities.

224. *The Los Angeles Times* of November 4, 1978, reported congressional testimony that a secret Weapons Evaluation Committee set up by the South Korean government had decided to proceed with the development of nuclear weapons in the early 1970s, but dropped the project after the United States learned of it (cited by Yager, p. 65). Premier Chiang Ching-kuo is reported to have claimed that Taiwan began research on nuclear weapons in the late 1950s but stopped the program upon the direct orders of President Chiang Kai-shek (see Lefever, p. 88).

225. Other examples are West Germany, Japan, Sweden, and Switzerland. Useful accounts of Canadian nuclear decision-making are provided by Quester, *The Politics of Nuclear Proliferation*, pp. 154–159; Beaton and Maddox, pp. 98–108; Arthur Steiner, *Canada: The Decision to Forego the Bomb*, Monograph No. 8, Report prepared for the Energy Research and Development Agency, (Los Angeles: Pan Heuristics, 1977).

226. See Steiner, *Canada*, p. 4, and Beaton and Maddox, pp. 98–99.

227. Quester, *The Politics of Nuclear Proliferation*, p. 54.

228. Steiner, *Canada*, p. 4.

229. James Eayrs, "Canada, NATO, and Nuclear Weapons," *RCAF Staff College Journal* (1960) cited by Beaton and Maddox, p. 101.

230. Steiner, *Canada*, p. 11. A poll taken in December 1974 indicated that 77 percent of the American public favored military involvment, including the use of U.S. troups, if Canada were invaded. Corresponding figures for Western Europe, West Berlin, and Israel were respectively 39 percent, 34 percent, and 27 percent (p. 11).

231. On this point see Quester, *The Politics of Nuclear Proliferation*, p. 155.

232. Blair Fraser, *The Search for Identity—Canada, 1945-1967* (Toronto: Doubleday, 1967), p. 50, cited by Steiner, p. 23. For further indications of Canada's early commitment to the international control of nuclear energy, see J. A. Munro and A. I. Inglis, "The Atomic Conference 1945 and the Pearson Memoirs," *International Journal* (Winter 1973-74), pp. 90-109.

233. Steiner, *Canada*, p. 21.

234. Quester, *The Politics of Nuclear Proliferation,* p. 156. For a useful analysis of the domestic politics of Canadian nuclear policy, see Howard Lenter "Foreign Policy Decision Making: The Case of Canada and Nuclear Weapons," *World Politics* (October 1976), pp. 29-66.

235. Quester (*The Politics of Nuclear Proliferation*, pp. 155-156) notes an interesting parallel between Canadian nonproliferation policy and Mexican support for a Latin American nuclear-free zone. Both countries, he argues, may exhibit the same "neighbor of the United States syndrome"—if an independent brandishing of such weapons is ludicrous in the shadow of such an enormous neighbor, one can perhaps show independence and moral superiority by making a fetish of renouncing such weapons."

236. Canada's unwilling contribution to India's nuclear weapons program has prompted the observation that Canada is the only country to give away nuclear weapons without making any for herself (see Quester, *The Politics of Nuclear Proliferation,* p. 154). Canada terminated all nuclear cooperation with India following the 1974 explosion and has refused to engage in nuclear cooperation with all nations, including the Euratom countries, that will not apply international safeguards to their entire nuclear program (see Steiner, *Canada*, pp. 25-26).

237. Beaton and Maddox, p. 108.

238. A partial exception to this conclusion is the absence of significant political prestige and influence incentives in the nuclear weapons decisions during World War II.

239. See Rosecrance, p. 300.

240. Ashok Kapur, *India's Nuclear Option,* and Lawrence Scheinman, *Atomic Energy Policy in France Under the Fourth Republic.*

241. Similar distinctions in terms of the process of nuclear decision-making are made by Kapur, *International Nuclear Proliferation,* pp. 54-55. For an effort to quantify the requisites for an atomic weapons manufacturing capability and a list of the dates when different states acquired that capability, see Meyer, pp. 223-241.

242. This deficiency in past research on nuclear proliferation is representative of a more general failure of students of comparative foreign policy to pay too much attention to the elaboration of factors that affect foreign policy outputs without adequate regard for the description of the dependent variable. (On this point see William Potter, "Issue Area and Foreign Policy Analysis," *International Organization* (Summer 1980), pp. 423-424.) Lewis Dunn and William Overholt make a similar plea for reconceptualizing proliferation in "The Next Phase in Nuclear Proliferation Research," in Overholt, pp. 1-2.

243. India was the first to challenge this conceptualization of "going nuclear." The Indian government insists that what counts is the intention behind an atomic test and that proliferation does not result from a peaceful test (see Kapur, *International Nuclear Proliferation,* p. 13). Argentina at times has adopted a similar posture (see Redick, "The Tlatelolco Regime," p. 121). The Carter administration's policy of equating, at least implicitly, the completion of the nuclear fuel cycle with nuclear proliferation constitutes a more recent challenge to the traditional definition.

244. See Dunn and Overholt (p. 4) for one version of a ladder measuring levels of nuclear capability.
245. See Dunn and Overholt (p. 3) on this point.

Chapter 6

Strategies for Control

Many strategies have been proposed to deal with the phenomenon of nuclear proliferation. Most can be distinguished in terms of their emphasis on affecting the *demand* for versus the *supply* of weapons. Demand-oriented approaches are intended to reduce the incentives and strengthen the disincentives of a party to acquire nuclear weapons. They include such "political-fix" strategies as security and fuel supply guarantees, conventional arms transfers, and sanctions, and arms control measures such as nuclear-free zones and a comprehensive test ban. Supply-oriented approaches, on the other hand, are designed to make it more difficult for a party seeking nuclear weapons to obtain them. Representative of this approach to nonproliferation are "technological fixes" (including export restrictions on sensitive technologies and safer fuel cycles) and international and domestic safeguards.

The general characteristics and strengths and weaknesses of these approaches are discussed below. An effort is then made to assess their relative utility with respect to several possible proliferation developments.

DEMAND POLICIES

Reducing Incentives

International security concerns represent the principal nuclear incentives for many states. This was the case for nine of the thirteen states surveyed in the preceding chapter. Among the most frequently proposed strategies to reduce security incentives to acquire nuclear weapons are the provision of conventional arms substitutes and the extension of superpower security guarantees.

1. Arms Transfers. The proposal to use non-nuclear arms transfers as an instrument of nonproliferation policy is founded on the premise that states sufficiently equipped with conventional arms will gain confidence in their ability to defend themselves and will consequently have less reason to covet nuclear arms. Advocates of this approach can point to recent breakthroughs in conventional weapons technology providing increased accuracy and firepower which may enable advanced conventional weapons to assume certain military missions previously reserved for nuclear arms.[1]

The applicability of the arms transfer approach to nonproliferation to specific *N*th countries is the subject of considerable debate. Among the states most frequently mentioned as possible targets for a selective arms transfer strategy are Taiwan, South Korea, Pakistan, and Israel.[2] For these and other countries, however, the goal of nonproliferation may come into conflict with other foreign policy objectives, including that of limiting regional arms races. The tension between the dual arms control goals of containing nuclear proliferation and slowing conventional arms transfers has been called the "dove's dilemma."[3]

The use of conventional arms as a nonproliferation tactic entails a number of risks. One of the most significant is the possibility that an influx of arms will increase regional instability by emboldening the recipient to assume a more belligerent posture and/or encouraging the recipient's adversary to escalate the arms race (perhaps even to the nuclear level) or to strike preemptively before the military balance has been changed.[4] Arms transfers also run the risk of exacerbating the supplier's relations with other countries in the region without necessarily satiating the recipient's appetite for nuclear arms.[5] This latter point is emphasized by Richard Betts, who argues that arms aid does not erase the attractiveness of nuclear weapons as an autonomous deterrent for a state with international security fears that is "dependent on foreign arms suppliers who retain leverage through the option to stop resupply in a crisis or embargo spare parts and cripple maintenance."[6] The possibility exists, moreover, that even if security pressures were reduced by arms transfers, other compelling proliferation incentives would remain.[7] There is also the risk that although the leaders of proliferation-prone countries may accept the logic of the arms transfers–nonproliferation linkage and the implied dependence, they may not be able to fulfill their end of the bargain because of domestic politics and intragovernmental opposition.[8]

Perhaps the most serious deficiency of most proposals to use arms transfers as an instrument of nonproliferation policy is the tendency to focus on narrow considerations of one Nth country's security dilemma in isolation from broader regional and international political issues. For example, as one perceptive analyst points out, "most of the restraints on the potential use of arms transfers to ease proliferation pressures in Taiwan, South Korea, Pakistan and South Africa result from U.S. policy goals rather than a desire to limit arms sales or aid."[9] In Taiwan, this is a concern for normalization of relations with the PRC; in South Korea, this is (or at least was until recently) the desire for a general reduction in the American presence in Asia; in Pakistan, this is the desire to avoid upsetting the South Asian balance by estranging India, the preeminent power; and in South Africa, this is (or again, until recently, was) the U.S. commitment to support the international arms embargo and the search for better relations with the black African nations.[10]

The preceding discussion of the risks of transferring arms as an instrument of nonproliferation policy does not point to a resolution of the dove's dilemma. Although the risks associated with arms transfers are certainly great, they may still be preferable to the introduction of nuclear weapons into a conflict-prone region.[11] Before a determination of these relative risks can be made, it is essential, at a minimum, that an analysis is undertaken of: (1) the Nth country's security perceptions and incentives to go nuclear; (2) its conventional defense capabilities and the impact arms transfers will have on them; and (3) its near-term capabilities to acquire nuclear weapons.[12] Unless a judgment can be made that the Nth country's proliferation incentives are principally security-related, can be alleviated by the infusion of more arms, and can be translated into an operational nuclear weapons capability, an arms transfer nonproliferation strategy is apt to entail great risks but holds little prospect of success.

2. Security Guarantees. Another approach to reducing the security incentives of potential proliferators, often discussed in conjunction with the provision of arms transfers, is the extension of security guarantees by one or more of the nuclear weapons states. These guarantees may be in the form of the deployment in the Nth country of the guarantor's troops, military facilities, and weaponry (including nuclear arms and their delivery vehicles), formal alliances which provide explicit binding guarantees, or less formal commitments to ensure the territorial integrity of the *N*th country.

Illustrative of the first form of security guarantee is the deployment in South Korea of U.S. troops and military facilities. These deployments are designed not only to bolster the host country's military capability, but to strengthen the credibility of the formal U.S. security commitment by providing a "tripwire" which increases the likelihood of American involvement should an attack occur. The extension of the American nuclear umbrella to Western Europe and Canada through NATO, the comparable Soviet nuclear guarantee to its Warsaw Pact allies, and the U.S. mutual assistance treaty with Japan are other examples of formal security assurances. A less formal but nevertheless firm pledge is the American commitment to the survival of Israel.[13]

The success of security guarantees, from a nonproliferation standpoint, has been mixed. On the one hand, security assurances from nuclear powers have been a prerequisite for the willingness of many states to adhere to the NPT and to justify their decisions in the face of domestic opposition.[14] Security guarantees appear to have been especially important for such isolated and insecure NPT parties as South Korea and Taiwan. Firm, if not formal, U.S. security assurances, on the other hand, have not kept Israel from moving to the threshold of nuclear weapons status. The formal American security commitment to Pakistan also has proved ineffective as a deterrent to the Pakistani quest for nuclear weapons.[15] American nuclear guarantees and the NATO umbrella, moreover, failed to deter Great Britain and France from developing their own nuclear arsenal.

Although the nonproliferation strategy of security guarantees may be successful in specific situations, the general applicability of the approach is constrained by a number of factors. Among the most important are the reluctance of potential guarantors to extend security guarantees that may entangle them in the *N*th country's foreign and domestic policy problems and the unwillingness of many *N*th countries to accept security guarantees if they entail the loss of control of certain aspects of their own domestic and external policies.[16] The utility of security guarantees may also be compromised if they are directed against other allies or states with whom the prospective guarantor seeks improved relations.[17] At the end of 1979, for example, the United States judged it necessary to terminate its defense treaty with the Republic of China in the interest of improving relations with Mainland China.

The difficulty of providing credible security guarantees should also be mentioned. Credibility is not something that can be produced by a treaty signature or solemn pledge. It results instead from past performance and the perception of strong and enduring common interests.[18]

Finally, the use of security guarantees as an instrument of non-proliferation policy is subject to two caveats made previously with respect to conventional arms transfers: (1) security-oriented approaches are irrelevant for *N*th countries whose primary motives for acquiring nuclear weapons are international prestige, the assertion of autonomy and influence, technological momentum, or domestic politics; and (2) security guarantees must not be viewed in isolation from broader foreign policy objectives, some of which may be at odds with the extension of security commitments.

It occasionally has been proposed that the nuclear powers jointly guarantee the security of states which renounce nuclear weapons. Some non-nuclear countries, in fact, sought this kind of assurance during the negotiations preceding the NPT.[19] The most that has been achieved in the form of joint obligations, however, is very limited. It consists of the nonspecific reference in the NPT preamble to the obligation of states under the U.N. Charter to refrain from the threat or use of force and a security guarantee to non-nuclear weapon state parties to the NPT by the depository governments of the NPT (i.e., the U.S., the USSR, and the U.K.) in the form of U.N. Security Council Resolution 255.[20] This latter pledge is generally regarded as meaningless since it provides that assistance to any non-nuclear nation threatened with nuclear aggression will be given in accordance with the U.N. Charter, that is, through the Security Council where each of the guarantors, as well as France and China, has a veto.

3. Arms Control Measures. International and regional arms control measures represent another approach to reducing proliferation incentives. They tend to be directed at both the security and prestige motivations of potential proliferators and to emphasize the obligations of the nuclear powers under Article VI of the NPT to work for a cessation of the nuclear arms race at an early date and for nuclear disarmament.[21] Among the more frequently proposed arms control measures are adoption of a comprehensive test ban and creation of nuclear-free zones.[22]

Proponents of a comprehensive test ban (CTB) cite both political and technical reasons why the complete cessation of nuclear weapons testing would serve the cause of nonproliferation.[23] Politically, they argue, a CTB would reduce the incentives for present non-nuclear weapons states to acquire nuclear weapons by demonstrating the nuclear powers' commitment to Article VI of the NPT (pursuit of "negotiations in good faith on effective measures relating to the cessation of the nuclear arms race at an early date"). Failure to make progress on the CTB front, it is argued, underscores the discriminatory aspect of the NPT and undermines the effectiveness of the nonproliferation regime.[24] The technical argument is more straightforward and simply notes that "non-nuclear nations could not with confidence develop a nuclear explosive without nuclear testing."[25] A corollary of this technical argument is that in the absence of testing, design of an explosive would have to be more conservative and would require more fissionable material per weapon.[25]

Those who oppose a CTB generally maintain that there is little, if any, connection between the arms race behavior of the superpowers and nonproliferation; in addition, they cite a litany of perceived adverse effects likely to accompany a comprehensive test ban.[26] This list includes: difficulties in verifying Soviet compliance with a CTB; problems of assuring the reliability of existing nuclear weapons without an on-going test program; the need to make weapons safer and more secure against accidents and misuse; the need to study the effects of nuclear explosives (e.g., in designing a ballistic missile defense system); the potential peaceful uses of nuclear explosives; the danger of losing trained personnel; and the problem of nuclear powers who refuse to take part in test ban negotiations.[27]

It is not possible here to examine in detail the competing charges of proponents and critics of a CTB. This task is performed admirably by Barry Blechman, Dan Caldwell, and Sidney Drell, who argue persuasively that many of the critic's charges are not well founded.[28] More relevant to our discussion is the fact that regardless of the merits of the critics' charges, few respond to the contentions of CTB proponents or pertain directly to the relationship of a CTB to nonproliferation. Indeed, there is much to Dan Caldwell's observation that "neither the claims of the ardent proponents nor the dire predictions of the hardline opponents accurately depict the most likely effect that a comprehensive test ban would have on proliferation [i.e., very little.] In all probability the 'near nuclear states' would remain ambiguously non-nuclear."[29]

If one assumes that a CBT would not affect those near-nuclear states such as Israel, South Africa, and Pakistan, its major promise lies in making the superpowers' call for nuclear restraint more credible to other states, thereby reducing at least the political excuse, if not the primary incentive, for some nations to pursue a nuclear weapons program.[30] For those parties that signed, the CTB would also raise the political costs of "going nuclear."

Nuclear-free zones constitute another arms control approach to strengthening the NPT regime. Unlike the CTB negotiations that the superpowers dominated,[31] most nuclear-free zone proposals have been initiated by the non-nuclear weapon states of the region concerned. Although the immediate impetus for nuclear-free zone proposals vary from region to region, proposals tend to share the general objective of promoting regional peace and stability and the more specific goal of removing the region from the sphere of competition and confrontation between current nuclear weapon states.[32]

The idea of strengthening regional security by establishing geographical zones in which nuclear weapons would be prohibited grew out of the German question in the 1950s and first found formal expression in the so-called Rapacki Plan to denuclearize Central Europe.[33] Subsequent proposals have been made for the denuclearization of the Middle East, the Mediterranean, the Nordic countries, South Asia, Africa, the Balkans, and the Indian Ocean.[34] The approach was also reflected in the Antarctic Treaty of 1959, the Outer Space Treaty of 1967, and the Seabed Treaty of 1971.[35] The most significant nuclear-free zone in existence and the only one to affect a major inhabited region applies to Latin America under the Treaty for the Prohibition of Nuclear Weapons in Latin America, commonly known as the Treaty of Tlatelolco. The current status of the Tlatelolco regime and nonproliferation in Latin America illustrates both the potential and the problems of a nuclear-free zone approach to nonproliferation.

Under the terms of the Treaty of Tlatelolco, open for signature in 1967 and currently in force for twenty-two Latin American states, parties pledge to keep their territories entirely free of nuclear weapons. The treaty also established an international agency to ensure compliance with the accord and a control system that includes the application of IAEA safeguards to all nuclear activities of the contracting parties.[36] The significance of this nonproliferation measure, sometimes viewed as a model for other regions, is mainly diluted by the absence as full parties to the treaty of the two countries generally regarded as the region's prime proliferation candidates, Argentina and Brazil.[37] Their abstinence tends to obscure the presence of three full parties to the treaty who have not ratified the NPT (Columbia, Barbados, and Trinidad and Tobago).

The major problems which have prevented the Tlatelolco Treaty from fully achieving its nonproliferation objective involve the issue of peaceful nuclear explosions (PNEs) and superpower attitudes. The PNE issue is complicated by the ambiguous language of the treaty, which in Article 18 speaks favorably of PNEs but stipulates in Article 5 that such explosives "appropriate for use for warlike purposes" are prohibited. Although most Latin American states have interpreted the treaty as not permitting indigenously produced PNEs, this interpretation has not been shared by Argentina and Brazil and is advanced as a major justification for their failure to adhere to the treaty.[38] Although the Brazilian position on PNEs has recently become more flexible, that of Argentina remains unaltered and is founded on the argument that the key factor distinguishing a PNE from a weapon is the intent of the user.[39] Argentine officials, moreover, cite the PNE issue as a prime example of a modification of the rights of Tlatelolco parties by nuclear weapon states.[40]

The issue of superpower attitudes is highlighted by two protocols to the treaty which: (1) require states having territorial interests in the region affected by the treaty to keep their possessions free of nuclear weapons; and (2) seek pledges by nuclear weapon states "not to use or threaten to use nuclear weapons" against the full parties of the treaty. The United States, the Soviet Union, Great Britain, France, and China have ratified Protocol II dealing with the "no first-use" pledge.[41] The United States and France, however, have yet to ratify Protocol I.[42] U.S. failure to ratify the protocol appears to be due more to domestic political concerns (about the brouhaha which might result if U.S. nuclear prerogatives for Puerto Rico, the Virgin Islands, and Guantanamo were surrendered) than to international strategic considerations. It is therefore significant that in his first major statement on nonproliferation President Reagan announced that he would promptly seek the Senate's advice and consent to ratify Protocol I.[43]

It is difficult to judge the applicability of the Tlatelolco experience to other regions. Progress toward the Latin American nuclear weapon free zone was certainly facilitated by the coincidence of a number of circumstances. John Redick includes among these: (1) the establishment of a legal instrument in advance of military-technological momentum (i.e., nuclear technology was not well established in Latin America in the 1960s); (2) the strong leadership and tenacity of Mexican Under-Secretary Garcia Robles; (3) the stimulus of the Cuban missile crisis in October 1962 (at which time the initial proposal for the Latin American nuclear-free zone was introduced); (4) the shared cultural and legal traditions of the region, as well as commonly held perceptions of a regional identity; and (5) the relative absence of superpower competition in the region.[44]

It is unlikely that the entire set of circumstances noted by Redick will be duplicated, although a number of the conditions may be found elsewhere. Perhaps most difficult to obtain will be a region relatively free of superpower competition and confrontation. The slow but steady progress toward completion of the Treaty of Tlatelolco system, nevertheless, suggests the possibility of success for a nuclear-free zone if it enjoys the general support of the states in the region concerned, is based on a genuine search for a common interest, and does not significantly alter the regional balance of power.[45]

4. Fuel Supply Assurances. So far our discussion of "demand policies" and means to reduce proliferation incentives has focused on considerations of international security. Although insecurity appears to be the dominant motive for the majority of states intent on the acquisition of nuclear weapons, a number of nonproliferation approaches focus on alternative motivations. One that has received considerable attention (especially after the 1974 Indian nuclear explosion) and is designed primarily to reduce incentives for premature use of plutonium and the development of nationally controlled sensitive technologies is the provision of nuclear fuel supply assurances.

Although there is little evidence that considerations of fuel supply assurances have, to date, had much bearing on national decisions to go or to refrain from going nuclear, the concept of assured supply has been fundamental to the nonproliferation regime that has evolved since the mid-1950s. The logic underlying the strategy of assured supply is clearly presented in a recent report of the Atlantic Council's Nuclear Fuels Policy Working Group:

> Supply alone, on an *ad hoc* basis, unaccompanied by assurances of its dependability on reasonable terms, would not have had the intended deterrent effect on the development of independent and potentially uncontrolled sources of nuclear materials and equipment. In normal markets, this assurance is supplied largely by the traditions of the market itself, and the self-interest of the supplier in maintaining his profitable supply arrangements. In the case of nuclear materials and equipment, the security sensitivity of the products, the absence of any orderly market tradition and the limited number of suppliers combined to make a new form of governmentally assured supply essential, if the objective of deterring independent sources was to be realized.[46]

This logic was endorsed by the International Nuclear Fuel Cycle Evaluation, which concluded that "assurance of supply and assurance of non-proliferation are . . . complementary and that greater assurance of supply can . . . contribute to non-proliferation objectives by reducing the pressures for a world-wide spread of enrichment and reprocessing facilities."[47]

Almost without exception, nuclear supplier and recipient states publicly acknowledge that because nuclear energy programs require enormous investments and long lead-times, there must be reasonable assurances of supply of fuel, equipment, and services. The tensions between supplier and recipient states stem from past attempts by suppliers to use their leverage to encourage compliance with more stringent nonproliferation measures. Canada in 1977, for example, imposed an embargo on the sale of uranium to members of the European Atomic Energy Community and Japan while negotiations were under way to incorporate stricter nonproliferation provisions in their fuel supply agreements. The U.S. Nuclear Non-Proliferation Act (NNPA) of 1978, with its imposition of new conditions on existing supply agreements, is also widely viewed abroad as an unjustified, unilateral action which jeopardizes the energy security of America's trading partners.[48] Skepticism about the motives underlying U.S. fuel supply policy also has strained relations among supplier states, the 1974 U.S. decision to suspend the signing of new foreign contracts for uranium enrichment services often being cited as an example of arbitrary U.S. supply policy unrelated to nonproliferation objectives.[49]

A number of methods have been proposed to remove security of supply as a driving force for the acquisition of nationally controlled sensitive technologies. These include both market mechanism and governmental control measures and range from the removal of all political restrictions on purchases of enriched or natural uranium fuels and reliance on a competitive market for protection against interruptions of supply to bilateral and multinational fuel cycle arrangements in which accession to full-scope safeguards would be a precondition for fuel supply guarantees.[50]

One of the most frequent proposals involves multinational agreements, or cross-guarantees, among several suppliers and consumers that provide for emergency allocation of either natural or low-enriched uranium. This kind of multinational fuel assurance arrangement might be modeled after the past practice of utilities in Europe (on both a national and multinational level) of assisting each other in cases of supply interruptions by making available loans of fuel out of inventories for limited periods.[51] For this plan to work, the suppliers entering into the agreement would need to have the capacity to increase their exports to meet emergency demands.[52] The practicability of the approach also depends on the nations to be involved and the nonproliferation conditions attached to fuel supply assurances. Involvement of the United States in a cross-guarantees network, for example, would require revision of the 1978 Nuclear Non-Proliferation Act, which sets strict conditions on any export of nuclear materials.[53]

As an alternative to the assurance of fuel supplies through cross-guarantees backed by national stockpiles, an international nuclear fuel bank has been proposed.[54] This institution would most likely have assets of physical stocks of natural and enriched uranium as well as claims on fuel held by other governmental and private entities and could distribute fuel to nations suffering from fuel supply interruptions which were unrelated to their nonproliferation obligations. Among the practical issues which might be contentious and would have to be resolved before an international fuel bank could be established are: Where should the bank be located? What assets should the bank hold? How should its operations be financed? What conditions should be attached to fuel supplies?[55]

The International Nuclear Fuel Cycle Evaluation noted both safety net arrangements such as cross-guarantees and an international nuclear fuel bank as possible short- to medium-term supply guarantee mechanisms. A competitive market, however, was identified as the preferred long-term solution to fuel supply problems.[56] A number of market-oriented approaches have received considerable attention recently.[57] Most approaches emphasizing market incentives, however, tend to be attuned more closely to supplier rather than consumer concerns.[58] In particular, they ignore consumers' fears that uranium supplies will be suspended for political reasons or that supply contracts will be unilaterally amended and new conditions applied retroactively.[59]

More generally, nonproliferation strategies which emphasize fuel supply assurances appear to be more appropriate for relatively low-risk *N*th countries that may move unintentionally up the nuclear weapons capability ladder (see Figure 5-2), than for states actively pursuing nuclear weapons because of international security considerations. This does not mean that efforts to establish reliable, long-term fuel supply assurances should be abandoned. Such assurances are probably both attainable and necessary for rebuilding international confidence in the nuclear nonproliferation regime. Measures that restore stability, predictability, and security to the fuel supply market, however, should not be regarded as treatment for the underlying causes of proliferation.

Strengthening Disincentives

To strengthen disincentives means to raise the perceived costs of acquiring nuclear weapons. A frequently proposed means to accomplish this task is to threaten to impose, and to impose, sanctions.

Sanctions can take a variety of forms; they range from low-level economic and political penalties such as the delay of economic assistance and diplomatic protest to the ultimate reprisal of the use of military force. Other sanctions often suggested include the termination of nuclear assistance and trade, imposition of a multilateral trade embargo, termination of military assistance and the supply of conventional arms, a ban on private investment in the country in question, and withdrawal of prior security guarantees.[60]

The effectiveness of sanctions depends on the nature of the incentives for an Nth country to go nuclear, the economic and political vulnerability of the proliferator, and the degree of support from the international community for specific sanctions. The nature of the Nth country's proliferation motives are critical since some, such as perceived threats to national survival, may not be susceptible to influence by any form of sanction but might be reduced by security guarantees. Some domestic political and international prestige pressures to proliferate, moreover, might actually be intensified rather than reduced by the imposition of sanctions which would produce a nationalist reaction. While unilateral action by a great power may work well in selected cases where overwhelming leverage can be exerted (e.g., U.S. success in inducing South Korea to rescind its order for a French reprocessing plant),[61] unilateral sanctions against other Nth countries are apt to be futile. For countries such as Brazil, Argentina, and South Africa, for example, even multilateral sanctions involving both superpowers probably could only raise the cost but not prevent the implementation of a decision to produce nuclear weapons.[62]

Historically, there is little evidence that economic and political sanctions have been very effective, whether applied unilaterally (e.g., by the United States against North Vietnam and Cuba) or collectively (e.g., against Rhodesia after its declaration of independence).[63] As one study notes, "Belief in the efficacy of sanctions, both in terms of the probability of their application in the event of violation and their effectiveness when applied, . . . suffered a major setback as the result of the Indian nuclear explosion."[64] Not only was international reaction generally mild, but India made clear it was not prepared to surrender the right which it asserted to construct its first nuclear explosive.[65]

The case of India illustrates another important point with respect to the utility of sanctions: policies designed for discouraging proliferation may not be appropriate for encouraging moderation once the nuclear threshold has been breached. This dilemma is well expressed by George Quester, who points out that instead of "punishing India for its decision to acquire what amounts to a nuclear weapon or making a last-ditch attempt to induce New Delhi to surrender these weapons, the more pressing concern may be to keep India on a moderate course on whether it brandishes or tests such explosives and on whether it shares the technology with any other aspiring nuclear weapons state."[66] Despite the apparent cynicism of the policy shift, therefore, "the last culprit may have to be aided as much as punished."[67]

SUPPLY POLICIES

Supply-oriented approaches to nonproliferation are designed to limit the nuclear weapons capabilities of states that do not now have nuclear weapons. They tend to focus on means to prevent the misuse of civil nuclear energy facilities for military purposes.[68] One of the most widely discussed and controversial supply-oriented mechanisms is the system of international and domestic safeguards.

The Safeguards Approach

Since the outset of the nuclear age, arguments have been made that nuclear energy must be subject to safeguards to ensure that it be used exclusively for peaceful purposes. What constitutes "safeguards," however, has never been defined very precisely, and the term has been used to describe a wide range of national and international nonproliferation measures. They include the Baruch Plan's call for international ownership, management, and control of atomic energy, the system of worldwide IAEA nuclear facility inspection and reports, national measures to guard against the loss of diversion of nuclear material, and nuclear export regulations and restraints.[69]

Our discussion focuses primarily on international safeguards, used here to mean the system of measures applied by the International Atomic Energy Agency to detect and deter national governments' diversion of nuclear material from peaceful uses to military purposes. National safeguards, in contrast, refer to measures undertaken by national governments "to detect, deter, prevent, or respond to the unauthorized possession or use of significant quantities of nuclear materials through theft or diversion and sabotage of nuclear facilities."[70] They tend to emphasize the provision of physical security and are directed at nonstate actors.[71]

According to Article III, A, 5 of the statute of the IAEA, the agency is:

> To establish and administer safeguards designed to ensure that special fissionable and other materials, services, equipment, facilities, and information made available by the Agency or at its request or under its supervision or control are not used in such a way as to further any military purpose; and to apply safeguards, at the request of the parties, to any bilateral or miltilateral arrangement, or at the request of a State, to any of that State's activities in the field of atomic energy.[72]

No authority is granted the agency to recover diverted material or to provide physical security for nuclear materials or facilities. The IAEA Statute and its safeguards system, it should also be emphasized, do not prohibit states from acquiring fissile material or making nuclear weapons. India, for example, did not technically violate any IAEA safeguards agreement when it exploded a nuclear device. The safeguards are simply intended to ensure that specific facilities, projects, and nuclear material are not diverted from peaceful to military uses.[73]

Until the entry into force of the NPT in March 1970, the IAEA's safeguards system was based on the idea of safeguards for specific projects. If a nation, for example, sought to obtain agency assistance for the operation of a nuclear power reactor, it would apply for approval of that specific project and would have to accept agency safeguards for the nuclear facility. In addition, a state might unilaterally submit some or all of its nuclear energy activities to the agency's safeguard system. Thus, as William Epstein points out, "a state might have one facility under agency safeguards while retaining, unsafeguarded, all or part of a nuclear fuel cycle."[74] Under the NPT, however, this project-specific focus on safeguards shifted to one designed to apply to all peaceful nuclear activities within non-nuclear weapon states. Article III of the NPT, moreover, requires that the IAEA system of safeguards be accepted by all non-nuclear weapon parties to the treaty (within twenty-four months for the original parties and eighteen months for states acceding later). As of February 14, 1981, seventy-eight non-nuclear weapon states party to the NPT had negotiated safeguards agreements with the IAEA.[75] Two nuclear weapon state parties to the NPT, the United States and the United Kingdom, and the non-NPT nuclear weapon state, France, also have agreed voluntarily to submit those nuclear installations "not directly significant for their national security" to IAEA safeguards.[76] Thirty-two NPT parties, however, still had not concluded the required safeguard negotiations with the IAEA (see Appendix B for a list of NPT parties with safeguards in effect). Although most of these countries did not have extensive nuclear activities, six non-nuclear weapon states at the end of 1980 operated significant nuclear facilities not subject to IAEA or bilateral safeguards. These states and their relevant nuclear facilities are indicated in Table 6.1. Two nuclear weapon states, the Soviet Union and the PRC, also have refused, to date, to submit their nuclear installations to IAEA safeguards.

The effectiveness of international safeguards is a subject of considerable controversy. Critics of the existing safeguards system point, in particular, to the nonuniversal scope of the NPT and its safeguards requirements; provisions of the NPT which tend to discriminate against non-nuclear weapon states (NNWS) party to the treaty by requiring "full-scope" safeguards on exports to NNWS parties, but only "project specific" safeguards to nonparties; the IAEA's commitment to nonintrusive safeguards and its unwillingness to insist on strict safeguards compliance; and problems regarding the physical security of nuclear material which is left exclusively to individual states.[77] The point is also sometimes made that although the safeguards system is useful in helping to build confidence in the nonproliferation regime, it does not prevent nations from moving within days or less of having nuclear explosives without violating existing safeguards.[78] As Henry Rowen notes, "It is not a violation of the NPT to have possession of nuclear explosive materials nor is it a violation to do experiments on rapidly crushing materials at very high pressures, i.e., to build the non-nuclear components of nuclear explosives."[79] Because Article X.1 of the NPT gives parties the right to withdraw from the treaty upon serving three months notice, any state that is concerned that detection of safeguard violations is imminent can withdraw and refuse controls.[80]

During the Carter administration, the United States also raised two additional critiques of the international safeguards system. As discerned by Pierre Lellouche, this twofold challenge entailed: (1) the charge that it was no longer sufficient to rely on the voluntary character of safeguards (i.e., all recipients of nuclear exports should be obliged to submit to full-scope safeguards); and (2) the assertion that certain nuclear fuel cycle facilities were too dangerous and should be denied even with safeguards.[81] Consistent with the first charge was the provision of the Nuclear Non-Proliferation Act, which required a cutoff of all U.S. nuclear exports to non-nuclear weapon states lacking full-scope safeguards. Illustrative of the second assertion was the position taken by the Carter administration (but modified by President Reagan) that plutonium reprocessing and breeder reactor development should be curtailed.

Table 6.1. Operating Nuclear Facilities Not Subject to IAEA or Bilateral Safeguards, as of 31 December 1980[a]

Country	Facility	Indigenous or Imported	First Year of Operation
Egypt	Inshas research reactor	Imported (USSR)[b]	1961
India	Apsara research reactor	Indigenous	1956
	Cirus research reactor	Imported (Canada/USA)[c]	1960
	Purnima research reactor	Indigenous	1972
	Fuel fabrication plant at Trombay	Indigenous	1960
	Fuel fabrication plant, CANDU-type of fuel elements, at the Nuclear Fuel Cycle complex, Hyderabad	Indigenous	1974
	Reprocessing plant at Trombay	Indigenous	1964
	Reprocessing plant at Tarapur	Indigenous	1977
Israel	Dimona research reactor	Imported (France/ Norway)[d]	1963
	Reprocessing plant at Dimona	Indigenous (in cooperation with France)[e]	
Pakistan	Fuel fabrication plant at Chashma	Indigenous (in cooperation with Belgium)[f]	1980
South Africa	Enrichment plant at Valindaba	Indigenous (in cooperation with FRG)[g]	1975
Spain	Vandellos power reactor	Operation in cooperation with France[h]	1972

Source: SIPRI, *World Armaments and Disarmament: SIPRI Yearbook 1981* (London: Taylor & Francis, and Cambridge, Mass: Oelgeschlager, Gunn & Hain, 1981), p. 310.

[a]Significant nuclear activities outside the five nuclear weapon states recognized by the NPT.

[b]Egypt also has a small-scale reprocessing facility not subject to safeguards. Operability and current status are unknown. In view of Egypt's recent adherence to the NPT, all its nuclear activities will have to be safeguarded by the IAEA.

[c]The reactor is of Canadian origin; some heavy water was supplied by the USA.

[d]French-supplied reactor running on heavy water from Norway.

[e]Assistance by Saint Gobain Techniques Nouvelles.

[f]Assistance at an early stage by Belgo-Nucleaire. In addition, Pakistan is about to establish significant reprocessing and enrichment capacities. The status of these programs is unknown.

[g]Cooperation between STEAG (FRG) and UCOR (South Africa).

[h]Negotiations with the IAEA on safeguarding of this reactor were being held.

Although much of the criticism of the existing safeguards system comes from those who believe it needs to be strengthened, one can also discern resistance to the upgrading of IAEA safeguards if that entails further spending by the agency. This resistance comes primarily from developing countries and involves the fundamental tension between Articles III and IV of the NPT and the difficulty of striking a balance between nuclear safeguards and the transfer of nuclear technology and peaceful purposes.[83] More specifically, a number of developing countries appear to worry that safeguards may come to dominate the IAEA's program to the detriment of the agency's technical assistance functions.[84]

There is widespread recognition among nonproliferation analysts that the international safeguards system is imperfect and needs improvement. Among the partial remedies often suggested are technological improvements such as advanced material accounting systems;[85] augmenting IAEA funding, staffing, and technical competence at a rate commensurate with the global expansion of civilian nuclear energy production;[86] closing the gap between the NPT and non-NPT safeguards regime (e.g., standardizing bilateral safeguard measures);[87] and moving toward compulsory full-scope and universal safeguards.[88] The last recommendation in the list is the most contentious and would require the greatest change in the existing safeguards system although steps in this direction have been taken by some members of the London Suppliers Group after 1975 and received considerable support among supplier states at the 1980 NPT Review Conference.[89] Both superpowers, significantly, have taken very similar positions on this issue.

One additional strategy for strengthening the nonproliferation regime, frequently discussed within the context of international safeguards, is the establishment of regional, multinational fuel cycle facilities (MFCFs) for uranium enrichment, fuel fabrication, reprocessing, spent fuel storage, and waste disposal.[90] From a nonproliferation standpoint, the primary intent of MFCFs is to remove sensitive fuel cycle facilities from national controls and to facilitate the safeguarding of nuclear material and sensitive technology.

The advantages usually attributed to MFCFs are: (1) the reduction of economic incentives and rationales for national facilities and the corresponding increase of political costs associated with a decision to develop national facilities; (2) the improvement of physical security and more effective safeguards against diversion of material, at lower cost; (3) movement away from the discriminatory nature of most nonproliferation measures by the participation of nuclear "have-nots"; and (4) a constructive approach to bridge considerations of nonproliferation, energy security, and international equity.[91] These possible advantages, however, may be offset by the potential of MFCFs to spread the disease they are designed to control (i.e., transfer sensitive technologies to nations which might not otherwise have obtained them) and to stimulate plutonium reprocessing and legitimize commerce in separated plutonium.[92] The criticism is also sometimes made that establishment of MFCFs would have no direct bearing on the problem of proliferation because the states intent on developing a nuclear weapons program would probably not forgo domestic facilities in order to participate in a MFCF.[93]

One cannot easily dismiss the arguments about the potential counterproductiveness of MFCFs. The critics' case, however, is much weaker for MFCFs devoted to certain fuel cycle activities than others and hinges, in part, on the philosophy guiding nonproliferation policy (i.e., technology denial or dissuasion). The establishment of multinational storage facilities for spent fuel, for example, would appear to avoid many of the disadvantages attributed to MFCFs generally and at the same time might provide a means of testing the viability of the MFCF concept.[94] This concept was endorsed by the INFCE Waste Management and Disposal Working Group, which concluded that "centralized facilities for the disposal of spent fuel and/or vitrified high-level waste would alleviate the concerns of countries with small nuclear power programs [and] could reduce the diversion risk . . . ."[95]

It is beyond the scope of this study to examine and assess the wide array of institutional arrangements for fuel cycle activities that have been described as multinational in conception. It is important to note, however, that a number of historical precedents exist for the establishment of multinational ventures in sensitive fuel cycle areas, although they have tended to involve technologically advanced states with common interests and have been primarily motivated by economic and technical considerations rather than nonproliferation concerns.[96] Principal ones include URENCO and EURODIF (uranium enrichment consortia) and EUROCHEMIC and United Reprocessors Group (spent fuel reprocessing and plutonium separation consortia).[97]

One can identify a number of practical problems with all multinational arrangements including such sensitive issues as membership, financing, voting arrangements, conditions of access, dispute settlement, and status of the host government. Agreement on the site for a MFCF is apt to be particularly troublesome since ideally it should be free of serious local or international political problems and in a host country (if a non-nuclear state) perceived as unlikely to seek nuclear weapons.[98] It may also be difficult to alleviate the suspicions of Third World countries that MFCFs will not be dominated by the industrialized nuclear supplier states. This problem will be accentuated if the principal criterion in selecting a MFCF site is one of safe and stable environment or, essentially, a Western industrial state.[99]

Despite these inherent difficulties, the concept of multinational fuel cycle arrangements has much merit, not as *the* solution to the problem of proliferation but as a means to bridge often competing nuclear considerations of nonproliferation, energy security, and nondiscrimination. The challenge, as Lawrence Scheinman points out, is to fashion "institutional arrangements so as to meet the political, economic, operational, and management concerns that inevitably will enter into any consideration of multinational activity and . . . to insure that multinationalism does not become a pretext or subterfuge for activities which could undermine the stability of the international nuclear regime."[100]

Export Controls

Export restrictions on sensitive technologies represent perhaps the most hotly disputed means of attempting to contain the spread of nuclear weapons. At the heart of the dispute are disagreements over the efficacy of technology denial measures and their justifiability under the terms of the NPT.

Proponents of export restraints on technologies such as enrichment and reprocessing plants generally do not regard controls as a potential solution to the problem of proliferation, but see them as a means to slow the spread of nuclear weapons capabilities and thereby buy time for the development of safer fuel cycle components and a stronger international nonproliferation regime. This perspective is well articulated by Joseph Nye, one of the architects of the Carter administration's nonproliferation policy:

> We are sometimes told that the goal is hopeless because the nuclear "horse is out of the stable." But proliferation is a matter of degrees, not absolutes. Our policy can affect the number of horses, which horses, and when horses leave the barn.[101]

Underlying the nonproliferation strategy articulated by Nye and the measures taken by the United States in the form of the Nuclear Non-Proliferation Act is the subordination of Article IV of the NPT (dealing with the promotion of nuclear energy for peaceful purposes) to the principle that some sensitive nuclear technologies should be denied even under safeguards. As two high-ranking nonproliferation spokesmen in the Carter administration put it, "By the late 1970s, it appeared to many, including the U.S. government, that the nonproliferation treaty was inadequate even for parties to it, because inspection alone might not provide 'timely warning' of diversions for nuclear-weapons purposes."[102]

Outside of the U.S. Congress, it is difficult to find strong support today for the NNPA. Many of its critics, however, do not dispute the need for export restraints, but simply regard the rigidity of the 1978 act and its imposition of new conditions on most of America's nuclear trading partners (in some cases retroactively) as counterproductive.[103] U.S. attempts to gain nonproliferation leverage through the denial of nuclear materials, it is argued, "only tightens near-term supply conditions and increases uncertainties abroad, adding to the pressure to decide in favor of the very activities the United States is trying to restrain."[104] A nonproliferation strategy emphasizing technology denial, in other words, may reduce confidence among importing states about access to materials and technology and give impetus to nuclear autarky. "The result," it is maintained, "is likely to be a short-term reduction in proliferation risks—e.g., South Korea will not soon acquire reprocessing capability ... —but an increase in such risks over the longer term."[105] The failure to consider nuclear export policy within a broader foreign policy context and the indiscriminate application of export controls, moreover, have aggravated U.S. relations with critical non-nuclear weapons states—many of whom have long had the technical capability to develop nuclear weapons but not the motivation to do so—without seriously affecting the weapons programs of overt nuclear aspirants.[106]

For other critics of the NNPA, opposition to nuclear export restraints is more fundamental. Many Third World states, for example, appear to regard U.S. export legislation, as well as the activities of the London Suppliers Group, as concerted efforts by the nuclear weapons states to flout the nuclear assistance provisions of the NPT. They are also inclined to view the restrictive measures taken by the nuclear supplier countries as serving the suppliers' economic interests rather than nonproliferation goals and protest that the technological restrictions introduced by the London Club was drawn up without consultation by other NPT parties.[107] At a more abstract level, Third World opposition to nuclear export controls sometimes also appears to be based on the premise that export restraints perpetuate the international nuclear status quo and the "have-not" status of most Third World countries.[108]

Efforts to regulate nuclear exports generally have been directed at two groups of industrialized states: the so-called "first-tier" nuclear suppliers capable of providing the entire range of advanced civilian nuclear technology, facilities, and services, and "second-tier" suppliers with a more limited range of nuclear exports. A "third-tier" of nuclear suppliers, however, has recently begun to emerge: developing states with advanced nuclear technologies. Argentina and India have already assumed the role of third-tier nuclear suppliers, and Brazil, Taiwan, Pakistan, and South Korea may well attempt to emulate their nuclear export programs in the future.[109] From a nonproliferation standpoint, this development is troubling since many of the third-tier suppliers are not NPT parties. The prospects for coopting third-tier suppliers into future nuclear supplier group arrangments, moreover, seems slim given the existing level of suspicion about export restraints by third-tier suppliers. India, for example, has expressed no interest in joining the suppliers group, although it has also taken the stance that it will not export sensitive technology.[110]

More generally, nonproliferation proposals involving supplier cooperation and coordination must overcome enormous political and economic obstacles. At a minimum, nuclear-exporting countries will have to perceive sufficient shared interests and dangers to overcome economic rivalries and the inclination to view nuclear exports as a source of political influence and prestige.[111] Export controls also must be sufficiently flexible and sensitive to consumer state concerns so as not to stimulate the development of national nuclear industries including enrichment and reprocessing facilities. In other words, not only must the opportunity costs of controls be perceived by the supplier states as equitably distributed, but the perception must also exist among importers that "controls do not unreasonably hinder diffusion of the benefits of civilian nuclear energy—either in terms of energy supply or cost."[112] These are difficult conditions to satisfy. As a consequence, as one U.S. government study points out, "the political viability of export controls for more than the short term is very much in doubt."[113]

Technical Measures

The potential impact of technical measures on proliferation is restricted by the widespread availability of the material and technical wherewithal to make nuclear weapons. The lack of a "technical fix" for the problem of proliferation is reflected in the findings of both the International Nuclear Fuel Cycle Evaluation (INFCE) and the U.S. Nonproliferation Alternative Systems Assessment Program

(NASAP). Although these two massive studies differ substantially in their operating assumptions and specific recommendations, they generally agree that technical measures by themselves can have only a limited impact on the full range of proliferation risks, particularly those above the level of subnational seizure threats.[114] Nevertheless, many proliferation analysts continue to search for technical ways of increasing fuel cycle proliferation resistance.

Technical measures aimed at making it more difficult for national governments or subnational groups to divert nuclear material generally fall into one of three categories. They are: (1) measures to reduce the presence and quantities of pure plutonium or highly enriched uranium in the fuel cycle; (2) measures to use radioactivity to protect those materials from diversion; and (3) measures to guard the materials by means of physical barriers.[115]

Among the more frequently proposed technical measures to reduce the presence of plutonium in the fuel cycle in separated form are co-location of reprocessing and mixed-oxide (MOX) fuel-fabrication plants, the storage and transportation of plutonium in dilute MOX form, co-processing (i.e., managing the plutonium extraction system in a reprocessing plant so that the product is a mixture of uranium and plutonium rather than just plutonium), and co-conversion (i.e., mixing the plutonium nitrate recovered during reprocessing with uranyl nitrate and co-converting them into mixed oxide.)[116] Co-location is generally regarded as the simplest and most feasible of these measures and would have the unambiguously positive effect of reducing both the need for transport between sites and the resources necessary for effective physical protection, nuclear material accountancy, and the application of other international safeguards.[117] Elimination of the transport of concentrated plutonium could also be accomplished by physically blending the oxide powders of plutonium and uranium to form a MOX material. Although this "technical fix" would not pose a major obstacle to national governments intent on diversion, the increased quantity of material that would have to be diverted and the need to separate the plutonium might increase proliferation resistance for nonstate actors. The retention of a chemical dilution barrier by co-processing or co-conversion would also probably reduce the risk of diversion by subnational groups. Co-processing and co-conversion techniques, however, are much less relevant as a means of increasing resistance to national proliferation, especially for countries possessing facilities for separating plutonium oxide from mixed plutonium/uranium oxide fuel.[118]

A second category of technical measures relies on the introduction of a radiation barrier in order to deter diversion. Among the methods that have been proposed for introducing this radiation barrier are spiking of fresh fuel with a highly radioactive material such as cobalt-60; pre-irradiation, in which the mixed uranium/plutonium oxide fuel element is irradiated before shipment to the reactor site; and partial processing or decontamination, in which the reprocessing plant is designed so that a portion of the fission products always remains associated with the plutonium.[119]

Spiking can take several forms ranging from the addition of small quantities of radioactive isotopes as tracers to facilitate detection and material containment to the introduction of lethal amounts of radioactive material to fresh reactor fuel for the purpose of disabling a potential divertor. Most studies now discount the utility of massive spiking, in part because of the economic, environmental, and safeguards disadvantages associated with its employment,[120] and also because of its dubious effectiveness against any group competent to separate plutonium from uranium in mixed-oxide fuel. Both the INFCE and NASAP reports, for example, conclude that while spiking may have some effectiveness against theft by nonstate actors, it would prove generally ineffective against diversion by national governments.[121]

Pre-irradiation of fabricated MOX fuel would probably be accomplished in a specially constructed neutron irradiation facility. This facility might be a reactor designed for rapid on-line refueling that would provide a small but significant burnup to the fresh fuel elements. At such a low burnup, the NASAP study suggests, "the fuel would be radioactive enough that it would require, in effect, a dedicated, shielded, and remotely operated chemical separation facility to recover the plutonium."[122] The major difficulties with this approach are the economic costs involved and the potential for increased population exposure to radiation and environmental hazards. Like spiking, pre-irradiation also poses difficulties for existing methods of nuclear material accounting and other safeguards procedures.[123]

Partial processing is a further variation on co-processing and co-conversion whereby some of the radioactive fission products would be kept with the recovered uranium and plutonium, thereby creating a radiation barrier throughout the fuel cycle. Although the technique is less well developed than spiking and irradiation, the principal advantages and disadvantages appear to be similar.[124] One additional limitation of the technique, however, stems from the short-lived nature of the fission products. Because they are short-lived, the protection given by them will decrease after about two years from the time the spent fuel was originally discharged from

Table 6.2. INFCE Evaluation of Technical Measures to Reduce Proliferation Risk[a]

Alternative Technology	Proliferation Risk				Effect on IAEA Safeguards	Other Assessment Factors		Effort Needed to Bring to Industrial Scale
	No National Reprocessing/ Refabrication	Proliferation Under Safeguards	Proliferation Not Under Safeguards	Subnational Theft		Economic[c]	Environmental[d]	
Co-location	N/A	+	0	++	+	+	+	None
Storage/transport as MOX	N/A	+	0	++	0	–	0	Small
Co-processing	N/A	+	+	++	0	0	0	Moderate
Pre-irradiation	+	0	0	++	0	–	–	Moderate
Spiking	+	0	0	++	–	–	–	Large
Partial processing	+	+[b]	+[b]	++	–	–	–	Large
Physical barriers	N/A	+	0	++	+	0	+	Moderate

Source: Reprocessing, Plutonium Handling, Recycle, Report of INFCE Working Group 4 (Vienna: IAEA, 1980), p. 144. For a similar evaluation see *Nuclear Proliferation and Civilian Nuclear Power,* Report of the Nonproliferation Alternative Systems Assessment Program (Washington, D.C., 1980), Vol. 1, p. 45.

[a] + indicates a net improvement or saving when compared with the reference technology; a large improvement is shown as ++. When there is a net deterioration or loss when compared with the reference technology this is shown as – ; a large deterioration is indicated by ––. When there is little or no change when compared with the reference technology, the symbol 0 is used. N/A means "not applicable."

[b] Only for out-of-pile recycle times of up to two to three years.

[c] For a discussion of this issue see *Reprocessing, Plutonium Handling, Recycle,* pp. 91–110.

[d] For a discussion of this issue see *Reprocessing, Plutonium Handling, Recycle,* pp. 73–90.

the reactor.[125] Partial processing, like the other methods to retain a radiation barrier in recycle materials, would seem to offer somewhat greater potential for increasing proliferation resistance than does co-processing or co-conversion of uranium and plutonium because of its requirement of more elaborate facilities (e.g., shielding and remote controls) to recover plutonium from diverted material.[126]

The physical isolation of the reprocessing and/or MOX fuel-fabrication process by means of structural barriers represents yet another category of technical measures designed to decrease the opportunities for diversion. Proposed techniques to create physical barriers include automatically or remotely controlled systems that reduce accessibility to sensitive materials and security devices which shut down or disable equipment under specified conditions. France and West Germany have shown particular interest in developing physical barrier techniques, one of the more promising of which is known as Pipex.[127]

An overall evaluation of the diversion resistance of the alternative technical measures discussed above is provided in Table 6.2. This list of technical measures, it should be emphasized, is by no means exhaustive. One might also have included proposals to adopt entirely different fuel cycles (e.g., the denatured thorium-uranium cycle discussed in Chapter 3,[128] the so-called CIVEX method of reprocessing which combines a number of the "Category One" techniques in a single operation,[129] and the radical measure, articulated most forcefully by Amory Lovins et al., to abandon civilian nuclear power altogether.[130] What is most apparent from our survey is the much greater potential deterrent impact of technical measures on subnational groups than national governments. This finding suggests the hazard of relying extensively on technical approaches if it obscures what is generally regarded as the greater danger of national proliferation and the need to reduce the political and security pressures for acquisition of nuclear weapons.

MANAGING PROLIFERATION

The discussion in this chapter so far has focused on the assets and liabilities of alternative strategies for limiting the spread of nuclear weapons to additional parties. Notwithstanding the implementation of the best of these approaches, some further proliferation may well occur. It is therefore relevant to consider how this might come about, the kinds of problems it would pose, the utility of previously identified demand and supply measures to moderate these difficulties, and additional steps that could be taken to minimize the dangers of proliferation.

Many scenarios have been proposed for the course of proliferation in the next two decades. One of the most interesting attempts to explore the dynamics of future proliferation is the work of Lewis Dunn and Herman Kahn. In a major study commissioned by the U.S. Arms Control and Disarmament Agency, *Trends in Nuclear Proliferation 1975–1995,* they develop ten basic alternative proliferation scenarios ranging from "limited but steady proliferation" (in which there are few new overt entries into the nuclear club) to "widespread, multi-regional, chain reaction proliferation" (in which the overt development of a nuclear bomb by India leads to an exponential rate of growth in the spread of nuclear weapons).[131] Based on this set of projections, they identify eleven countries which they regard to be most critical in terms of the impact of their proliferation posture on the scope and pace of future proliferation: Argentina, Brazil, India, Iran, Israel, Japan, Libya, Pakistan, South Korea, Taiwan, and West Germany.[132]

Although the anticipated impact of a decision to proliferate by each of these *N*th countries varies, an underlying premise of the Dunn–Kahn projections is a nuclear proliferation chain reaction. In all the projections, for example, the overt development of an Indian nuclear bomb produces a reciprocal response by Pakistan and, in most cases, also Iran.[133] These developments, in turn, are assumed in most instances to precipitate an overt Israeli nuclear weapons posture and also the avowed interest in or actual overt development of nuclear weapons by Iraq, Egypt, and Saudi Arabia.[134] Similar chain reactions are postulated for other regions.

One may find fault with a number of the projections made by Dunn and Kahn. Some of the implicit assumptions in their nuclear chain model are also questionable.[135] Nevertheless, the states they single out as critical *N*th countries generally correspond to those identified by most analysts.[136] What is not adequately explored, however, are the proliferation routes likely to be taken by these critical *N*th countries should they decide to move toward a nuclear weapons capability. Will they, for example, seek to divert weapons material from safeguarded nuclear fuel cycle facilities or instead choose to follow the example of the existing nuclear weapons states and manufacture weapons at "dedicated facilities" designed specifically for the production of weapons-grade plutonium or uranium? Alternatively, they might attempt to purchase or steal existing nuclear explosives, or manufacture them by the overt use of weapons material produced in the operation of nuclear power and research facilities in the absence of, after withdrawal from, or in disregard of international agreements prohibiting such behavior.[137]

The relative attractiveness of alternative proliferation routes is the subject of considerable dispute among proliferation analysts since it has direct bearing on the relevance of alternative nonproliferation strategies.[138] To the extent that a consensus exists, it is that the theft or purchase route is least likely.[139] Much more contentious is the thesis, most frequently advocated by exponents of rapid nuclear power development, that the dedicated facility route pursued by the first five nuclear weapon states will remain the dominant route for the foreseeable future. This interpretation is challenged, in particular, by those who see the production of weapons material from nuclear fuel cycle facilities as increasingly attractive to prospective proliferators as the diffusion of civilian nuclear power progresses and as technical and economic barriers to weapons proliferation are reduced. According to the perspective, many states, without actually making a conscious decision to build nuclear weapons, will drift toward a weapons capability and find themselves in a position where it is much easier to cross the nuclear threshold in response to various transient incentives.[140]

Because so little is known about the decision-making processes for nuclear issues in most Nth countries, one cannot adequately resolve the paths to proliferation dispute. As a consequence, any assessment of alternative nonproliferation stratergies must be very tentative. Our profile of proliferation factors in thirteen countries, however, suggests that the selection of a proliferation route is probably linked closely to the kind of primary motivating and constraining factors present and the status of existing domestic nuclear fuel cycle facilities.

The direct dedicated facilities approach, for example, would appear to be attractive primarily to states that perceive security threats to be acute, regard nuclear weapons as a means to alleviate them, are relatively unconcerned about the reactions of other states (i.e., are either great powers or pariahs), and lack in-place fuel cycle facilities to serve as a basis for a covert weapons program. The dedicated facilities route is likely to be preferred by this category of potential proliferator because it can yield weapons material more quickly and at less cost than a nuclear power program conceived with covert weapons production in mind. Although most past proliferators (including Israel, if it has nuclear weapons) fit this profile, it corresponds to few present non-nuclear weapons states. Pakistan is probably the closest match, although its apparent indifference to the reaction of other states to its quest for nuclear weapons cannot be explained by its international power status or diplomatic standing. The Republic of China and South Korea are other states where pressures to proliferate are closely linked to perceived security threats. Both countries, however, are sensitive to the reaction of their superpower patron and are unlikely to engage in overt efforts to manufacture nuclear weapons as long as they perceive the United States to be a credible guarantor of their security.[141]

The two proliferation routes associated with the production of weapons material from nuclear fuel cycle facilities clearly are possible only for those states committed to at least the appearance of a civilian nuclear power program. Whether or not a would-be proliferator proceeds down the clandestine or overt diversion route is likely to hinge on the domestic and international costs and benefits of being seen as moving toward a bomb and the urgency with which a nuclear weapon is sought.[142] It is reasonable to anticipate, for example, that given similar disincentives, the more acute the underlying pressures to acquire nuclear weapons, the more direct and overt the proliferation route. If this hypothesis is correct and based on our prior summary of underlying pressures and constraints for select *N*th countries, one would expect Brazil and Argentina to avoid any overt misuse of civilian fuel cycle facilities and to mask any move toward a weapons option under the guise of a peaceful nuclear explosions program. Development of such a program would certainly be facilitated by the acquisition of a complete nuclear fuel cycle including reprocessing and enrichment technologies.[143]

Before discussing the adequacy of alternative demand and supply strategies to cope with "life in a nuclear armed crowd," to use Albert Wohlstetter's vivid expression, it is first necessary to specify the new conditions apt to be associated with the spread of nuclear weapons to additional states. Rather than reiterate the discussion provided in the first chapter of the general effects of proliferation on international stability,[144] the focus is restricted to some of the problems most likely to confront the United States directly.[145]

An intensification of the superpower arms race is one possible consequence of further nuclear proliferation. This may arise due to the increased perception of threat by Soviet and U.S. leaders to the military capabilities of new nuclear weapon states and consequent efforts by the superpowers to bolster their security. Although these measures initially might not be directed against each other, it would be difficult for one superpower to ignore the other's strategic force adjustments. Strong pressures to augment U.S. forces, for example, might be expected to follow an increase in Soviet strategic capabilities, even if the Soviet force increases were based on new targets

and threats posed by the nuclearization of such U.S. allies or potential allies as South Korea, Taiwan, South Africa, Israel, Japan, and
West Germany. This relationship tends to be ignored by those who
are complacent about proliferation because they regard more potential *N*th countries as likely to target the Soviet Union than the
United States.[146]

One possible change in the superpower strategic relationship to
result from further proliferation is abrogation or substantial modification of the 1972 ABM Treaty—an arms control accord which
has encouraged nuclear deterrence by denying each superpower the
ability to ward off a massive retaliatory strike. Should the superpowers deploy ballistic missile defenses about their cities to guard
against the threat of an *N*th country force, the premise of mutual
assured destruction between the United States and the Soviet Union
would also be undermined and the deterrent value of the much
smaller nuclear arsenals of the other nuclear weapons states
negated.[147]

To the extent that nuclear proliferation exacerbates regional conflicts, it might also increase the prospect of a U.S.–Soviet confrontation. The region where this is generally regarded as most likely to
occur is the Middle East. This is due to the already high level of confrontation and conflict in the area, the presence in the region of several would-be and could-be proliferators, the high stakes for both the
United States and the Soviet Union in the region, and the likelihood
that the superpowers would find themselves allied with opposing
*N*th countries.[148] Notwithstanding the likely desire by both superpowers to avoid confrontation, it might come about as a result of
circumstances beyond either's control. The United States or the
Soviet Union, for example, might come under attack through the
precipitous action of an ally.[149] A similar scenario has been
proposed for Northeast Asia, in which an attack by a South Korean
force equipped with nuclear weapons against the North leads to a
response by the Soviet Union against South Korea (and U.S. forces
stationed there).[150]

The possibility of inadvertent superpower involvement in a
regional conflict among nuclear armed parties is increased by the
absence in most *N*th countries of many of the technical and political
conditions which in the United States and Soviet Union limit the
unauthorized and unintended use of nuclear weapons. Most significant among these are systems of command, control, and communication; effective intelligence-gathering and -processing capabilities;
reliable early warning systems; and domestic political stability. The
absence of these conditions, together with the lack of secure and

reliable second-strike forces, would undermine deterrence stability in a crisis situation involving Nth countries and would increase pressures for one of the parties to preempt. As Lewis Dunn and Herman Kahn point out:

> Both sides would fear that the opponent by striking first could sever command and control links, degrading the system and reducing the weight of retaliation. Both would be tempted by the possibility that by striking first they could have that effect upon the opponent. Reciprocal fears of surprise attack would rise and, each side, knowing what the other side was thinking, would be under increasing pressure to "strike second, first."[151]

Some of the same factors which make inadvertent nuclear war more probable as nuclear weapons proliferate also might increase the risk of seizure and use of nuclear weapons by subnational terrorists.[152] Domestic political instability in some potential Nth countries, for example, might create opportunities for different factions to seize weapons for their own use or for sale on a black market. Inexperience with the physical security of nuclear weapons and the lack of sophisticated built-in protective mechanisms would exacerbate this threat.

The principal danger to the United States of this development (i.e., the seizure of nuclear weapons by terrorists abroad) is that a revolutionary group might attempt to direct its nuclear threat against the United States to obtain certain demands (e.g., cessation of support for the government in power). Unlike most other kinds of nuclear threats which, if implemented, would likely be counterproductive for a revolutionary organization because of the indiscriminate and massive destruction they would bring, a nuclear threat against an external power might not provoke overwhelming opposition from those the group sought to govern.[153] A crude bomb delivered in a small vessel to a U.S. harbor might be the means chosen to back up the threat. Alternatively, a well-publicized nuclear hoax, made credible by the knowledge of the feasibility of nuclear theft, might accomplish the terrorist's objectives without entailing the costs of actual seizure. This is not to say that small groups of extremists with nihilistic or anarchistic ideologies and without large constituencies would hesitate to use nuclear violence if they could. For the moment, however, it appears to be the case that those nonstate entities most likely to undertake acts of nuclear violence are the ones least able to acquire nuclear weapons and that those groups most able to gain access to nuclear explosives would be inclined to use them, if at all, in a fashion calculated to minimize destruction.[154]

Another possible consequence of proliferation, at first glance, may appear to be far-fetched but has been suggested by a number of analysts: the erosion of domestic civil liberties.[155] Civil liberties, it is argued, may be affected by activities designed to prevent nuclear terrorist incidents or by activities undertaken in response to them. Preventive measures might include increased domestic surveillance of potential terrorists (perhaps broadly defined to include most dissidents) and the expanded use of security checks and physical searches. In response to terrorist threats or knowledge that nuclear materials or weapons had been stolen, there might also be forced evacuations, blanket searches, and detention and interrogation without legal counsel or probable cause. The fear is also expressed that after the crisis is past some tactics employed in the crisis might persist. This risk is noted by the authors of the Ford–Mitre study who are concerned that "strong public sentiment that such a crisis should never be allowed to happen again, and widespread fear of society's vulnerability to nuclear terrorism" might prompt the extension of crisis tactics to routine law enforcement operations.[156] Dunn and Kahn suggest that pressures for an authoritarian political shift might also result from "the increased insecurity, hostility, and competitiveness that could accompany the emergence of a world of as many as forty nuclear weapon states by 1995."[157]

Mention should also be made of the problems associated with an additional form of proliferation, or more precisely, quasi-proliferation. This is the global spread of nuclear energy facilities and the potential they present as surrogate nuclear weapons in time of war.

The implications of the destruction of nuclear energy facilities in war are not well understood and until recently received surprisingly little attention in the public literature.[158] What is known suggests that nuclear energy plants pose some of the same threats as nuclear bombs. In particular, they pose the danger of releasing highly radioactive nuclear products over a wide area, although an actual nuclear explosion is impossible.[159] These latent weapons also have the unusual property of conferring a variety of nuclear destructive power not to the host of the nuclear installation but to any party able to target it with the proper type of conventional penetrating weapon.[160] Although this is not an easy task given the normal containment of commercial nuclear reactors in structures made of reinforced concrete designed to withstand the impact of a jetliner, it is made possible by the existence of conventional penetrating weapons able to burrow through yards of concrete before releasing their charge.[161] Israel's attack on Iraq's nuclear facility demonstrated that this scenario is not merely a theoretical possibility, but a very real policy option. It also underscored the "lightning rod effect" that vulnerable nuclear reactors may have in common with poorly defended nuclear forces, both of which present a tempting first-strike target. There is little reason to expect that U.S. nuclear power plants are any less vulnerable to destruction than was Iraq's nuclear research center.[162]

The failure of most nonproliferation studies even to recognize the problem of the destruction of nuclear energy facilities in war, much less propose solutions, may be an atypical oversight and not a fair measure of the adequacy of existing nonproliferation strategies to cope with the problems of life in a world of continuing proliferation.[163] A legitimate criticism of most nonproliferation approaches, however, is their fixation on stopping additional states from "going nuclear" (defined as the detonation of a single nuclear device) to the neglect of possible methods for managing the proliferation process in order to moderate its most threatening characteristics.

It is, of course, much easier to note this deficiency of prior research than to remedy it. Some tentative conclusions regarding the utility of alternative demand and supply strategies for influencing the proliferation process, however, may be drawn from the preceding analysis.

The first point that can be made is that none of the nonproliferation strategies identified above can provide much assurance that "timely warning" will be given prior to the entry of a new nation into the nuclear weapons club. This is the case even though international safeguards are justified primarily as an alerting mechanism and even though some of the most frequently proposed approaches to control proliferation (e.g., sanctions) assume the need for adequate warning of movement toward a bomb in order to organize an effective international response.[164] The length of the warning period, moreover, continues to shrink with the global proliferation of plutonium separation and uranium enrichment facilities as well as research reactors using highly enriched uranium.[165] At best, improved safeguards and the convergence of international views on appropriate sanctions in anticipation of possible proliferation developments may make it more difficult for a prospective proliferator to count on announcing a *fait accompli* and thereby raise the political costs of embarking on a nuclear weapons program.

The traditional nonproliferation strategies discussed in this chapter, including both demand and supply approaches, also do not appear to be very helpful in reducing the risk of an inadvertent or unintended nuclear war initiated by a nuclear weapons novice. One alternative and controversial strategy that has been proposed to deal with this contingency is the provision by existing nuclear weapon states of technical assistance to *N*th countries, designed to influence the characteristics of their future nuclear forces and strategic doctrine.[166] Technical assistance, for example, could be provided to improve early warning system and command and control reliability, weapons safety, and force suvivability.[167] The existing nuclear powers could also attempt to influence doctrine and reinforce the nuclear taboo by encouraging the assessment of nuclear war outcomes and the study of deterrence theory.

Unfortunately, although such assistance might promote development of a more secure *N*th country nuclear force and reduce the risk of war by accident, miscalculation, or unauthorized use, or as the result of preemption due to fear of strategic vulnerability, it might also have several counterproductive effects. Assistance which reduces the danger of preemptive attack by increasing force survivability, for example, might remove what otherwise would be a compelling proliferation disincentive. Efforts to improve weapons reliability and safety and command and control performance also run the risk of making nuclear forces more usable. An additional danger is that such assistance would be perceived by other potential *N*th countries as a reward for going nuclear.

The risks of attempting to influence *N*th country nuclear postures and policy to reduce the probability of inadvertent or unintended war illustrates the basic tension that exists between efforts to manage proliferation and attempts to retard it. The proper nonproliferation emphasis, moreover, is apt to vary from case to case and to depend on such factors as the anticipated proliferation impact of a given country, other national security policy objectives, the means available for retarding a particular *N*th country's movement toward nuclear weapons, and the means available for influencing the characteristics of that state's nuclear program at the margin.

Careful consideration of the means available for retarding or managing proliferation is itself a necessary first step toward adoption of an effective nonproliferation strategy. There is a need, in other words, to assess nonproliferation measures not only in terms of the extent to which they address the most important proliferation problems (however they are defined) but also with respect to their relevance for problems that are susceptible to manipulation, prevention, and cure. From this perspective, the source of recent U.S. nonproliferation policy difficulties is principally one of misconception, not implementation. Far too much emphasis was placed on supply-oriented approaches in pursuit of the improbable task of restructuring other countries' domestic nuclear energy programs. Inadequate attention, on the other hand, was given to the implementation of fuel supply assurances—a less pivotal factor with respect to nuclear weapons decision-making, but one over which the United States could have exercised significant influence.

Two additional proliferation problem areas appear to be susceptible to manipulation and treatment, if not prevention: nuclear theft and terrorism by nonstate actors and vertical proliferation. Most applicable to the former problem are domestic safeguards and more diversion-resistant fuel cycle technologies. The limited effectiveness of safeguards and so-called technological fixes with respect to national proliferation should not detract from their potential utility as means to curb subnational proliferation threats. Similarly, although superpower-initiated arms control measures such as a CTB may have only a limited direct impact on the decision-making calculus of potential *N*th countries, this should not obscure their potential for moderating vertical proliferation and restoring the credibility and acceptability of other nonproliferation measures, some of which may be necessarily discriminatory in nature. A failure to moderate U.S.-Soviet arms competition and the postponement of serious strategic arms control negotiations, on the other hand, can only increase pressures in both the United States and the Soviet Union to subordinate nonproliferation policy objectives to other foreign policy goals defined more narrowly in East–West terms. One likely consequence of this kind of preoccupation is the reliance on security guarantees and conventional arms transfers not as measures to reduce proliferation incentives, but as enticements to resist the advances of the other superpower. Potential nonproliferation measures utilized in this fashion may whet rather than satiate the appetites of potential *N*th countries for nuclear weapons by emphasizing security threats and the perceived utility of weapons.

CONCLUSION

It would be convenient to conclude this study by identifying a single culprit responsible for proliferation and a simple nonproliferation remedy in need only of faithful implementation. What is most apparent from the preceding chapters, however, is the multicausal nature of the spread of nuclear weapons and the need to tailor nonproliferation measures to specific cases.

This does not mean that patterns of proliferation are nonexistent or that we should abandon efforts to model the proliferation process. Indeed, Stephen Meyer's careful application of quantitative methods to explore the correlates of proliferation is a useful reminder of an underutilized approach to test contending proliferation hypotheses.[168]

Particularly noteworthy is his demonstration of the inadequacy of the "technological imperative" model to account for the scope and pace of past proliferation. This conclusion is consistent with the findings from our survey of thirteen past and potential proliferators, which reveals the predominance of international political and security incentives for and constraints on proliferation.

One of the most disturbing findings of our study is the recurrent tension between nonproliferation objectives and other domestic and foreign policy goals and priorities. This policy dilemma is further complicated by the tendency for priorities in both foreign and domestic sectors to vary substantially across countries. Illustrative of this variation is the greater importance in recent years attached to energy independence in most West European states and Japan than in the United States and the resulting discrepancy in these countries' views toward plutonium reprocessing and early commercialization of the breeder. The attractiveness to different states of alternative nonproliferation measures such as nuclear export restraints, multinational fuel cycle facilities, fuel supply assurances, and diversion-resistant fuel cycle technologies also can be explained, in many instances, in terms of each country's individual energy demands and resources. Our survey of the economics of nuclear power and the politics of nonproliferation, however, cautions against automatically assuming the operation of economic rationality in nuclear decision-making and indicates the necessity of accounting for additional military, political, and psychological factors. An understanding of these variables, unfortunately, is more easily recommended than accomplished.

Much more attention could also profitably be given the study of competing international perspectives on nuclear power and nonproliferation. What is apparent from the brief examination undertaken in this study is the existence of profound differences which divide the international community on most of the major issues pertaining to nuclear energy and proliferation. The task of forging a consensus among nations about these nuclear issues or restoring a strong international nuclear nonproliferation regime would therefore appear to be enormous. The very different interpretations given to the conclusions of the International Nuclear Fuel Cycle Evaluation, released in 1980, reinforce this pessimistic interpretation.[169] The INFCE experience, moreover, seems to indicate that it is unlikely that any new nuclear consensus that may emerge will reflect fully or even in large part what has been the U.S. position for most of the last decade.[170] The objectives of future U.S. nonproliferation policy, therefore, may have to be redefined more modestly. This may mean shifting attention away from unilateral measures to deny sensitive nuclear material and technology to more cooperative efforts aimed at influencing at the margin the nuclear programs and ambitions of critical *N*th countries.

The relationship between the growth of nuclear power and nonproliferation is still evolving. Unfortunately, the relationship to date has been an antagonistic one. This has led even sophisticated observers sometimes to pose the necessity of choice between "the avoidance of nuclear weapons spread and the provision of additional energy sources."[171] To pose the dilemma in this fashion, however, is to exaggerate the technological component of the proliferation problem. More to the point is Richard Rosecrance's observation almost two decades ago that the dispersion of nuclear weapons is "eminently a problem in strategy and politics."[172] To this one might add that no nonproliferation policy is a substitute for a sound foreign policy and that major nonproliferation successes are probably attainable by the United States only at substantial cost to other domestic and foreign policy goals.

NOTES

1. See Richard Burt, "Nuclear Proliferation and Conventional Arms Transfers: The Missing Link," The California Seminar on Arms Control and Foreign Policy, September 1977; James Digby, "Precision Guided Weapons," Adelphi Paper No. 118 (London: International Institute for Strategic Studies, 1975); and John Mearsheimer, "Precision-guided Munitions and Conventional Deterrence," *Survival* (March/April 1979), pp. 68–76.
2. See, for example, Lewis Dunn, "Some Reflections on the Dove's Dilemma," *International Organization* (Winter 1981), pp. 183–184; Ted Greenwood, "Discouraging Proliferation in the Next Decade and Beyond," in Ted Greenwood, Harold A. Feiveson, and Theodore B. Taylor, *Nuclear Proliferation: Motivations, Capabilities, and Strategies for Control* (New York: McGraw-Hill, 1977), p. 61; and Burt, pp. 23–24.
3. A particularly good discussion of the dilemma is provided by Jo Husbands, "Arms Transfers and Nuclear Proliferation: Policy Implication of the 'Dove's Dilemma'" (Paper delivered at the Annual Meeting of the International Studies Association, Los Angeles, March 19–22, 1980). See also Dunn.
4. See Dunn, pp. 185–186.
5. Ibid., p. 187.
6. Richard K. Betts, "Paranoids, Pygmies, Pariahs and Nonproliferation," *Foreign Policy* (Spring 1977), p. 177.
7. See Husbands, p. 39, and Dunn, p. 185. These other incentives may have been less visible while security concerns were paramount.
8. This point is discussed by Husbands, p. 35.
9. Ibid., p. 42.
10. Ibid.
11. See Dunn, p. 188, on this point.

12. Husbands, p. 37.
13. See Yager, p. 409. It should be noted that nuclear nonproliferation was not the original or primary objective of these guarantees.
14. This point is made by Philip J. Farley, "Nuclear Proliferation," in Henry Owen and Charles Schultze, eds., *Setting National Priorities: The Next Ten Years* (Washington, D.C.: The Brookings Institution, 1976), p. 150.
15. The nonproliferation relevance of the U.S. security commitment to Pakistan, it should be noted, is diluted by the failure of the guarantee to apply to an attack by India.
16. See Greenwood, pp. 58–59.
17. Ibid., p. 58.
18. See, for example, Greenwood, p. 59, and Alan Dowty, *The Role of Great Power Guarantees in International Peace Agreements* (The Hebrew University of Jerusalem, February 1974), p. 21.
19. Beverly Rowen and Henry Rowen, *In the Face of Nuclear Proliferation—An Assessment of Policy Options for the United States,* Report prepared for the U.S. Arms Control and Disarmament Agency (Los Angeles: Pan Heuristics, 1977), p. 12.
20. For a discussion of this resolution see William Epstein, *The Last Chance: Nuclear Proliferation and Arms Control* (New York: The Free Press, 1976), pp. 139–143, and Stockholm International Peace Research Institute, *World Armaments and Disarmament: SIPRI Yearbook 1981* (London: Taylor & Francis and Cambridge, Mass: Oelgeschlager, Gunn & Hain, 1981), p. 331.
21. See William Epstein, "NPT Article VI: How Have the Parties Met Their Obligations? (Including a List of Recommendations for Possible Amendments to the NPT or for Inclusion in a Declaration Signed to Strengthen the NPT)," in Anne W. Marks, ed., *NPT: Paradoxes and Problems* (Washington, D.C.: Arms Control Association and the Carnegie Endowment for International Peace, 1975), pp. 74–91.
22. Additional measures proposed to reduce the prestige attached to nuclear weapons and to strengthen the security of potential *N*th countries are "no-first-use" declarations, curtailment of "vertical proliferation" (i.e., the further development, accumulation, and deployment of nuclear weapons), and a cessation of the production of fissionable material for weapons purposes. For a discussion of these measures, see the Office of Technology Assessment study, *Nuclear Proliferation and Safeguards* (New York: Praeger, 1977), pp. 63–65, and Epstein, *The Last Chance,* pp. 181–194.
23. Our discussion focuses on the effects of a CTB on horizontal proliferation (i.e., the spread of nuclear weapons to additional states). It does not address the effects that a CTB might have on the development of new nuclear weapons by existing nuclear weapon states.
24. See, for example, Gerard Smith and George Rathjens, "Reassessing Nuclear Nonproliferation Policy," *Foreign Affairs* (Spring 1981), p. 890; *Nuclear Power Issues and Choices* (Cambridge, Massachusetts: Ballinger, 1977), pp. 290–291; Barry M. Blechman, "The Comprehensive Test Ban Negotiations: Can They Be Revitalized?" *Arms Control Today* (June 1981), p. 3; Dan Caldwell, "CTB: An Effective SALT Substitute," *Bulletin of the Atomic Scientists* (December 1980), p. 31; Sidney D. Drell, "The Case for the Test Ban," *The Washington Post* (July 4, 1978), and Herbert York and G. Greb, "The Comprehensive Nuclear Test Ban," The California Seminar on Arms Control and Foreign Policy, June 1979, p. 12.
25. Wolfgang Panofsky, cited by York and Greb, p. 12.

26. A few go as far as to contend that the vertical–horizontal proliferation relationship is negative and that a CTB would be interpreted as a sign of weakness by the allies of the superpowers who would be encouraged to develop weapons of their own. See George Will, "The Test Ban Quest," *The Washington Post* (June 4, 1978).

27. See, for example, Will; Donald G. Brennan, "A Comprehensive Test Ban: Everybody or Nobody," *International Security* (Summer 1976), pp. 92–117; and Michael May "Do We Need a Nuclear Test Ban?" *Wall Street Journal* (June 28, 1976).

28. See Blechman; Caldwell; and Drell.

29. Caldwell, p. 31.

30. A number of near-nuclear powers (e.g., Brazil, Israel, and South Africa) which have refused to ratify the NPT are nevertheless parties to the Limited Test Ban Treaty whose preamble commits parties to subscribe to a CTB.

31. Negotiations for a CTB have taken place in various formats. The latest round of negotiations, initiated in 1977 and involving the United States, the Soviet Union, and Great Britain, was concluded in the fall of 1980 without producing an agreement. The next round of talks had yet to be scheduled as of mid-1981.

32. *Nuclear-Weapon-Free Zones* (Vantage Conference Report, The Stanley Foundation, 1975), p. 26.

33. See Epstein, p. 55, and *Comprehensive Study of the Question of Nuclear-Weapon-Free Zones in All Its Aspects* (Special Report of the Conference on the Committee of Disarmament, United Nations, 1976), pp. 20–22.

34. See Epstein, pp. 207–220, and *Nuclear-Weapon-Free Zones.*

35. For texts of these treaties, see *Arms Control and Disarmament Agreements: Texts and History of Negotiations* (Washington, D.C.: U.S. Arms Control and Disarmament Agency, 1975).

36. *Comprehensive Study,* p. 13.

37. Argentina has signed the treaty and announced its intention to ratify. Brazil has signed and ratified the agreement, but because of the treaty's complex implementation conditions is not yet a full party to the accord. For a discussion of the treaty and the provisions by which it can come into force, see John Redick, "The Tlatelolco Regime and Nonproliferation in Latin America," *International Organization* (Winter 1981), pp. 106–107.

38. *Nuclear-Weapon-Free Zones,* p. 13.

39. See George Quester, "Brazil and Latin American Nuclear Proliferation: An Optimistic View" (ACIS Working Paper No. 17, University of California, Los Angeles, 1979), p. 28, and Redick, p. 121.

40. Redick, p. 122.

41. Quester (p. 14) notes, however, that U.S. adherence to Protocol II was accompanied by an "interpretation" that leaves open the option of "transit" through the Canal Zone, an interpretation shared by France and Great Britain.

42. The two other countries affected by Protocol I, Great Britain and the Netherlands, have completed ratification.

43. "Reagan Statement on Spread of Atomic Arms," *New York Times* (July 17, 1981).

44. Redick, p. 111.

45. For a similar conclusion, see *Nuclear Proliferation and Safeguards,* p. 82.

46. *Nuclear Power and Nuclear Weapons Proliferation,* Report of the Atlantic Council's Nuclear Fuels Policy Working Group, Vol. I (Boulder, Colorado: Westview Press, 1978), p. 82.

47. *INFCE Summary Volume* (Vienna: IAEA, 1980), p. 122. The objective of Working Group 3 of INFCE was "to assess alternatives for assuring reliable long-term supplies of the fuel, heavy water, reactors and services, and their related equipment and technology, which are needed to make nuclear energy widely available as a credible, long-term energy source in the interest of national needs, consistent with non-proliferation."

48. For a discussion of the new conditions imposed by the Nuclear Non-Proliferation Act, see Neff and Jacoby, "Nonproliferation Strategy in a Changing Nuclear Fuel Market," *Foreign Affairs* (Summer 1979), pp. 1127–1130. A brief review of the act is also provided in Chapter 2 of this book.

49. See Nuclear Energy Policy Study Group, *Nuclear Power Issues and Choices* (Cambridge, Massachusetts: Ballinger, 1977), p. 373.

50. For a survey of alternative and governmental mechanism approaches, see *INFCE Summary Volume*, pp. 125–132, and *Nuclear Proliferation and Civilian Nuclear Power*, Report of the Nonproliferation Alternative Systems Assessment Program, (U.S. Department of Energy, June 1980), Vol. 7, pp. 2–7 to 2–22; and Joseph A. Yager, *International Cooperation in Nuclear Energy* (Washington, D.C.: The Brookings Institution, 1981), pp. 41–82.

51. *Nuclear Proliferation and Civilian Nuclear Power*, p. 2-12.

52. For a discussion of the development of national stockpiles to make a system of cross-guarantees more effective, see Yager, pp. 58–59.

53. Ibid., p. 57.

54. A good discussion of this institutional alternative is provided by Yager, pp. 60–66. See also *Nuclear Proliferation and Civilian Nuclear Power*, pp. 2-12 to 2-13, and *The Nuclear Fuel Bank Issue as Seen by Uranium Producers and Consumers* (London: Uranium Institute, 1979).

55. These questions are addressed by Yager, pp. 61–66.

56. *INFCE Summary Volume*, p. 130. See also *Assurances of Long-Term Supply of Technology, Fuel and Heavy Water and Services in the Interest of National Needs, Consistent with Non-Proliferation*, Report of INFCE Working Group 3, (Vienna: IAEA, 1980).

57. See, for example, Ted Greenwood and Robert Haffa, Jr., "Supply-Side Non Proliferation," *Foreign Policy* (Spring 1981), pp. 125–140; Steven J. Baker, "Why Not a Nuclear Fuel Cartel?" in William H. Kincade and Jeffrey D. Porro, eds., *Negotiating Security: An Arms Control Reader* (Washington, D.C.: The Arms Control Association and the Carnegie Endowment for International Peace, 1979), pp. 152–156; and Amory Lovins, L. Hunter Lovins, and Leonard Ross, "Nuclear Power and Nuclear Bombs," *Foreign Affairs* (Summer 1980), pp. 1137–1177. Lovins et al. believe that reliance on the market mechanism would ultimately move nations away from nuclear power altogether.

58. Greenwood and Haffa recognize this problem, p. 138.

59. See *Nuclear Proliferation and Civilian Nuclear Power*, p. 2-20.

60. See, for example, *Nuclear Power and Nuclear Weapons Proliferation*, Report of the Atlantic Council's Nuclear Fuels Policy Working Group, Vol. II (Boulder, Colorado: Westview Press, 1978), pp. 22–23; Ted Greenwood, "Discouraging Proliferation in the Next Decade and Beyond," in Ted Greenwood, Harold A Feiveson, and Theodore B. Taylor, *Nuclear Proliferation: Motivations, Capabilities, and Strategies for Control* (New York: McGraw-Hill, 1977), pp. 78–79; *Nuclear Proliferation and Safeguards*, p. 67; and Rowen and Rowen, p. 37.

61. For a discussion of U.S. sanctions in this case, see Ernest W. Lefever, *Nuclear Arms in the Third World* (Washington, D.C.: The Brookings Institution, 1979),

p. 130, and Leslie Gelb, "Arms Sales," *Foreign Policy* (1977), pp. 11-13.

62. Combined U.S. and Soviet pressures on South Africa appear to have prevented that country, to date, from demonstrating a nuclear weapon but not from acquiring the capability. *Nuclear Power and Nuclear Weapons Proliferation*, Vol. II, p. 27. See also Ashok Kapur, *International Nuclear Proliferation* (New York: Praeger, 1979), pp. 233-272, and Richard Betts, "South Africa," in Joseph Yager, ed., *Nonproliferation and U.S. Foreign Policy* (Washington, D.C.: The Brookings Institution, 1980), pp. 283-308.

63. *Nuclear Power and Nuclear Weapons Proliferation*, Vol. II, p. 27.

64. Ibid., p. 23.

65. Ibid.

66. George Quester, "Introduction: In Defense of Some Optimism," *International Organization* (Winter 1981), p. 11.

67. Ibid. An alternative view is that the threat of strong sanctions kept India from exploding a second device. This interpretation was suggested to me by Thomas Graham in a personal communication.

68. As will be discussed below, an alternative focal point might be so-called dedicated facilities, i.e., plants designed specifically for the production of weapons-grade uranium or plutonium.

69. See Epstein, *The Last Chance*, p. 147, and *Nuclear Proliferation Factbook*, 3rd edition (Washington, D.C.: U.S. Government Printing Office, September 1980), pp. 390-391.

70. *Nuclear Proliferation and Safeguards*, p. 194.

71. See ibid., p. 206, and Gene I. Rochlin, *Plutonium, Power, and Politics* (Berkeley: University of California Press, 1979), p. 151. An excellent discussion of national safeguards is provided by Mason Willrich and Theodore Taylor in *Nuclear Theft: Risks and Safeguards* (Cambridge, Massachusetts: Ballinger, 1974).

72. Reprinted in Epstein, *The Last Chance*, pp. 148-149.

73. Ibid., p. 149. See also Ralph Mabry, "The Present International Nuclear Regime," in Joseph Yager, *International Cooperation in Nuclear Energy* (Washington, D.C.: Brookings Institution, 1981), pp. 145-171. For a discussion of the technical means used by the IAEA in implementing its safeguards system, see Kapur, pp. 125-133, and *Nuclear Proliferation and Safeguards*, pp. 205-211.

74. Epstein, *The Last Chance*, p. 151.

75. *IAEA Bulletin*, March 1981, p. 32.

76. SIPRI, *SIPRI Yearbook 1981*, p. 311.

77. See, for example, Rochlin, p. 145, Epstein, *The Last Chance*, p. 153; and *Nuclear Power Issues and Choices*, p. 292.

78. See Henry S. Rowen, "How to Develop Nuclear Power While Limiting Its Dangers: Proposed Changes in the International Nuclear System," Mimeo, August 23, 1977, pp. 5-6.

79. Ibid., p. 6.

80. See Mabry, p. 167, and Paul C. Szasz, "The Inadequacy of International Nuclear Safeguards," *Journal of International Law and Economics*, Vol. 10 (1975), p. 434.

81. Pierre Lellouche, "Internationalization of the Nuclear Fuel Cycle and Nonproliferation Strategy" (SJD Dissertation, Harvard Law School, 1979), pp. 182-187.

82. President Reagan, in his first major statement on nuclear proliferation, indicated that his administration would not "inhibit or set back civil reprocessing under breeder-reactor development abroad in nations with advanced nuclear power programs *where it does not constitute a proliferation risk*" (emphasis

added). *New York Times* (July 17, 1981). The magnitude of change in U.S. policy is obscured by the last phrase.

83. Opposition to safeguards by states with large commercial nuclear activities on the grounds that they compromise industrial secrets and inflict commercial penalties is now rarely raised. (See SIPRI, *SIPRI Yearbook 1981*, p. 306.) For a discussion of French and German resistance to the principle of the automatic extension of full-scope safeguards to clients purchasing nuclear goods, see Lellouche, pp. 188–189.

84. Mabry, p. 171.

85. See Mabry, p. 171, and David Fischer, *International Safeguards 1979,* Working Paper of the International Consultative Group of Nuclear Energy (New York: The Rockefeller Foundation and The Royal Institute of International Affairs, 1979), pp. 33–34. Mabry reports that the in-plant dynamics material control system (Dymac) currently being developed in the United States is expected to provide near real-time material control by performing nearly continuous measurements of all materials being stored, transferred, or processed.

86. *Nuclear Proliferation and Safeguards,* p. 80.

87. Mabry, p. 171; Fischer, p. 31; Feiveson and Taylor, p. 157; and *Nuclear Proliferation and Safeguards,* p. 80.

88. Epstein, *The Last Chance,* p. 160 and SIPRI, *SIPRI Yearbook 1981,* p. 309. For lists of additional measures to strengthen safeguards see *Nuclear Proliferation and Safeguards,* pp. 80–81; Epstein, *The Last Chance,* pp. 160–161; Rochlin, pp. 174–180; Fischer, pp. 31–35; and Feiveson and Taylor, pp. 155–158.

89. See Lellouche, p. 186, and SIPRI, *SIPRI Yearbook 1981,* pp. 307–308. At the conference, most opposition to the imposition of full-scope safeguards as a condition of supply to non-NPT parties came from the Group of 77, a body of principally developing and nonaligned states.

90. Excellent reviews of multinational institutional arrangements for nonproliferation are provided by Lellouche; Rochlin, pp. 189–308; Lawrence Scheinman, "Multinational Alternatives and Nuclear Proliferation," *International Organization* (Winter 1981), pp. 77–102; the collection of essays in Abram Chayes and W. Bennett Lewis, eds., *International Arrangements for Nuclear Fuel Reprocessing* (Cambridge, Massachusetts: Ballinger, 1977). The most comprehensive examination of the subject is the two-volume IAEA study, *Regional Nuclear Fuel Cycle Centres: 1977 Report of the IAEA Study Projects* (Vienna: IAEA, 1977).

91. See, for example, Michael Guhin, *Nuclear Paradox: Security Risks of the Peaceful Atom* (Washington, D.C.: American Enterprise Institute for Public Policy Research, 1976), pp. 48–49; Albert Wohlstetter et al., *Swords from Plowshares* (Chicago: University of Chicago Press, 1979), p. 31; *Nuclear Proliferation and Safeguards,* p. 219; and Scheinman, pp. 98–99. Economies of scale is another potential advantage not directly related to proliferation considerations often attributed to MFCFs.

92. Scheinman, p. 98.

93. *Nuclear Weapons Proliferation and the International Atomic Energy Agency* (Report prepared by the Congressional Research Service for the U.S. Senate Committee on Government Operations, March 1976), p. 127.

94. See Rochlin, pp. 315–328, for an attempt to assess the relative advantages and disadvantages of multinational centers for different fuel cycle activities and the relative difficulty of negotiating arrangments for them. See especially the summary chart on p. 323.

95. *INFCE Summary Volume,* p. 48.

96. Scheinman, pp. 82–83.
97. For a discussion of these multinational ventures as possible models for MFCFs, see Scheinman, pp. 82–92; Lellouche, pp. 402–417; and *Nuclear Power and Nuclear Weapons Proliferation*, Vol. I, pp. 98–110.
98. Mabry, pp. 125–126.
99. Scheinman, p. 97.
100. Ibid., p. 101. For two innovative proposals that attempt to meet this challenge, see Bennett Ramberg, "Preventative Medicine for Global Nuclear Energy Risks: A Proposal for an International Nuclear Export Review Board," paper presented to the California Seminar on Arms Control and Foreign Policy, July 1979, and John H. Barton, ed., *Evaluation of an Integrated International Fuel Authority* (Institute for Energy Study, Stanford University, 1978).
101. Joseph S. Nye, "Nonproliferation: A Long-Term Strategy," *Foreign Affairs* (April 1978), p. 602.
102. Smith and Rathjens, p. 877.
103. See, for example, Neff and Jacoby, pp. 1141–1143.
104. Smith and Rathjens, p. 887.
105. Ibid.
106. Japan and West Germany are examples of the first category of states; Pakistan is the prime example of the second category.
107. See *SIPRI Yearbook 1981*, pp. 317–318, for a discussion of these and other complaints by Third World states raised at the Second NPT Review Conference.
108. For a discussion of these views, see Charles K. Ebinger, "International Politics of Nuclear Energy," *The Washington Papers*, No. 57, pp. 82–83.
109. Useful discussions of possible third-tier suppliers are provided by Lewis A. Dunn, "After INFCE: Some Next Steps for Nonproliferation Policy," Hudson Institute Paper, October 22, 1969, pp. 11–13, and Henry Rowen and Richard Brody, "Nuclear Potential and Possible Contingencies," in Joseph Yager, ed., *Nonproliferation and U.S. Foreign Policy* (Washington, D.C.: The Brookings Institution, 1980), pp. 220–225.
110. See Kapur, p. 118. India has provided technical nuclear assistance and training to Egypt, Vietnam, Argentina, and Libya. See Dunn, p. 12.
111. This point is made in *Nuclear Proliferation and Safeguards*, p. 75.
112. Ibid.
113. Ibid., p. 76.
114. For a discussion of this point, see Scheinman, p. 79.
115. See *Reprocessing, Plutonium Handling, Recycle*, Report of INFCE Working Group 4 (Vienna: IAEA, 1980), p. 145.
116. For a discussion of those "Category One" technical measures, see *Reprocessing, Plutonium Handling, Recycle*, pp. 60–64 and 146; *Nuclear Proliferation and Safeguards*, pp. 200–201; and *Nuclear Proliferation and Civilian Nuclear Power*, Vol. 1, pp. 143–148 and Vol. 2, pp. 2-25 and 2-35.
117. *Reprocessing, Plutonium Handling, Recycle*, p. 60. For a less positive assessment, see *Nuclear Proliferation and Safeguards*, pp. 40 and 202.
118. See *Nuclear Proliferation and Civilian Nuclear Power*, Vol. 2, pp. 2-26, and *Reprocessing, Plutonium Handling, Recycle*, pp. 26 and 61–65.
119. Useful discussions of these techniques are provided in *Nuclear Proliferation and Civilian Nuclear Power* Vol. 1, p. 42; Rochlin, pp. 215–216; *Nuclear Proliferation and Safeguards*, pp. 200–201; and *Reprocessing, Plutonium Handling, Recycle*, p. 147.
120. These difficulties are discussed in *Nuclear Proliferation and Civilian Nuclear Power*, Vol. 1, pp. 42 and 148.
121. See *Reprocessing, Plutonium Handling, Recycle*, p. 147, and *Nuclear Prolifera-

tion and Civilian Nuclear Power, Vol. 2, p. 42.

122. *Nuclear Proliferation and Civilian Nuclear Power,* p. 144.

123. See ibid., pp. 146 and 148.

124. The INFCE report indicates that the effects of retaining the fission products in the fabrication process is not known and that "it is unlikely that partial process-ing could be developed to the point where it could be introduced into industrial plants until some time after the end of the century." *Reprocessing Plutonium Handling, Recycle,* p. 66.

125. Ibid. See also *Nuclear Proliferation and Civilian Nuclear Power,* Vol. 1, p. 144.

126. See *Nuclear Proliferation and Civilian Nuclear Power,* Vol. 2, p. 2-27.

127. For a discussion of the Pipex concept, see *Reprocessing, Plutonium Handling, Recycle,* pp. 68–69, and INFCE/DEP/W64/64, "Pipex—A Model of Design Concept for Reprocessing Plants with Improved Containment and Surveillance Features," France/Federal Republic of Germany, March 15, 1979.

128. See p. 88 above.

129. For a discussion of the CIVEX process, recently advanced as an alternative to the PUREX method of reprocessing, see Rochlin, pp. 218–219; *Nuclear News* (April 1978), pp. 31–37; and "Fuel Reprocessing Still the Focus of U.S. Nonproliferation Policy," *Science* (August 1978), p. 697.

130. See Lovins et al., pp. 1137–1177.

131. Lewis Dunn and Herman Kahn, *Trends in Nuclear Proliferation, 1975–1995* (Croton-on-Hudson, N.Y.: Hudson Institute, 1976), pp. 23–75. The other basic scenarios are: Early to Mid-1980's Latin American Proliferation; Libyan-Triggered Early 1980's Middle East Proliferation; Early to Mid-1980's Emer-gence of a Nuclear Exports "Grey Market"; More Extensive Global Prolifera-tion: Repercussions of Growing Perceptions of American Unreliability; Explo-sive Late 1980's-Early 1990's European Proliferation: A West German Nuclear Weapon Program; Widespread Mid- to Late 1980's Proliferation in Asia: Japan "Goes Nuclear"; Late 1980's Erosion of Technical Constraints and of the NPT System; and Mid- to Late 1980's Proliferation in Eastern Europe.

132. Ibid., p. 73.

133. See ibid., pp. 24–66.

134. Ibid.

135. For a critique of their nuclear chain model, see Kapur, pp. 187–196.

136. A more up-to-date list would probably omit Iran because its regional military influence and commitment to nuclear power have been significantly reduced since the Islamic Revolution. Iraq, on the other hand, should probably be added to the list since it is now generally regarded as a major proliferation threat in the Middle East, even after the destruction of its nuclear reactor facility by Israel. South Africa is another state which might be added to the critical country list on the basis of the probability of its going nuclear, although the direct im-pact of a South African bomb on the nuclear policies of other states is difficult to judge. Japan and West Germany appear on the list, it should be emphasized, not because they are apt to seek nuclear weapons in the near future but because of the enormous international repercussions should they do so.

137. A similar list of alternative proliferation routes is provided in *Nuclear Power Issues and Choices,* pp. 279–280.

138. Compare, for example, C. Starr and E. Zebroski, "Nuclear Power and Weapons Proliferation," paper presented to American Power Conference, April 18–20, 1977; Wohlstetter et al., p. 45; George Rathjens and Albert Carnesale, "The Nu-clear Fuel Cycle and Nuclear Proliferation," in Abram Chayes and W. Bennett Lewis, pp. 3–7.

139. For a forceful argument about the dangers of theft, however, see Mason Willrich

and Theodore Taylor, *Nuclear Theft: Risks and Safeguards* (Cambridge, Massachusetts: Ballinger, 1974).

140. See Wohlstetter et al., p. 45.

141. A diplomatically isolated Taiwan might well move in the direction of proliferation by dedicated facilities if it believed the United States had abandoned it.

142. Following the INFCE definition, "diversion" refers to those activities, whether overt or covert, to implement a decision by a national government or subnational group to misuse nuclear fuel cycle facilities or nuclear materials in order to attempt the manufacture of nuclear weapons." See *Reprocessing, Plutonium Handling, Recycle,* p. 126.

143. For a more thorough discussion of likely proliferation routes for the countries mentioned in this section, see the source material cited in the case studies in Chapter 5.

144. See pp. 10-12. See also Enid C. B. Schoettle, *Postures for Non-Proliferation* (London: Taylor & Francis, 1979), pp. 5-7.

145. For informed discussions of the problems of proliferation, see Dunn and Kahn, pp. 114-139, and Wohlstetter et al., pp. 126-150.

146. The illogic of this position is discussed by Quester, pp. 11-12.

147. Private conservations with informed Chinese indicate that this is not unnoticed by the leadership in Peking, even though the Chinese have refused to sign the NPT and were among the harshest critics of the ABM Treaty.

148. For a list of potential nuclear confrontations in which the United States and Soviet Union might find themselves, see Dunn and Kahn, pp. 111-113.

149. The possibility that Israel could have targeted Soviet territory as well as the Soviet fleet in the Mediterranean with nuclear weapons in the 1970s is suggested by Avigdor Haselkorn, "Israel: From an Option to a Bomb in the Basement," in Robert M. Lawrence and Joel Larus, eds., *Nuclear Proliferation Phase II* (Lawrence: University Press of Kansas, 1974), p. 170.

150. Wohlstetter et al., p. 146.

151. Dunn and Kahn, pp. 91-92.

152. Useful discussions of nuclear terrorism are provided by Epstein, *The Last Chance,* pp. 259-273; Ted Greenwood, "Discouraging Proliferation in the Next Decade and Beyond," pp. 99-108; *Nuclear Power Issues and Choices,* pp. 301-315; Brian K. Jenkins, "Will Terrorists Go Nuclear?" RAND Paper P-5546 (Santa Monica, Calif.: Rand Corporation, November 1975); and *Nuclear Proliferation and Safeguards,* pp. 115-138.

153. This argument is developed by Greenwood, "Discouraging Proliferation in the Next Decade and Beyond," p. 102.

154. This point is made in ibid., p. 104, and by Jenkins, p. 7.

155. For a discussion of this issue, see Dunn and Kahn, p. 132; *Nuclear Power Issues and Choices,* pp. 312-315; and *Nuclear Proliferation and Safeguards,* pp. 127-136.

156. *Nuclear Power Issues and Choices,* p. 313.

157. Dunn and Kahn, p. 132.

158. The most comprehensive study on this topic is Bennett Ramberg's *Destruction of Nuclear Energy Facilities in War: The Problem and the Implications* (Lexington, Massachusetts: Lexington Books, 1980). See also Conrad V. Chester and Rowena O. Chester, "Civil Defense Implications of the U.S. Nuclear Power Industry During a Large Nuclear War in the Year 2000," *Nuclear Technology* (December 1976), pp. 326-338. No mention of the subject appears in such comprehensive analyses of nuclear power and proliferation issues as Wohlstetter et al., *Swords from Plowshares;* Nuclear Energy Policy Study Group, *Nuclear Power*

Issues and Choices; and Office of Technology Assessment, *Nuclear Proliferation and Safeguards.*
159. See Ramberg, pp. 30–61.
160. For a discussion of military acts capable of exploiting nuclear facility vulnerability, see ibid., pp. 62–68.
161. See ibid., pp. 64–66, and Lee Dembart, "Vulnerability of U.S. A-Plants Cited: Israeli Raid Raises Issue; Nuclear Industry Doubts Attack," *Los Angeles Times* (June 11, 1981).
162. See Dembart.
163. For a discussion of possible means to diminish the wartime vulnerability of nuclear energy facilities, see Ramberg, pp. 113–160.
164. For a discussion of the concept of "timely warning," see Wohlstetter et al., pp. 24–25; *Nuclear Power and Nuclear Weapons Proliferation,* Vol. II, pp. 20–22; Rochlin, pp. 146–149; and Mabry, pp. 167–168.
165. The Iraqi reactor bombed by the Israelis utilized 93-percent enriched uranium. The lesson of the Iraqi nuclear program for "timely warning" is mixed. Although the Israelis struck before Iraq had developed a bomb, *post hoc* analyses of the program reveal mixed intelligence estimates of the time Iraq required for construction of a nuclear explosive, no evidence of unambiguous Iraqi violations of IAEA safeguards, and few clues to how the United States or other Western nations would have responded had they been convinced, as were the Israelis, that Iraq would soon have begun the manufacture of nuclear weapons. See "Israeli Attack on Iraqi Nuclear Facilities," Hearings before the Committee on Foreign Affairs, U.S. House of Representatives, June 17 and 25, 1981.
166. See, for example, Dunn and Kahn, p. 144, and Harold W. Maynard, "In Case of Deluge: Where Nuclear Proliferation Meets Conventional Arms Sales," (Mimeo, USAF Acedemy, July 29, 1977). For a critique of this approach, see Thomas A. Halsted, "Nuclear Proliferation: How to Retard It, Live With It," a Workshop Report of the Aspen Institute for Humanistic Studies, 1977, pp. 19–20.
167. See Dunn and Kahn, pp. 89–94.
168. Stephen M. Meyer, "Probing the Causes of Nuclear Proliferation: An Empirical Analysis, 1940–1973" (Ph.D. Dissertation, University of Michigan, 1978).
169. For a much more optimistic outlook on nonproliferation, see George Quester, "Introduction: In Defense of Some Optimism," *International Organization* (Winter 1981), pp. 1–14.
170. This point is also made by Lewis A. Dunn, "The Proliferation Policy Agenda: Taking Stock," Report of the World Peace Foundation Conference on Managing in a Proliferation-Prone World (Dedham, Massachusetts, December 9–11, 1977).
171. This is George Quester's formulation in "Nuclear Proliferation: Linkages and Solutions," *International Organization* (Autumn 1979), p. 566.
172. Richard Rosecrance, "International Stability and Nuclear Diffusion," in Rosecrance, ed., *The Dispersion of Nuclear Weapons* (New York: Columbia University Press, 1964), p. 314.

Treaty on the Non-Proliferation of Nuclear Weapons

Signed at London, Moscow, and Washington July 1, 1968
Entered into force March 5, 1970

The States concluding this Treaty, hereinafter referred to as the "Parties to the Treaty,"

Considering the devastation that would be visited upon all mankind by a nuclear war and the consequent need to make every effort to avert the danger of such a war and to take measures to safeguard the security of peoples,

Believing that the proliferation of nuclear weapons would seriously enhance the danger of nuclear war,

In conformity with resolutions of the United Nations General Assembly calling for the conclusion of an agreement on the prevention of wider dissemination of nuclear weapons,

Undertaking to cooperate in facilitating the application of International Atomic Energy Agency safeguards on peaceful nuclear activities,

Expressing their support for research, development and other efforts to further the application, within the framework of the International Atomic Energy Agency safeguards system, of the principle of safeguarding effectively the flow of source and special fissionable materials by use of instruments and other techniques at certain strategic points,

Affirming the principle that the benefits of peaceful applications of nuclear technology, including any technological by-products which may be derived by nuclear-weapon States from the development of nuclear explosive devices, should be available for peaceful purposes to all Parties to the Treaty, whether nuclear-weapon or non-nuclear weapon States.

Convinced that, in furtherance of this principle, all Parties to the Treaty are entitled to participate in the fullest possible exchange of scientific information for, and to contribute alone or in cooperation with other States to, the further development of the applications of atomic energy for peaceful purposes,

Declaring their intention to achieve at the earliest possible date the cessation of the nuclear arms race and to undertake effective measures in the direction of nuclear disarmament,

Urging the cooperation of all States in the attainment of this objective,

Recalling the determination expressed by the Parties to the 1963 Treaty banning nuclear weapon tests in the atmosphere in outer space and under water in its Preamble to seek to achieve the discontinuance of all test explosions of nuclear weapons for all time and to continue negotiations to this end,

Desiring to further the easing of international tension and the strengthening of trust between States in order to facilitate the cessation of the manufacture of nuclear weapons, the liquidation of all their existing stockpiles, and the elimination from national arsenals of nuclear weapons and the means of their delivery pursuant to a treaty on general and complete disarmament under strict and effective international control,

Recalling that, in accordance with the Charter of the United Nations, States must refrain in their international relations from the threat or use of force against the territorial integrity or political independence of any State, or in any other manner inconsistent with the Purposes of the United Nations, and that the establishment and maintenance of international peace and security are to be promoted with the least diversion for armaments of the world's human and economic resources,

Have agreed as follows:

ARTICLE I

Each nuclear-weapon State Party to the Treaty undertakes not to transfer to any recipient whatsoever nuclear weapons or other nuclear explosive devices or control over such weapons or explosive devices directly, or indirectly; and not in any way to assist, encourage, or induce any non-nuclear-weapon State to manufacture or otherwise acquire nuclear weapons or other nuclear explosive devices, or control over such weapons or explosive devices.

ARTICLE II

Each non-nuclear weapon State Party to the Treaty undertakes not to receive the transfer from any transferor whatsoever of nuclear weapons or other nuclear explosive devices or of control over such weapons or explosive devices directly, or indirectly; nor to manufacture or otherwise acquire nuclear weapons or other nuclear explosive devices; and not to seek or receive any assistance in the manufacture of nuclear weapons or other nuclear explosive devices.

ARTICLE III

1. Each non-nuclear-weapon State Party to the Treaty undertakes to accept safeguards, as set forth in an agreement to be negotiated and concluded with the International Atomic Energy Agency in accordance with the Statute of the International Atomic Energy Agency and the Agency's safeguards system for the exclusive purpose of verification of the fulfillment of its obligations assumed under this Treaty with a view to preventing diversion of nuclear energy from peaceful uses to nuclear weapons or other nuclear explosive devices. Procedures for the safeguards required by this article shall be followed with respect to source or special fissionable material whether it is being produced, processed or used in any principal nuclear facility or is outside any such facility. The safeguards required by this article shall be applied on all source or special fissionable material in all peaceful nuclear activities within the territory of such State, under its jurisdiction, or carried out under its control anywhere.

2. Each State Party to the Treaty undertakes not to provide: (a) source or special fissionable material, or (b) equipment or material especially designed or prepared for the processing, use or production of special fissionable material, to any non-nuclear-weapon State for peaceful purposes, unless the source or special fissionable material shall be subject to the safeguards required by this article.

3. The safeguards required by this article shall be implemented in a manner designed to comply with article IV of this Treaty, and to avoid hampering the economic or technological development of the Parties or international cooperation in the field of peaceful nuclear activities, including the international exchange of nuclear material and equipment for the processing, use or production of nuclear material for peaceful purposes in accordance with the provisions of this article and the principle of safeguarding set forth in the Preamble of the Treaty.

4. Non-nuclear-weapon States Party to the Treaty shall conclude agreements with the International Atomic Energy Agency to meet the requirements of this article either individually or together with other States in accordance with the Statute of the International Atomic Energy Agency. Negotiation of such agreements shall commence within 180 days from the original entry into force of this Treaty. For States depositing their instruments of ratification or accession after the 180-day period, negotiation of such agreements shall commence not later than the date of such deposit. Such agreements shall enter into force not later than eighteen months after the date of initiation of negotiations.

ARTICLE IV

1. Nothing in this Treaty shall be interpreted as affecting the inalienable right of all the Parties to the Treaty to develop research, production and use of nuclear energy for peaceful purposes without discrimination and in conformity with articles I and II of this Treaty.

2. All the Parties to the Treaty undertake to facilitate, and have the right to participate in, the fullest possible exchange of equipment, materials and scientific and technological information for the peaceful uses of nuclear energy. Parties to the Treaty in a position to do so shall also cooperate in contributing alone or together with other States or international organizations to the further development of the applications of nuclear energy for peaceful purposes, especially in the territories of non-nuclear-weapon States Party to the Treaty, with due consideration for the needs of the developing areas of the world.

ARTICLE V

Each Party to the Treaty undertakes to take appropriate measures to ensure that, in accordance with this Treaty, under appropriate international observation and through appropriate international procedures, potential benefits from any peaceful applications of nuclear explosions will be made available to non-nuclear-weapon States Party to the Treaty on a non-discriminatory basis and that the charge to such Parties for the explosive devices used will be as low as possible and exclude any charge for research and development. Non-nuclear-weapon States Party to the Treaty shall be able to obtain such benefits, pursuant to a special international agreement or agreements, through an appropriate international body with adequate representation of non-nuclear-weapon States. Negotiations on this subject shall commence as soon as possible after the Treaty enters into force. Non-nuclear-weapon States Party to the Treaty so desiring may also obtain such benefits pursuant to bilateral agreements.

ARTICLE VI

Each of the Parties to the Treaty undertakes to pursue negotiations in good faith on effective measures relating to cessation of the nuclear arms race at an early date and to nuclear disarmament, and on a treaty on general and complete disarmament under strict and effective international control.

ARTICLE VII

Nothing in this Treaty affects the right of any group of States to conclude regional treaties in order to assure the total absence of nuclear weapons in their respective territories.

ARTICLE VIII

1. Any Party to the Treaty may propose amendments to this Treaty. The text of any proposed amendment shall be submitted to the Depositary Governments which shall circulate it to all Parties to the Treaty. Thereupon, if requested to do so by one-third or more of the Parties to the Treaty, the Depositary Governments shall convene a conference, to which they shall invite all the Parties to the Treaty, to consider such an amendment.

2. Any amendment to this Treaty must be approved by a majority of the votes of all the Parties to the Treaty, including the votes of all nuclear-weapon States Party to the Treaty and all other Parties which, on the date the amendment is circulated, are members of the Board of Governors of the International Atomic Energy Agency. The amendment shall enter into force for each Party that deposits its instrument of ratification of the amendment upon the deposit of such instruments of ratification by a majority of all the Parties, including the instruments of ratification of all nuclear-weapon States Party to the Treaty and all other Parties which, on the date the amendment is circulated, are members of the Board of Governors of the International Atomic Energy Agency. Thereafter, it shall enter into force for any other Party upon the deposit of its instrument of ratification of the amendment.

3. Five years after the entry into force of this Treaty, a conference of Parties to the Treaty shall be held in Geneva, Switzerland, in order to review the operation of this Treaty with a view to assuring that the purposes of the Preamble and the provisions of the Treaty are being realized. At intervals of five years thereafter, a majority of the Parties to the Treaty may obtain, by submitting a proposal to this effect to the Depositary Governments, the convening of further conferences with the same objective of reviewing the operation of the Treaty.

ARTICLE IX

1. This Treaty shall be open to all States for signature. Any State which does not sign the Treaty before its entry into force in accordance with paragraph 3 of this article may accede to it at any time.

2. This Treaty shall be subject to ratification by signatory States. Instruments of ratification and instruments of accession shall be deposited with the Governments of the United States of America, the United Kingdom of Great Britain and Northern Ireland and the Union of Soviet Socialist Republics, which are hereby designated the Depositary Governments.

3. This Treaty shall enter into force after its ratification by the States, the governments of which are designated Depositaries of the Treaty, and forty other States signatory to this Treaty and the deposit of their instruments of ratification. For the purposes of this Treaty, a nuclear-weapon State is one which has manufactured and exploded a nuclear weapon or other nuclear explosive device prior to January 1, 1967.

4. For States whose instruments of ratification or accession are deposited subsequent to the entry into force of this Treaty, it shall enter into force on the date of the deposit of their instruments of ratification or accession.

5. The Depositary Governments shall promptly inform all signatory and acceding States of the date of each signature, the date of deposit of each instrument of ratification or of accession, the date of the entry into force of this Treaty, and the date of receipt of any requests for convening a conference or other notices.

6. This Treaty shall be registered by the Depositary Governments pursuant to article 102 of the Charter of the United Nations.

ARTICLE X

1. Each Party shall in exercising its national sovereignty have the right to withdraw from the Treaty if it decides that extraordinary events, related to the subject matter of this Treaty, have jeopardized the supreme interests of its country. It shall give notice of such withdrawal to all other Parties to the Treaty and to the United Nations Security Council three months in advance. Such notice shall include a statement of the extraordinary events it regards as having jeopardized its supreme interests.

2. Twenty-five years after the entry into force of the Treaty, a conference shall be convened to decide whether the Treaty shall continue in force indefinitely, or shall be extended for an additional fixed period or periods. This decision shall be taken by a majority of the Parties to the Treaty.

ARTICLE XI

This Treaty, the English, Russian, French, Spanish and Chinese texts of which are equally authentic, shall be deposited in the archives of the Depositary Governments. Duly certified copies of this Treaty shall be transmitted by the Depositary Governments to the Governments of the signatory and acceding States.

Non-Nuclear Weapon States Party to NPT (as of May 14, 1981)[a]

1. **Afghanistan**
2. **Australia**
3. **Austria**
4. *Bahamas (10 January 75)**
5. *Bangladesh (27 March 81)*
6. *Barbados (21 August 81)*
7. **Belgium**
8. *Benin (30 April 74)*
9. *Bolivia* (5 March 72)*
10. *Botswana (5 March 72)*
11. **Bulgaria**
12. *Burundi (19 September 72)*
13. **Canada**
14. *Cape Verde (15 May 81)*[b]
15. *Central African Republic (25 April 72)*
16. *Chad (10 September 72)*
17. *Congo (23 April 80)*
18. **Costa Rica**
19. **Cyprus**
20. **Czechoslovakia**
21. *Democratic Kampuchea (2 December 73)*
22. *Democratic Yemen (1 December 80)*
23. **Denmark**
24. **Dominican Republic**
25. **Ecuador**
26. *Egypt (26 August 82)*
27. **El Salvador**
28. **Ethiopia**
29. **Figi**
30. **Finland**
31. *Gabon* (7 August 75)*
32, **Gambia**
33. **German Democratic Republic**
34. **Germany, Federal Republic of**
35. **Ghana**
36. **Greece**
37. *Granada (19 February 76)*
38. *Guatemala* (22 March 72)*
39. *Guinea Bissau (20 February 78)*
40. *Haiti* (2 June 72)*
41. **Holy See**
42. **Honduras**
43. **Hungary**
44. **Iceland**
45. **Indonesia**
46. **Iran**
47. **Iraq**
48. **Ireland**
49. **Italy**

(continued on next page)

50. *Ivory Coast (6 September 74)*
51. **Jamaica**
52. **Japan**
53. **Jordan**
54. *Kenya (5 March 72)*
55. **Korea, Republic of**
56. Lao People's Democratic *Republic (5 March 72)*
57. **Lebanon**
58. **Lesotho**
59. *Liberia (5 March 72)*
60. **Libyan Arab Jamahiriya**
61. **Liechtenstein**
62. **Luxembourg**
63. **Madagascar**
64. **Malaysia**
65. **Maldives**
66. *Mali (5 March 72)*
67. *Malta (5 March 72)*
68. **Mauritius**
69. **Mexico**
70. **Mongolia**
71. **Morocco**
72. **Nepal**
73. **Netherlands**
74. **New Zealand**
75. **Nicaragua**
76. *Nigeria (5 March 72)*
77. **Norway**
78. *Panama (13 July 78)*
79. **Paraguay**
80. **Peru**
81. **Philippines**
82. **Poland**
83. **Portugal**
84. **Romania**
85. *Rwanda (20 November 76)*

86. *St. Lucia (29 June 81)*
87. **Samoa**
88. *San Marino* (5 March 72)*
89. **Senegal**
90. *Sierra Leone* (26 August 76)*
91. **Singapore**
92. *Somalia (5 March 72)*
93. *Sri Lanka* (5 September 80)*
94. **Sudan**
95. **Suriname**
96. **Swaziland**
97. **Sweden**
98. **Switzerland**
99. *Syrian Arab Republic (5 March 72)*
100. **Thailand**
101. *Togo (5 March 72)*
102. *Tonga* (7 January 73)*
103. *Tunisia (5 March 72)*
104. *Turkey (17 October 81)*
105. *Tuvalu (19 July 1980)*
106. *United Republic of Cameroon (5 March 72)*
107. *Upper Volta (5 March 72)*
108. **Uruguay**
109. *Venezuela* (26 March 77)*
110. **Yugoslavia**
111. **Zaire**
112. *"Republic of China"—5 March 72. The "Republic of China" has ratified the NPT.*

Source: *IAEA Bulletin* (June 1981), p. 50

[a]The date in parentheses after the name of the state indicates the time by which the NPT safeguards agreement should have entered or should enter into force.

[b]Cape Verde does not appear in the *IAEA Bulletin* list but is regarded by the U.S. Arms Control and Disarmament Agency as a party to the NPT.

Note: Bold: States having NPT safeguards agreement in force.
Italics: States not having NPT safeguards in force.
*: Safeguards agreement approved by the IAEA Board of Governors and awaiting entry into force.

Selected Bibliography

The Annals of the American Academy of Political and Social Sciences. Issue
on "Nuclear Proliferation: Prospects, Problems, and Proposals," edited
by Joseph I. Coffey (March 1977).

Excellent collection of essays which address three aspects of nuclear proliferation: the prospect that new nuclear weapons states will come on the
scene, the problems that their arrival may create, and means of coping
with those problems.

Atlantic Council of the United States, *Nuclear Fuels Policy,* Report of the
Atlantic Council's Nuclear Fuel Policy Working Group (Washington,
D.C.: Atlantic Council, 1976).

An analysis of the U.S. nuclear fuel supply situation with policy recommendations.

Atlantic Council of the United States, *Nuclear Power and Nuclear Weapons
Proliferation,* Report of the Atlantic Council's Nuclear Fuels Policy Working Group, Vols. 1 and 2 (published by the Atlantic Council and distributed
by Westview Press, Boulder, Colorado, 1978).

Examines the relationship between the production of nuclear electric
power and the proliferation of nuclear weapons capability. Provides ex-

For a more extensive annotated bibliography, see U.S. Congress, Library of Congress, Congressional Research Service, *Bibliography: Nuclear Proliferation,* prepared
for the Senate Committees on Governmental Affairs and International Relations
and the House Committee on Science and Technology (Washington, D.C.: U.S. Government Printing Office, April 1978).

tended discussion of alternative nonproliferation strategies and extensive policy recommendations. Appendixes in Volume 2 include examination of the legislative basis for U.S. nonproliferation policy and institutional models and precedents for multinational nuclear fuel center facilities.

Bader, William B. *The United States and the Spread of Nuclear Weapons* (New York: Pegasus, 1968).

A historical treatment of U.S. policy toward nuclear proliferation up to the NPT.

Barber, Richard J. Associates, Inc. *LDC Nuclear Power Prospects 1975–1990: Commercial, Economic, and Security Implications.* (Prepared for U.S. Energy Research and Development Administration, Division of International Security Affairs, 1975).

Analysis of the market potential for U.S. nuclear exports to the Third World and the political, economic, and security implications of exports to developing countries.

Barnaby, Frank C. (ed.). *Preventing the Spread of Nuclear Weapons* (London: Souvenir Press, 1969).

A collection of papers and discussions from the first Pugwash Symposium on nuclear proliferation. Papers focus on nuclear technology, safeguards, and the political aspects of proliferation.

Beaton, Leonard, and John Maddox. *The Spread of Nuclear Weapons* (London: Chatto & Windus, 1962).

The first book-length treatment of the *N*th country problem. Thorough examination of the technical problems of becoming a nuclear power and examination of the nuclear programs and postures of nine past and potential proliferators.

Connolly, Thomas J., et al. *World Nuclear Energy Paths* (New York: The Rockefeller Foundation and The Royal Institute of International Affairs, 1979). Report prepared for the International Consultative Group on Nuclear Energy.

Review and analysis of alternative world supply-demand energy projections.

Duffy, Gloria. *Soviet Nuclear Energy: Domestic and International Policies* (Santa Monica: RAND Report R-236-2-DOE, December 1979). Prepared for the U.S. Department of Energy.

The most comprehensive study of recent Soviet nuclear energy policy.

Dunn, Lewis A. "The Proliferation Policy Agenda: Taking Stock," Report of the World Peace Foundation Conference on Managing in a Proliferation-Prone World (Boston: World Peace Foundation, 1978).

Concise and perceptive discussion of means to influence and manage the scope and pace of future proliferation.

Dunn, Lewis A., and Herman Kahn. *Trends in Nuclear Proliferation 1975–1995: Projections, Problems, and Policy Options* (Croton-on-Hudson, New York: Hudson Institute, 1976).

Major study of the problems of proliferation prepared for the U.S. Arms Control and Disarmament Agency. Study includes sections on the general pressures for and constraints on proliferation, alternative projections of future proliferation, the parameters of *N*th country nuclear weapons programs and postures, the problems and risks of proliferation, and possible U.S. nonproliferation policy options.

Epstein, William. *The Last Chance: Nuclear Proliferation and Arms Control* (New York: The Free Press, 1976).

A wide-ranging survey and analysis of problems pertaining to nuclear proliferation. One of the best overviews of the subject by a strong proponent of arms control and a long-time director of the Disarmament Division of the U.N. Secretariat.

Fischer, Georges. *The Non-Proliferation of Nuclear Weapons* (New York: St. Martin's Press, 1971). Translated from French by David Willey.

Review of the origins, negotiations, and provisions of the NPT.

Goldschmidt, Bertrand, and Myron B. Kratzer. *Peaceful Nuclear Relations: A Study of the Creation and the Erosion of Confidence* (New York: The Rockefeller Foundation and The Royal Institute of International Affairs, 1978). Report prepared for the International Consultative Group on Nuclear Energy.

Analysis of the underlying factors leading to the pre-1974 period of relative stability in international nuclear relations and the events and process by which this trust was eroded.

Gray, John E., et al. *International Cooperation on Breeder Reactors* (New York: The Rockefeller Foundation, May 1976).

Excellent survey of nuclear perspectives and breeder reactor programs in seven countries and the potential for international cooperation on breeders. Very extensive appendixes on the technology of alternative nuclear reactors and reactor and resource economics.

Greenwood, Ted, Harold A. Feiveson, and Theodore B. Taylor. *Nuclear Proliferation: Motivations, Capabilities, and Strategies for Control* (New York: McGraw-Hill, 1977).

Council on Foreign Relations "1980s Project" volume divided into two parts: an excellent review of proliferation incentives, disincentives, and nonproliferation strategies by Greenwood and an assessment of three alternative fission futures by Taylor and Feiveson.

Greenwood, Ted, George Rathjens, and Jack Ruina. *Nuclear Power and Weapons Proliferation,* Adelphi Paper 130 (London: The International Institute for Strategic Studies, 1976).

Excellent overview of the technological aspects of the nuclear power-weapons proliferation controversy. Extremely useful introduction to nuclear weapons technology and the nuclear fuel cycle.

Guhin, Michael A. *Nuclear Paradox: Security Risks of the Peaceful Atom* (Washington, D.C.: American Enterprise Institute, 1976).

Short monograph on measures that could be taken on an international level to reduce the security risks associated with the peaceful uses of atomic energy.

Halperin, Morton H. *China and the Bomb* (New York: Praeger, 1965).

Early study of the Chinese nuclear program and Chinese perspectives on nuclear weapons.

Halsted, Thomas A. *Nuclear Proliferation: How to Retard It, Manage It, Live with It,* workshop report of the Aspen Institute for Humanistic Studies Program in International Affairs (Princeton, New Jersey: Aspen Institute, 1977).

Summary of Aspen Institute's 1976 workshop on proliferation. Good introduction to subject with sections titled: "Incentives and Paths to Acquire Nuclear Weapons," "Strategies for Control," "Managing a Proliferated World," and "Future Policy Options."

Harkavy, Robert E. *Spectre of a Middle Eastern Holocaust: The Strategic and Diplomatic Implications of the Israeli Nuclear Weapons Program* (Graduate School of International Studies, University of Denver, Monograph Series in World Affairs, Volume 14, 1977).

Examines the impending strategic and political implications of the Israeli nuclear weapons program.

Hewlett, Richard G., and Oscar E. Anderson, Jr. *The New World, 1939–1946: A History of the U.S. Atomic Energy Commission,* Vol. 1 (University Park: Pennsylvania State University Press, 1962).

A comprehensive, official history of the wartime atomic bomb program in the United States, written by the Historical Advisory Committee of the U.S. Atomic Energy Commission. Very well researched.

Holloway, David. "Entering the Nuclear Arms Race: The Soviet Decision to Build the Atomic Bomb, 1939–45," Working Paper No. 9, The Wilson Center International Security Studies Program (Washington, D.C., 1979).

The most comprehensive analysis of Soviet decision-making with respect to the atomic bomb.

Imai, Ryukichi, and Henry S. Rowen. *Nuclear Energy and Nuclear Proliferation: Japanese and American Views* (Boulder, Colorado: Westview Press, 1980).

An unusual dialogue between two leading Japanese and U.S. experts on nuclear power and nonproliferation.

International Nuclear Fuel Cycle Evaluation. Reports of INFCE Working Groups in 8 volumes with 1 Summary Volume (Vienna: International Atomic Energy Agency, 1980).

Public reports of the eight INFCE working groups on: Fuel and Heavy Water Availability; Enrichment Availability; Assurances of Long-term Supply of Technology, Fuel and Heavy Water and Services in the Interest of National Needs Consistent with Non-proliferation; Reprocessing, Plutonium Handling, Recycle; Fast Breeders; Spent Fuel Management; Waste Management and Disposal; and Advanced Fuel Cycle and Reactor Concepts. Useful review of eight working group reports in Summary Volume.

International Organization. Special issue on "Nuclear Proliferation: Breaking the Chain," edited by George Quester (Winter 1981).

A very useful collection of eleven essays on how the global problems of nuclear proliferation will unfold in the 1980s and 1990s. Specific topics covered include European perspectives on the Carter administration's nonproliferation policy, the Tlatelolco regime in Latin America, pariah states and proliferation, multinational approaches to nonproliferation, and Indian–Pakistani nuclear rivalry.

Jabber, Fuad. *Israel and Nuclear Weapons: Present Option and Future Strategies* (London: Chatto & Windus, 1971).

The first major study of Israel's nuclear program. Focus on both Israeli capabilities and the requirements for nuclear weapons production and Israeli strategic doctrine.

Jensen, Lloyd. *Return from the Nuclear Brink: National Interests and the Nuclear Non-Proliferation Treaty* (Lexington, Massachusetts: Lexington Books, 1973).

Examination of the postures toward nonproliferation taken by various states prior to the entry into force of the NPT in March 1970.

Jones, Gregory. *South African Proliferation Prognosis and U.S. Policy Options* (Los Angeles: Pan Heuristics, 1977). Report prepared for the U.S. Energy Research and Development Administration.

Examination of South Africa's nuclear program and U.S. policy options for influencing it.

Kapur, Ashok. *India's Nuclear Option: Atomic Diplomacy and Decision Making* (New York: Praeger, 1976).

Examination of Indian nuclear decision-making from a bureaucratic politics perspective.

Kapur, Ashok. *International Nuclear Proliferation: Multilateral Diplomacy and Regional Aspects* (New York: Praeger, 1979).

A provocative treatment of the determinants of proliferation and means for its control. Especially useful sections on the role of the Zangger Committee in multilateral nonproliferation diplomacy and the methodology of nuclear proliferation research.

Khalilzad, Zalmay. *Pakistan: The Nuclear Option* (Los Angeles: Pan Heuristics, 1977). Report prepared for the U.S. Energy Research and Development Administration.

Examination of Pakistan's nuclear program and its proliferation incentives and disincentives.

Khan, Munir Ahmad. *Nuclear Energy and International Cooperation: A Third World Perception of the Erosion of Confidence* (New York: The Rockefeller Foundation and The Royal Institute of International Affairs, 1979). Report prepared for the International Consultative Group on Nuclear Energy.

Study by the chairman of Pakistan's Atomic Energy Commission on Third World energy needs and perceptions of nuclear power and proliferation.

King, John Kerry (ed.). *International Political Effects of the Spread of Nuclear Weapons* (Washington, D.C.: U.S. Government Printing Office, 1979).

A collection of ten essays written for a colloquium on the potential international political consequences of rapid nuclear proliferation sponsored by the Central Intelligence Agency and Department of Defense. Especially interesting chapter by Kenneth Waltz with the unorthodox theme that a world with more nuclear states could be desirable.

Kramish, Arnold. *Atomic Energy in the Soviet Union* (Stanford: Stanford University Press, 1959).

The standard work on the development of the Soviet atomic eneregy program.

Lawrence, Robert M., and Joel Larus (eds.). *Nuclear Proliferation Phase II* (Lawrence: University Press of Kansas, 1974).

A collection of nine essays, most of which focus on the proliferation perspectives of different countries. Particularly provocative essay by Haselkorn on Israel's nuclear posture.

Lefever, Ernest W. *Nuclear Arms in the Third World.* (Washington, D.C.: The Brookings Institution, 1979).

Examines the technical foundations and incentives for nuclear power and weapons programs in India, Pakistan, Iran, Israel, Egypt, South Korea, Taiwan, Argentina, and Brazil. Reviews U.S. policy options to deter nuclear arms acquisition in these countries.

Lellouche, Pierre. "Internationalization of the Nuclear Fuel Cycle and Non Proliferation Strategy: Lessons and Prospects" (Harvard Law School SJD Dissertation, 1979).

Very thorough study of past and present approaches to the internationalization of nuclear activities with recommendations for the future.

Lönnroth, Mans, and William Walker. *The Viability of the Civil Nuclear Industry* (New York: The Rockefeller Foundation and The Royal Institute of International Affairs, 1979). Report prepared for the International Consultative Group on Nuclear Energy.

Brief but excellent study of the structure and characteristics of the civil nuclear industry, constraints on nuclear expansion, and the prospects for the reactor industry. The best publication on the subject.

McGarvey, David, Bryan Jack, and David Snyder. *South Korea and Nuclear Weapons* (Los Angeles: Pan Heuristics, 1977). Report prepared for the U.S. Energy and Research Administration.

Examination of South Korean nuclear program with special attention to the decision not to acquire a reprocessing plant after pressure by the United States and possible Japanese reaction to a ROK nuclear capability.

Marks, Anne W. (ed.). *NPT: Paradoxes and Problems* (Washington, D.C.: The Arms Control Association and the Carnegie Endowment for International Peace, 1975).

Good collection of papers from a pre–NPT Review Conference meeting of the Arms Control Association and the Carnegie Endowment for International Peace. Topics discussed include peaceful nuclear explosions, the status and prospects of the NPT, and measures to strengthen the NPT.

Marwah, Onkar, and Ann Schulz (eds.). *Nuclear Proliferation and the Near-Nuclear Countries* (Cambridge, Massachusetts: Ballinger, 1975).

Good collection of conference papers on the nuclear programs and perspectives of potential nuclear weapons states.

Meyer, Stephen M. "Probing the Causes of Nuclear Proliferation: An Empirical Analysis 1940–1973" (Ph.D. Dissertation, University of Michigan, 1978).

Sophisticated empirical examination of two contending models of proliferation: the "technological imperative" and "motivational" models. Notable for ingenious operationalization of variables and novel methodological approach to the subject.

Nero, Anthony V., Jr. *A Guidebook to Nuclear Reactors* (Berkeley: University of California Press, 1979).

A very useful introduction to nuclear reactors, fuel cycles, and the connection of nuclear power and weapons proliferation. Excellent diagrams.

Nuclear Energy Policy Study Group. *Nuclear Power Issues and Choices* (Cambridge, Massachusetts: Ballinger, 1977).

Very influential and comprehensive Ford-Mitre study on the major issues pertaining to nuclear power and proliferation, especially their overlap. A number of the study group's recommendations, summarized in introductory chapter, found expression in the Carter administration's nonproliferation policy.

Overholt, William H. (ed.). *Asia's Nuclear Future* (Boulder, Colorado: Westview Press, 1977).

A collection of seven essays which appraise the nuclear future of Asia from a number of different vantage points. Also includes useful methodological chapter by Lewis Dunn and William Overholt on "The Next Phase in Nuclear Proliferation Research."

Quester, George. *The Politics of Nuclear Proliferation* (Baltimore: The Johns Hopkins University Press, 1973).

Sophisticated discussion of seventeen countries' perspectives on nuclear proliferation and the NPT and the domestic and international determinants of these views.

Ramberg, Bennett. *Destruction of Nuclear Energy Facilities in War: The Problem and the Implications* (Lexington, Massachusetts: Lexington Books, 1980).

Comprehensive analysis of the problems posed by the destruction of nuclear energy facilities in war and possible options to reduce their wartime vulnerability.

Rochlin, Gene I. *Plutonium, Power, and Politics: International Arrangements for the Disposition of Spent Nuclear Fuel* (Berkeley: University of California Press, 1979).

Excellent study of possible international arrangements for the management or control of the back end of the nuclear fuel cycle. Interesting application of social science theory to explore nuclear power and proliferation issues.

Rosecrance, Richard N. (ed.). *The Dispersion of Nuclear Weapons: Strategy and Politics* (New York: Columbia University Press, 1964).

Excellent collection of essays on the national nuclear experience of the United States, Great Britain, France, and the PRC and on the impact of future technology. Perceptive synthesis of case studies by Rosecrance in concluding chapter.

Rowen, Beverly C., and Henry S. Rowen. "In the Face of Nuclear Proliferation: An Assessment of Policy Options for the United States" (Los Angeles: Pan Heuristics, 1977).

Brief but well-documented study of proposed antiproliferation policies since 1946 and possible measures that could now be taken by the United States and other countries to affect the supply of and demand for nuclear weapons. Study prepared for the U.S. Arms Control and Disarmament Agency.

Schoettle, Enid C. B. *Postures for Non-Proliferation: Arms Limitation and Security Policies to Minimize Nuclear Proliferation* (London: Taylor & Francis, 1979). Published for the Stockholm International Peace Research Institute.

Careful study of alternative strategies for limiting proliferation and an analysis of the 1975 NPT Review Conference and the negotiations on the NPT between 1965 and 1968.

Smyth, Henry. *Atomic Energy for Military Purposes: The Official Report on the Development of the Atomic Bomb under the Auspices of the United States Government* (Princeton, New Jersey: Princeton University Press, 1945).

The first officially authorized account of the Manhattan Project. Summarizes the administrative history and the unclassified technical details of the development of the atomic bomb.

Starr, Chauncey, and E. Zebroski. "Nuclear Power and Weapons Proliferation," paper prepared for the American Power Conference, April 18, 1977. (Available from Electric Power Research Institute, Research Reports Center, P.O. Box 10090, Palo Alto CA 94303.)

Analysis of the linkage between nuclear power and weapons proliferation. Suggests measures to promote nuclear energy development without impeding nonproliferation efforts.

Steiner, Arthur. *Canada: The Decision to Forego the Bomb.* (Los Angeles: Pan Heuristics, 1977). Report prepared for the U.S. Energy Research and Development Agency.

Study of the factors responsible for the Canadian decision not to acquire nuclear weapons.

Steiner, Arthur. *Great Britain and France: Two Other Roads to the Atomic Bomb* (Los Angeles: Pan Heuristics, 1977). Report prepared for the U.S. Energy Research and Development Administration.

Survey of the British and French paths to nuclear weapons.

Stockholm International Peace Research Institute. *Nuclear Energy and Nuclear Weapons Proliferation* (London: Taylor & Francis, and New York: Crane, Russak & Co., 1979).

Collection of papers from a SIPRI-sponsored conference in 1978 devoted to the technical aspects of the control of fissionable materials. Includes chapters on peaceful applications of nuclear explosions, safeguards technology, breeder reactors, and enrichment and waste-disposal technologies.

Stockholm International Peace Research Institute. *Safeguards Against Nuclear Proliferation* (Cambridge, Massachusetts: MIT Press, 1975).

Reviews the operation of IAEA safeguards.

U.S. Congress. Library of Congress, Congressional Research Service (Environment and Natural Resources Policy Division). *Nuclear Proliferation Factbook.* (Washington, D.C.: Government Printing Office, September 1980). Prepared for the House Committee on Governmental Affairs.

Third edition of extremely valuable and wide-ranging selection of documents and data pertaining to nuclear power and nuclear weapons proliferation.

U.S. Department of Energy. *Nuclear Proliferation and Civilian Nuclear Power*, Report of the Nonproliferation Alternative Systems Assessment Program, 9 volumes with Executive Summary (Washington, D.C.: U.S. Department of Energy, June 1980).

Comprehensive and enormous government study designed to provide recommendations for the development of more proliferation-resistant civilian nuclear power systems and institutions. Study was initiated in late 1976 and restructured in 1977 to respond to President Carter's April 1977 policy statement on nuclear power. NASAP volumes on: Program Summary; Proliferation Resistance; Resources and Fuel Cycle Facilities; Commercial Potential; Economics and Systems Analysis; Safety and Environmental Consideration for Licensing; International Perspectives; Advanced Concepts; Reactor and Fuel Cycle Descriptions.

U.S. Office of Technology Assessment. *Nuclear Proliferation and Safeguards.* Vol. 1 (New York: Praeger, 1977); Vol. 2, Appendices (Washington, D.C.: U.S. Government Printing Office, 1977).

The most comprehensive study available of nuclear power and nonproliferation issues and their policy implications. Includes discussion of the technology of nuclear power and nuclear explosives, incentives and disincentives for proliferation, the nature of nonstate adversaries, safeguards technology, and the international nuclear industry.

Warnecke, Steven J. *Uranium, Nonproliferation and Energy Security* (Paris: The Atlantic Institute for International Affairs, 1979).

Analysis of the politicization of uranium supplies and its implications for nuclear power and nonproliferation policy in the United States and abroad.

Wilrich, Mason (ed.). *International Safeguards and Nuclear Industry* (Baltimore: The Johns Hopkins University Press, 1973).

A detailed study of the history, operation, and problems of the IAEA/NPT safeguards system.

Willrich, Mason, and Theodore B. Taylor. *Nuclear Theft: Risks and Safeguards* (Cambridge, Massachusetts: Ballinger, 1974).

The standard reference in the area of nuclear terrorism and safeguards.

Wohlstetter, Albert, et al. *Moving Toward Life in a Nuclear Armed Crowd?* (Los Angeles: Pan Heuristics, 1976).

Commissioned by the U.S. Arms Control and Disarmament Argency, a very influential and wide-ranging study of technological, political, and economic aspects of nuclear proliferation. Arguments made against plutonium recycle especially significant. Subsequently released commercially in condensed form as *Swords from Plowshares* (Chicago: University of Chicago Press, 1979).

Yager, Joseph A. (with the assistance of Ralph T. Mabry, Jr.). *International Cooperation in Nuclear Energy* (Washington, D.C.: The Brookings Institution, 1981).

Examines broad range of measures for international cooperation to exploit nuclear energy for peaceful purposes while controlling the spread of nuclear proliferation. Useful appendices by Mabry on the IAEA and the present nuclear safeguards system and on the export policies of major suppliers.

Yager, Joseph A. (ed.). *Nonproliferation and U.S. Foreign Policy* (Washington, D.C.: The Brookings Institution, 1980).

Very good collection of essays by Richard Betts, Henry Rowen and Richard Brody, William Courtney, and Joseph Yager on the present and possible future proliferation incentives for India, Pakistan, Iran, South Africa, Japan, South Korea, Taiwan, Argentina, Brazil, Israel, and the Middle Eastern Arab countries. Examines measures to reduce incentives and limit capabilities and the susceptibility of *N*th countries to U.S. influence.

Appendix D

Chronology of Events in Nuclear Weapons Development and Nonproliferation

July 1945	The United States detonates first atomic bomb at Alamogordo, New Mexico.
August 1945	The United States drops atomic bomb on Hiroshima and Nagasaki.
January 1946	The United Nations Atomic Energy Commission is established.
June 1946	The United States submits the Baruch Plan for international control of nuclear activities to the United Nations.
August 1946	The U.S. Congress passes the Atomic Energy Act of 1946 (also known as the McMahon Act).
September 1949	The Soviet Union explodes its first atomic bomb.
October 1952	The United Kingdom explodes its first atomic bomb.
November 1952	The United States explodes its first hydrogen bomb.
August 1953	The Soviet Union explodes its first hydrogen bomb.

December 1953	President Eisenhower makes his "Atoms for Peace" proposal to the United Nations.
May 1957	The United Kingdom explodes its first hydrogen bomb.
July 1957	The International Atomic Energy Agency (IAEA) is established under UN auspices.
December 1959	The Antarctic Treaty banning nuclear tests and military bases in Antarctica is opened for signatures.
February 1960	France explodes its first atomic bomb.
August 1963	The Partial Test Ban Treaty is opened for signatures.
October 1964	The People's Republic of China explodes its first atomic bomb.
January 1967	The Outer Space Treaty banning nuclear weapons in outer space is opened for signatures.
February 1967	The Treaty of Tlatelolco is opened for signatures.
June 1967	The People's Republic of China explodes its first hydrogen bomb.
July 1968	The Treaty on the Non-Proliferation of Nuclear Weapons (NPT) is opened for signatures.
August 1968	France explodes its first hydrogen bomb.
November 1969	The Strategic Arms Limitation Talks (SALT) begin.
March 1970	The NPT enters into force.
February 1971	The Seabed Treaty banning the emplacement of nuclear weapons on the seabed or ocean floor is opened for signatures.
May 1972	The SALT ABM Treaty and Interim Agreement on Offensive Arms are signed by the United States and the Soviet Union.
May 1974	India explodes its first nuclear device.
June 1974	The Zangger Committee decides to adopt trigger list for nuclear exports.
July 1974	The United States and the Soviet Union sign the Threshold Test Ban Treaty limiting un-

derground nuclear weapons tests to a yield of 150 kilotons each after March 31, 1976.

May 1975	The first NPT Review Conference is held.
January 1976	The London Suppliers Group endorses a uniform code for conducting international nuclear sales.
October 1976	President Ford announces deferral of commercial reprocessing.
May 1976	The United States and the Soviet Union sign treaty restricting peaceful nuclear explosions to 150 kilotons.
April 1977	Seven-point nuclear program is announced by President Carter.
October 1977	The International Nuclear Fuel Cycle Evaluation (INFCE) is organized.
March 1978	The Nuclear Non-Proliferation Act of 1978 is signed into law.
April 1979	Nuclear reactor accident occurs at Three Mile Island.
February 1980	Final report of INFCE is issued.
June 1980	Final report of the Nonproliferation Alternative Systems Assessment Program (NASAP) is issued.
August–September 1980	The second NPT Review Conference is held.
June 1981	Israel attacks Iraq nuclear facility.
July 1981	President Reagan makes major policy statement on nuclear proliferation.

Index

About the Author

William C. Potter is Assistant Director of the Center for International and Strategic Affairs, University of California, Los Angeles. He is coauthor of *SALT and Beyond: A Handbook on Strategic Weapons and Means for Their Control* (1977) and editor of *Verification and SALT: The Challenge of Soviet Strategic Deception* (1980). His current research focuses on Soviet nuclear export policy.